THE UNITED STATES–
SOUTH KOREA ALLIANCE

A COUNCIL ON FOREIGN RELATIONS BOOK

The Council on Foreign Relations (CFR) is an independent, nonpartisan membership organization, think tank, and publisher dedicated to being a resource for its members, government officials, business executives, journalists, educators and students, civic and religious leaders, and other interested citizens in order to help them better understand the world and the foreign policy choices facing the United States and other countries. Founded in 1921, CFR carries out its mission by maintaining a diverse membership, with special programs to promote interest and develop expertise in the next generation of foreign policy leaders; convening meetings at its headquarters in New York and in Washington, DC, and other cities where senior government officials, members of Congress, global leaders, and prominent thinkers come together with CFR members to discuss and debate major international issues; supporting a Studies Program that fosters independent research, enabling CFR scholars to produce articles, reports, and books and hold roundtables that analyze foreign policy issues and make concrete policy recommendations; publishing *Foreign Affairs*, the preeminent journal on international affairs and U.S. foreign policy; sponsoring Independent Task Forces that produce reports with both findings and policy prescriptions on the most important foreign policy topics; and providing up-to-date information and analysis about world events and American foreign policy on its website, www.cfr.org.

The Council on Foreign Relations takes no institutional positions on policy issues and has no affiliation with the U.S. government. All views expressed in its publications and on its website are the sole responsibility of the author or authors.

SCOTT A. SNYDER

THE UNITED STATES–
SOUTH KOREA
ALLIANCE

Why It May Fail and Why It Must Not

Columbia University Press / *New York*

Columbia University Press
Publishers Since 1893
New York   Chichester, West Sussex
cup.columbia.edu

Library of Congress Cataloging-in-Publication Data
Names: Snyder, Scott, 1964– author.
Title: The United States-South Korea alliance : why it may fail and why
it must not / Scott A. Snyder.
Description: New York : Columbia University Press, 2023. | Series: A Council
on Foreign Relations book | Includes bibliographical references and index.
Identifiers: LCCN 2023020867 (print) | LCCN 2023020868 (ebook) |
ISBN 9780231208680 (hardback) | ISBN 9780231208697 (trade paperback) |
ISBN 9780231557559 (ebook)
Subjects: LCSH: United States—Foreign relations—Korea (South) |
Korea (South)—Foreign relations—United States. | Korea (South)—Foreign
relations. | United States—Foreign relations—21st century. | Military assistance,
American—Korea (South)
Classification: LCC E183.8.K6 S59 2023 (print) | LCC E183.8.K6 (ebook) |
DDC 327.7305195—dc23/eng/20230519
LC record available at https://lccn.loc.gov/2023020867
LC ebook record available at https://lccn.loc.gov/2023020868

Cover image: Shutterstock

In appreciation of my parents, Dowen "Buck"
and Carol Snyder, and my sister, Joy Snyder

CONTENTS

CONTENTS

PART II

EXTERNAL THREATS TO THE ALLIANCE

PART III

THE CREDIBILITY OF THE AMERICAN ALLIANCE
COMMITMENT AND THE IMPLICATIONS OF
ALLIANCE BREAKDOWN

PREFACE

To mark the seventieth anniversary of the U.S.–South Korea alliance in April 2023, U.S. president Joe Biden hosted South Korean president Yoon Suk-yeol for a state visit during which President Yoon addressed a joint meeting of Congress and held numerous meetings across a broad range of sectors with U.S. and South Korean business leaders. The leaders' joint statement acknowledged over $100 billion of South Korean investments in the United States and deepened policy coordination between the two governments across a broad range of functional areas encompassing not only security cooperation but also technology, space, public health, and international development. The U.S.–South Korea alliance "forged in blood" during the Korean War in the 1950s appeared set to be powered by cooperation on chips, batteries, and clean technology through the 2020s and beyond.

Yet despite the clear resiliency and broadened scope of cooperation on display between the United States and South Korea, it would be a mistake to ignore emerging domestic political vulnerabilities that threaten alliance cooperation resulting from a combination of narrow nationalism and deepening domestic political polarization in both countries that became visible during the Trump and Moon administrations only a few years earlier. These domestic developments in both countries suggest that the U.S.–South Korea alliance faces its greatest vulnerability not from external threats such as North Korea's nuclear development or China's desire to refashion a Sino-centric world order but rather from within.

As domestic political drama unfolded in both countries under the Trump and Moon administrations, it became clear that the resiliency of a U.S.–South Korea relationship that had been tested and transformed over seven decades was potentially vulnerable to political developments in both countries that had previously been unimaginable. Long-standing assumptions underpinning alliance cooperation were challenged by a combination of domestic political polarization and narrowing conceptions of national interest in both the United States and South Korea. This book reflects my effort to systematically consider the impact and consequences of domestic political developments in both countries on the resiliency and effectiveness of the U.S.–South Korea alliance.

ACKNOWLEDGMENTS

I was aided in research and drafting of the manuscript by two able research associates, Ellen Swicord and Jennifer Ahn, with additional research support from Seojung Kim, Dokyoung Koo, Heemin Ahn, Edward Kim, Dennis Kim, Chris Park, and Doyeong Jung. I benefited from constructive comments by three blind reviewers and the editorial support of Stephen Wesley at Columbia University Press. I am thankful to Trish Dorff, James Lindsay, and Richard Haass at the Council on Foreign Relations for providing institutional support for this project and for reading and making invaluable suggestions that improved the manuscript. I am grateful to Al Song and his colleagues at the Smith Richardson Foundation for their generous support for this project.

Finally, I thank SoRhym, Elliana, and Elyssa Snyder for their love, support, and encouragement.

PART I

THE U.S.–SOUTH KOREA ALLIANCE UNDER TRUMP AND MOON AND SOUTH KOREAN DOMESTIC CHALLENGES

1

THE THREAT TO THE U.S.–SOUTH KOREA ALLIANCE FROM WITHIN

The security alliance between the United States and South Korea (also known as the Republic of Korea, or ROK) has guaranteed South Korea's security alongside the Korean Armistice Agreement, outlasted the Cold War, evolved through South Korea's transition from authoritarianism to democracy, and been reinforced by the threat from North Korea's persistent nuclear development over the past two decades. The U.S.–South Korea alliance has long served as a model of stability and longevity, playing an essential role in the U.S.-led security architecture that has kept the peace in Northeast Asia.

Moreover, the alliance has secured regional stability along the fault line across the Korean Peninsula that has divided the Western and communist world. North Korea's expanding nuclear arsenal, China's growing influence, and the return of major power competition between the United States and China make the alliance more necessary than ever before. Yet, despite the resiliency the U.S.–South Korea alliance has shown under the Joe Biden administration with both the Moon Jae-in and Yoon Suk-yeol administrations, the alliance remains vulnerable to threats from within, in the form of narrow and exclusive definitions of national interest in each country that could pit the United States and South Korea against each other in opposition to common interests that justify coordination between the alliance partners. Thus, internal threats to the U.S.–South Korea alliance have revealed themselves as a source of vulnerability against the backdrop of deepening political polarization and rising nationalism-infused critiques of the value of the alliance to both nations. The simultaneous emergence of leaderships in the United States and South Korea that define national interests to the exclusion of a shared interest in upholding mutual security interests might weaken the alliance, regardless of the seriousness of external threats that have justified close security cooperation between the two countries.

The threat to alliance interests posed by exclusive forms of self-interested nationalism was most recently prevalent in the Donald Trump administration's "America-First" extortionist demands toward South Korea for dramatically increased financial contributions in support of a continued U.S. troop presence on the peninsula. More broadly, the outlines of Trump's "America-First" foreign policy involved reducing U.S. commitments abroad while insisting on global deference to and support for American interests and objectives. Although such sentiments had not been part of the mainstream American foreign policy debate for decades, these themes have resonated on both sides of the political spectrum, increasing the likelihood that debates over the significance and utility of the alliance with South Korea will be a part of U.S. policy discussions in the future.

Trump's view of the U.S.–South Korea alliance revolved around the characterization of South Korea as a wealthy free rider that had conned the United States into defending it from attack. When top U.S. military commanders stationed in the country showed Trump the revamped and gleaming Camp Humphreys, a U.S. military base about forty-five miles south of Seoul that was expanded with an almost $10 billion investment from South Korea, Trump used it as evidence that South Korea should and could pay even more for the presence of U.S. forces in South Korea rather than as evidence of South Korean commitment to the alliance. Trump's first director of the National Economic Council, Gary Cohn, reportedly blocked Trump from tearing up the U.S. trade agreement with South Korea in August 2017

4

by pocketing the order on Trump's desk at the Oval Office.[1] Trump publicly expressed his intent to end the U.S.–South Korea alliance if he won a second term.[2] It is entirely plausible that a future presidential candidate may revive and adhere to populist Trumpian themes that could again weaken the alliance or place it in danger of degradation.

By the same token, North Korea–first progressives in South Korea, who place reconciliation with North Korea as South Korea's top foreign policy priority over the U.S.–South Korea alliance, lobbied then President Moon to pursue policies of appeasement toward North Korea that generated frictions in the U.S.–South Korea alliance throughout his administration. Ultimately, the Moon administration adhered to policies that prioritized and reinforced alliance cooperation with the United States, but advocacy within the administration for pro–North Korea policies generated frictions with the Trump and Biden administrations and catalyzed progressive fears of entrapment around U.S. opposition to reconciliation with a nuclear-armed North Korea. The presidential standard-bearer for Moon's Democratic Party in the March 2022 presidential election Lee Jae-myung—who relied on policy advisors such as the former national security advisor and prominent North Korea–first progressive Lee Jong-seok and who was even more inclined than Moon to prioritize inter-Korean reconciliation over U.S.–South Korea alliance coordination—lost by only 0.7 percentage points to the conservative Yoon Suk-yeol in the closest presidential election in South Korea's history. South Korean progressives will be strongly motivated to recapture power in 2027 following five years out of power, opening the possibility of a return to both appeasement policies toward North Korea and frictions over North Korea policy within the U.S.–South Korea alliance.

In the meantime, although the conservative Yoon administration has made the "comprehensive strategic alliance" with the United States a centerpiece of South Korea's foreign policy, it is possible that South Korean conservatives may challenge the alliance by pursuing a Korea-first foreign policy from the right. This could happen if South Korean conservatives lose faith in U.S. pledges and policies of deterrence toward North Korea. The credibility of U.S. commitments to the defense of South Korea could come under question if the United States is perceived as restraining South

Korea from retaliating against North Korean military provocations out of fear of conflict escalation. Or they could be challenged by a failure to stand up to North Korean nuclear blackmail, leaving South Korea vulnerable to the North's extortionary demands. For instance, the criticism by some South Korean conservatives of the Yoon administration for agreeing to the April 26, 2023, Washington Declaration, which they viewed as "shackling" South Korea to greater reliance on the United States through its reaffirmation of South Korean commitments to the NPT, provides a clear example of such a challenge.[3]

In the event of a return to Trumpism, the rekindling of an unconventional Trump-style "bromance" with Kim Jong-un might induce conservative fears of abandonment that would motivate a South Korea no longer confident in U.S. defense commitments to pursue its own independent nuclear capability. The steady increase in South Korean public support for an independent nuclear capability over the past decade underscores the plausibility that a conservative South Korean president might pursue such a course of action. There have been considerable efforts to revitalize U.S.–South Korea alliance coordination under the Biden administration with the Moon and Yoon administrations, but these efforts remain vulnerable to growing domestic political polarization and the emergence of exclusively self-interested forms of nationalism in both countries. To the extent that political leadership in the two countries becomes susceptible to such influences, the potential for conflict within the alliance could exceed previous levels.

Under the management of Trump and Moon, the alliance faced a moment when both leaders harbored narrow desires influenced by their own respective versions of nationalism that might have led them to place national self-interest above the shared challenges of dealing with threats from North Korea and China. For Trump, the political costs of overriding the counsel of his own advisors and challenging congressional and American public support for South Korea to appease Kim Jong-un and abandon long-standing alliance commitments to South Korea were high. But they might easily have been worn down over time or by the need to feed Trump's ego via sustained summitry with Kim. For Moon, the dream of Korean unification was fueled by the euphoric experience of speaking to over 150,000

North Koreans at the May Day stadium in Pyongyang in September 2018. But the impediments imposed by international sanctions on North Korea and the security risks generated by North Korea's refusal to denuclearize remained as obstacles to Moon's realization of that dream. If it was possible for American and South Korean political leadership to weaken the alliance under Trump and Moon, it is possible that a similar combination of narrowly nationalist political leadership could happen again.

The challenge to the alliance faced by the Trump and Moon administrations involved the risk of a simultaneous rise of opposition from domestic sources in both the United States and South Korea. To the American public, the argument for reducing U.S. responsibilities abroad may tempt some to shed the additional burdens the United States has long carried for the provision of regional stability in East Asia on the Korean Peninsula. For some South Koreans, there is an opportunity to unshackle South Korea from perceived obstacles to inter-Korean reconciliation associated with the U.S. military presence in South Korea and alleged U.S. interests in keeping the peninsula divided. A virulent combination of deepening political polarization and rising nationalism in both countries might under the right circumstances put at risk almost seven decades of cooperation against rising threats from North Korea and China.

In addition, North Korea and China may exploit South Korean domestic political polarization to weaken the alliance, or interest divergence between the United States and South Korea might emerge as a consequence of China's rising power and regional influence. As part of the unfinished competition for legitimacy between North and South Korea, North Korea has attempted to influence South Korea's domestic politics to achieve its own objectives, whether it be to sow internal dissension and foment revolution in South Korea or to drive a wedge in the U.S.–South Korea alliance. South Korea's domestic political polarization has been reflected in debates over the future of China–South Korea relations along with the impact of China's economic influence both on South Korea's perceptions of political opportunity with China and the impact of the securitization of technology on the economic dimension of the U.S.–South Korea alliance.

This book presents the possible costs of alliance degradation to the respective foreign policies of the United States and South Korea. Alliance degradation is not necessarily a likely outcome for the U.S.–South Korea alliance, but following developments during the Trump and Moon administrations, it has now become a plausible outcome. The exercise of imagining a world with no U.S.–South Korea alliance provides a deeper appreciation of the sources of resilience within the alliance and the alliance's impact on and contributions to both regional security and the national security interests of the two countries.

THE DURABILITY OF THE U.S.–SOUTH KOREA ALLIANCE AND SOURCES OF VULNERABILITY

A study of all international security alliances formed since 1800 shows that the average security alliance has lasted a little over a decade.[4] But the U.S.–South Korea alliance has lasted almost seven decades, providing evidence of its utility and resilience. The U.S. alliance with South Korea, along with the U.S. alliance with Japan, has done more than meet tactical security needs of the moment; it is part of an architecture that has successfully deterred conflict and enabled prosperity, markets, and growth across Northeast Asia over half a century. The U.S.-led alliance system outlasted the Cold War, rewarded export-led industrialization while supplying American consumer markets, and supported South Korea's political transition from authoritarianism to democracy.

The alliance theorist Stephen Walt describes factors that enable alliances to endure despite the weakening of external threats, including hegemonic leadership, sustenance of the alliance as a symbol of credibility, high degrees of institutionalization, elite manipulation, and ideological solidarity.[5] Alexander Lanoszka adds that alliances appear to have proven more durable in the nuclear age, when the stakes and potential costs of military conflict have become much higher, and that alliances may endure or dissolve regardless of the persistence or diminution of the immediate threat justifying alliance formation.[6] J. J. Suh observed in his study of the durability of the U.S.–South Korea alliance that the end of the Cold War, famine in North Korea during the 1990s, and inter-Korean rapprochement in the early 2000s raised questions among many in South Korea about whether the alliance remained an essential instrument for maintaining South Korea's security. But the highly institutionalized structures of coordination, the sunk costs from decades of alliance cooperation, and the convergence of shared values and approaches to major international security issues kept the alliance going in the face of debate over its continued necessity and viability.[7]

The habits of cooperation in the U.S.–South Korea alliance that were built over decades have provided a buffer against external security threats. They have enabled the alliance to adapt to new challenges, to evolve, and to grow in strength. The alliance partnership that exists today is a far cry from the patron-client relationship resulting from the difference in power between the United States and South Korea at the moment of the alliance's founding in 1953. At that time, South Korea was truly dependent on the United States as its primary patron and security guarantor in the face of external threats from more powerful neighbors, including North Korea. South Korea's economic development since then and its acquisition of world-class technology and military capabilities have enabled it to contribute to the alliance as well as to its own defense, allowing the United States to transition responsibilities for significant aspects of South Korean defense into Korean hands. The scope of U.S.–South Korea alliance cooperation has extended beyond the peninsula to include contributions to global health, international security, and international development. The Biden administration's efforts to revitalize U.S.–South Korea alliance cooperation and the posture of the Yoon administration in support of the "comprehensive strategic alliance" has suggested that these leaders would maintain a high degree of ideological solidarity as the basis for expanding alliance ties and its application to local, regional, and global security challenges. One might argue, based on these trends, that the U.S.–South Korea alliance has never been more effective, constructive, or global than it is today.

But despite the gains and contributions of the alliance to international security in recent years, the alliance's Achilles' heel is rising domestic political divisions in both countries. Walt identifies changing threat perceptions, declining alliance credibility, and domestic politics as factors that may lead to alliance collapse. Specifically, he asserts that alliances may be put in jeopardy "if influential elites decide that they can improve their internal positions by attacking the alliance itself . . . or if the terms of the alliance involve measures that are seen as an affront to national sovereignty."

Past studies of internal challenges to the U.S.–South Korea alliance involved studying local expressions of anti-Americanism, anti–U.S. base protests, and public resentments over the local impact of the U.S. military and misconduct of U.S. soldiers in South Korea.[8] But these studies focus primarily on alliance frictions that arose from the bottom up, rather than top-down frictions arising from elite-driven politically motivated attacks on the alliance. Such is the nature of the challenge to the U.S.–South Korea alliance posed by the intersection of America-First and Korea-first forms of nationalism.

This challenge is different from prior domestic challenges to the alliance in at least three critical respects. First, the exclusive nationalism that Trump favored reflected top-down influence by top political decision makers to the bureaucratic managers under their leadership, whereas previous bottom-up threats to the U.S.–South Korea alliance from civil society actors had to overcome resistance from government bureaucrats and an elite consensus in favor of the alliance. Second, dissatisfaction with the alliance has usually been most vocally expressed during periods of relative decline in perceptions of external threats, but under the Trump and Moon administrations the North Korean and Chinese security threats were expanding rather than diminishing. Third, despite extensive institutionalization of U.S.–South Korea alliance cooperation based on habits of cooperation and customary practices built up over seven decades, the legal underpinnings of the alliance are built on the same narrow base as when the alliance was promulgated, with both countries able to terminate the alliance by formal notice of only one year.

In the face of deepening political polarization and an increased willingness to disrupt past precedents in both countries, the gap between the customary and normative practices of the alliance should not be casually dismissed. In the same way that Americans came to realize under Trump that many facets of democratic practice relied on convention rather than formal legal frameworks and procedures, it is plausible that a calculated and determined effort by a future populist leader in either the United

States or South Korea might succeed in exploiting the relatively weak and dated legal framework underpinning the alliance. For this reason, although the advances in U.S.–South Korea alliance cooperation made under the Biden administration and the Moon and Yoon administrations suggested a strong recovery from the challenges the alliance faced under Trump and Moon, the possibility of degradation of the alliance may seem implausible, but it should no longer be regarded as unthinkable.

Table 1.1 illustrates the likely impact of challenges to alliance cooperation that would result from the emergence of leadership in either country that is motivated primarily by exclusive forms of nationalism. Under pro-alliance presidents regardless of political party, a convergence of interests

TABLE 1.1 Influence of Leadership and Ideology on U.S.–South Korea Alliance Management

PRO-ALLIANCE AMERICAN LEADERSHIP PRO-ALLIANCE KOREAN LEADERSHIP	PRO-ALLIANCE AMERICAN LEADERSHIP KOREA FIRST LEADERSHIP
Deepened institutional coordination within alliance; broadened scope of alliance to regional and global objectives Effective combined approaches to deterrence and engagement toward North Korea Cooperative approach to addressing the security and economic implications of China's rise	Tensions over the management of differing security and economic priorities Gaps in threat perception of North Korea generate tensions in alliance management Gaps in perceptions of China generate frustration and complicate alliance coordination on regional security policy
AMERICA FIRST LEADERSHIP **PRO-ALLIANCE KOREAN LEADERSHIP**	**AMERICA FIRST LEADERSHIP** **KOREA FIRST LEADERSHIP**
Tensions over the management of differing security and economic priorities Gaps in perceptions of North Korea lead to doubts about the credibility of American commitment to alliance Differing priorities toward China lead to friction within the alliance; coordination difficulties with other U.S. security partners	Divergence of priorities and conflict over policy preferences Political frictions over priority and value of alliance diminish the ability to jointly respond to peninsular and regional threats Weakened alliance coordination

in the face of common threats provides opportunities for both sides to deepen institutionalization of alliance cooperation. But the emergence of exclusivist strains of nationalist leadership in either the United States or South Korea inevitably generate tensions resulting from a divergence in national priorities between the two sides. In addition, domestic political polarization that has arisen alongside these forms of exclusive nationalism in both the United States and South Korea has both enabled the influence of ideology and constrained the ability of government officials on both sides to effectively address problems within the alliance. In the event that leaders of both countries were to prioritize exclusive nationalist priorities over alliance cooperation, the ability of the alliance to perform effectively would be eviscerated, leaving institutional forms of alliance cooperation as a hollow shell.

ASIAN CASES OF ALLIANCE DEGRADATION

In his study of military alliances, Lanoszka posits five reasons for the dissolution of alliances: (1) success in overcoming the threat, making the alliance obsolete; (2) military defeat of the alliance; (3) downgrading and marginalization of the alliance as a priority for one or both partners; (4) divergence of interests leading to abrogation of the alliance; and (5) transformation of the alliance, most probably due to its absorption into a multilateral security framework that reinforces and expands efforts to meet security needs of the countries concerned.[9] Among these scenarios, the most likely forms of a weakened U.S.–South Korea alliance that would result from America-First and/or South Korea-first challenges to cooperation are the downgrading of alliance priorities in which alliance forms continue in a "zombie" state without real effectiveness or capabilities, or a decision to abandon the alliance in favor of more pressing interests with an alternative strategic partner.

The few post–Cold War cases in which bilateral alliances have been abrogated will lead some to argue that predictions of alliance dissolution themselves are alarmist and unrealistic. However, the cases themselves provide support for the proposition that either domestic political differences or the emergence of diverging interests between alliance partners are factors that can lead to alliance degradation.

The termination of U.S.–New Zealand alliance arrangements in the 1980s in response to the antinuclear New Zealand government's refusal to allow nuclear-powered U.S. vessels to enter into New Zealand waters shows how political leaders with agendas that conflict with alliance practices can lead to the evisceration of alliance cooperation. Likewise, the withdrawal of U.S. forces from the Clark and Subic bases in the Philippines following the failure of the Philippine Senate to ratify new basing agreements in the early 1990s reveals the challenge to alliance durability posed by domestic political realities. But domestic political challenges are also variable. U.S. forces returned to the Philippines in the late 1990s both for counterterrorism purposes and in the face of a growing Chinese military presence in the South China Sea around disputed maritime features under a newly established Visiting Forces Agreement. Park Jae-jeok argues that a rationale for the endurance of alliance arrangements is to provide a form of insurance intended to support the existing regional order through the preservation of the status quo.[10] In both cases, alliance arrangements were neutralized as a result of domestic politics and the alliance became an empty shell that existed in form alone, even if the alliance itself was not formally dissolved.

The demise of the U.S.–Taiwan alliance, in contrast, occurred primarily as a result of interest divergence, based on the U.S. strategic decision to normalize diplomatic relations with mainland China. China's insistence on the One China principle and the U.S. acknowledgment of China's view made it impossible for the United States to continue formal diplomatic relations with both Beijing and Taipei, but the United States and the leaders of Taiwan have since maintained an active quasi-official relationship.[11] The U.S.–Thailand alliance has become virtually dormant in part due to interest divergence in the aftermath of the Vietnam War and in part as a result of successive military coups that have continuously thwarted democratic rule in Thailand.[12] While it does not appear likely that the U.S.–South Korea alliance is in immediate danger of following any of these pathways to demise, the alliance degradation cases referenced above underscore the possibility that domestic political polarization and possible divergence of interests between alliance partners are factors that could dramatically weaken the U.S.–South Korea alliance.

THE U.S. STAKE IN MAINTAINING
THE U.S.–SOUTH KOREA ALLIANCE

The stakes for the United States that would accompany the weakening of the alliance are rising. If the U.S.–South Korea alliance were beset by a drift or divergence of threat perceptions, the United States would cede vital influence over a geopolitical linchpin and pivot point in Northeast Asia. Its capacity to project power in the region would diminish and generate an opening for a rising China to assume regional leadership. The Chinese president Xi Jinping in recent years has been straightforward in proposing a China-led regional order that would be characterized by mutual prosperity, regional cooperation, and limited U.S. influence.[13] A weakened U.S.–South Korea relationship would curtail the U.S. role in Asia, placing greater pressure on the U.S. alliance with Japan. South Korea might attempt to resist China's rising influence for a short period of time, but it remains plausible that the Korean Peninsula would eventually be absorbed into a continental strategic orbit reminiscent of Korea's previous peripheral role as a tributary state to China. The balance of power in the region would shift demonstrably toward China, opening the way for an expanded Chinese role across Asia that might facilitate and deepen decoupling trends, impeding the long-standing U.S. objective of keeping Asia open to free trade.

THE INFLUENCE OF KOREAN NATIONALISM

Korean expressions of nationalism have been defined by Korea's unique historical narrative and modern experiences and have represented an ongoing source of underlying tension with the concept of alliances, which involves dependence on an outside party to achieve national security. Professor Kang Jin-woong identifies Japanese colonialism, national division, as well as concepts of Korean exceptionalism and multiculturalism, modern national identity, and aspirations for future national reunification as formative experiences in the development of Korean nationalism.[14] The Stanford University sociologist Shin Gi-wook defines nation as "a product of social and historical construction, especially as the result of contentious politics, both within and without, in historically embedded and structurally contingent contexts."[15] This definition implies that it is impossible to understand nationalism without first examining a group's historical experience and the process by which political forces and powers have attempted to define and utilize national identity for their own purposes.

Efforts to conceptualize, formulate, and harness nationalism and mobilize national identity in South Korean politics have been shaped by three primary historical debates: (1) the debate over the relationship between race and nation, especially in the context of experiencing a loss of nationhood under colonial domination; (2) competing twentieth-century North and South Korean state-building efforts to mobilize and harness opposing ideologically defined concepts of national identity to overcome division by laying exclusive claim to a self-justifying concept of pan-national identity; and (3) a competition at the popular level between exclusive ethnically centered and multicultural nationalist narratives, especially in a South Korea strongly influenced since the 1990s by both the Korean diaspora and other forces of globalization.

The initial emphasis on an ethnically centered conception of Korean identity in modern nationalist historiography is a product of Korean subjugation under Japanese colonial rule. The early twentieth-century Korean nationalist Shin Chae-ho's writings emphasized distinctive ethnic unity as a response to both Japanese colonial rule and Japanese efforts to assimilate Korean ethnicity as part of a broader Japanese nationalist project. Shin's emphasis on ethnically defined concepts of Korean nationhood became an almost universal conceptual framework in the context of postwar divided Korea for imagining the rationale for a unified nation that has exerted a powerful effect on Korean thinking about national identity to this day.

Koreans witnessed a second form of nationalist discourse with the post-liberation establishment in 1948 of two separate states on the peninsula, each intent on harnessing ideologically based nationalism for their own nation-building purposes. Appeals to Korean nationalism in both the North and the South were largely about providing legitimation to rival concepts of nation building. Both North and South Korea constructed frameworks for appealing to nationalist political loyalties based on diametrically opposed ideological foundations. State-based competition for legitimacy based on nationalism, fed by the geopolitics of the Cold War, has contributed to contestation around the concept, purpose, and identity of progressive, and conservative, nationalism in South Korea. For authoritarian leaders, the task of nation building became a powerful tool for mobilizing popular support among the citizenry as well as for defining political loyalty and punishing political opposition to the state. But prodemocracy activists in South Korea mobilized counternarratives that challenged state constructions of national identity by defining a people-centered nationalist narrative around democracy and human rights.

South Korea's modern development and integration with the outside world have generated tensions between ethnic and civic forms of Korean nationalism. These tensions have come into relief as South Korea's national experience has evolved based on its successful economic development, cosmopolitan orientation and global experience of the South Korean diaspora, and relative openness to engagement with foreigners. South Korean polls show a remarkable shift in domestic conceptions of national identity as a result of South Korea's modern experiences with globalization and participation in international affairs. Conceptions have shifted from a view of Korean nationalism centered around ethnicity to a view of civic nationalism and state-centered nationalism built around democratic values and South Korea's distinctive contributions to the world.[16]

South Korean progressive nationalism builds on an ethnically centered vision of Korean national unification as the basis for elevating pro–North Korea policies as a top national priority.[17] But an ethnically centered framework for pursuing national identity is damaged by its association with North Korea's more virulent form of xenophobic nationalism, which is based on an ethnically exclusive rejection of foreign influences and a concept of ethnic purity as a basis for legitimation of the North Korean regime.[18] South

Korean progressive nationalism envisions a reunification of the Korean people that sets aside ideological divisions and is rooted in reconciliation and grand ethnic unity. But this vision of unification can only occur through integration with North Korea's family-based rule and totalitarian system. Such an approach is deeply contested between South Korean conservatives and progressives and is contradictory to the trend in thinking among younger South Koreans toward civic nationalism, which defines South Korea's national contributions in a broader global context and anticipates that the cosmopolitan impact of South Korean globalization will ultimately have a more powerful influence on South Korean conceptions of identity than the ethnocentric framing motivated primarily by a vision of an ethnically homogeneous single Korean state.

In contrast, South Korean conservative nationalism envisions South Korea as a major power on the world stage and assumes a South Korean–led unification of the Korean Peninsula. While most South Korean conservatives identify the U.S.–South Korea alliance as a platform that invaluably strengthens South Korean influence and global status, conservative nationalism could become a source of contention to the extent that the alliance is regarded by South Korean conservatives as constraining or adverse to South Korean national interests. Since South Korean conservative nationalism is shaped by realist thought, it would become operative either if South Korea is perceived to have achieved the capabilities to guarantee its security independently of external assistance from the United States or in the event that U.S. security assurances to defend South Korea from external aggression are no longer credible.

SOUTH KOREAN NATIONALIST SENTIMENTS AND U.S.–SOUTH KOREA ALLIANCE TENSIONS

South Korean concepts of ethnocentric national unity have been implicit in progressive attempts to generate dialogue, cooperation, and peaceful coexistence in inter-Korean relations. It is these concepts, rooted in the idea of national brotherhood and ethnic homogeneity, that have constituted the primary driving force underpinning South Korean progressive aspirations to recover national unity by pursuing inter-Korean reconciliation through dialogue and gradual integration of the two systems. These concepts have generated tensions in the U.S.–South Korea alliance under progressive political leadership because of the need to balance South Korea's defense needs with efforts to pursue national reconciliation with North Korea.

Manifestations of friction with the United States have been less visible under conservative South Korean political leaders, despite the emergence of periodic frictions involving U.S. advocacy for South Korean restraint so as to avoid escalation of tensions with North Korea. Though muted, these frictions could worsen if U.S. policies are perceived as the primary obstacle to South Korean efforts to defend itself against North Korean provocations, and especially against the asymmetric threat posed to a nonnuclear South Korea by the nuclear-armed North.

ALLIANCE TENSIONS DURING SOUTH KOREAN AUTHORITARIAN RULE

The U.S. discovery of South Korea's covert nuclear weapons program under Park Chung-hee in the mid-1970s led to a direct ultimatum by the Jimmy Carter administration for South Korea to abandon its nuclear program or face the withdrawal of U.S. security protections afforded by the alliance. Alongside this challenge, born of Park's deepening distrust in the credibility of U.S. security commitments to South Korea, domestic political developments on the U.S. side that put the alliance at risk included Carter's campaign pledges to withdraw U.S. troops from South Korea due to Park's oppressive human rights record and a lobbying scandal involving cash payments from a Korean national in Washington that ensnared many members of the U.S. Congress.

Park's assassination and the subsequent usurpation of military power by General Chun Doo-hwan involved the use of military force to violently suppress public prodemocracy demonstrations in the southwestern city of Gwangju. The circumstances surrounding Chun's use of the military to suppress the demonstrators generated criticisms and protests against the United States, which came to be regarded as having supported Chun to shore up South Korean internal stability against the threat from the North rather than standing for South Korean democracy. The incoming Ronald Reagan administration's invitation to Chun as one of the first foreign leaders to meet with Reagan further reenforced such perceptions, fanning the flames of anti-American activism among prodemocracy protesters in South Korea for decades.

POST-DEMOCRATIZATION ALLIANCE TENSIONS UNDER PROGRESSIVE AND CONSERVATIVE SOUTH KOREAN RULE

Following South Korea's democratic transition from authoritarianism to democracy, the alliance has continued to face challenges. Initial strains of friction within the alliance between the United States and progressive South Korean leaders date back to the late 1990s and early 2000s. At that time, anti-American sentiment became more openly expressed under the Kim Dae-jung administration—South Korea's first political transition from conservative to progressive rule—than had been possible under South Korea's authoritarian governments. Such sentiments were fanned by the euphoria of the first inter-Korean summit in June 2000 and shared among progressives who imagined that inter-Korean reconciliation would soon obviate the need for a U.S. troop presence and diminish the restraining role of U.S.–South Korea alliance ties. A historical revisiting of previously untouchable topics such as the Rogun-ri massacre of Korean civilians by U.S. airpower in the early stages of the Korean War and highly publicized incidents involving U.S. off-duty soldiers and their families roiled the emotional dynamics around the U.S.–South Korea security relationship.

Following the Rogun-ri story, the South Korean media dug into Korean claims of compensation for injury from the wartime use of Agent Orange and reported that a U.S. Forces Korea (USFK) employee had discharged formaldehyde into the Han River, a source of drinking water for the citizens of Seoul.[19] There were also damage claims for errant live bombs dropped on the Koon-ni training range near the village of Maehyang-ri, which exacerbated negative emotions about the United States among the Korean public.[20] Further stirring negative sentiments toward the United States, South Koreans were aggrieved by a judging dispute over a short-track skating event during the 2002 Winter Olympics in Salt Lake City, Utah; growing evidence of public differences over North Korea highlighted by President George W. Bush's reference in his 2002 State of the Union address to North Korea as part of an "axis of evil" along with Iran and Iraq; and the June 2002 accidental killing of two middle-school Korean girls by a U.S. military vehicle returning from training on a highway north of Seoul.

The introduction of these incidents into discussions about the U.S.–South Korea alliance stoked concerns in Washington and Seoul about anti-Americanism in South Korea and catalyzed South Korean desires to assert greater autonomy over their own affairs, or at least to demand more rapid changes in the management of what had been for decades a patron-client relationship in which the United States held predominant power. A 2002 survey of national attitudes in forty-two countries conducted by the Pew Research Center revealed that 44 percent of South Koreans held unfavorable views of the United States, which represented the highest level in Asia. Almost 57 percent of South Koreans favored the U.S. withdrawal of forces from South Korea by the end of 2002, a figure exceeded only by polling taken immediately following the historic first inter-Korean summit in June 2000.[21]

Negative views of the United States indirectly contributed to the 2002 election of the progressive Roh Moo-hyun as Kim Dae-jung's successor, though the main campaign issues involved desires for domestic reforms that would address regional inequalities and promote social equity. Nonetheless, Roh publicly asked during his presidential campaign "What's wrong with being anti-American?"[22]

Under Roh, South Korea's push for greater autonomy and cultivation of an independent image under the guise of anti-Americanism brought about alliance frictions but also catalyzed a careful examination within his administration of the challenges and opportunities associated with alliance cooperation. Roh's national security policy incorporated populist themes and rhetoric but ultimately was pragmatic in its efforts to enhance South Korea's independent political and military capabilities within the bounds of the alliance.[23] Roh's push for revised operational command and control arrangements for the South Korean military was motivated by a desire to assert greater autonomy and independence in defense and foreign policy. These demands stimulated careful joint examination of the future of the U.S.–South Korea alliance and coincided with both the withdrawal of a combat brigade from the Korean Peninsula for transfer to Iraq and the implementation of the Global Posture Review under then secretary of defense Donald Rumsfeld. Roh raised the level of South Korean defense spending and invested in the construction of a blue-water naval capacity that subsequently partnered with the United States and other nations in antipiracy operations in the Gulf of Aden. The United States and South Korea discussed how they might use USFK for off-peninsula operations, but this matter was sensitive to autonomy-desiring progressives who were worried that such deployments would imply South Korean political support for U.S. military operations that would inevitably entrap South Korea in potential regional conflicts.[24]

The apparent tensions between the Bush and Roh administrations implied the possibility of the weakening or degradation of the U.S.–South Korea alliance but ultimately became opportunities to expand the scope and application of alliance cooperation beyond the Korean Peninsula. The key to this evolution was the Roh administration's decision to pursue its aspirations for greater autonomy within the framework and boundaries of the alliance with the United States. By the end of the Roh administration, the outlines of a shared vision for enduring alliance cooperation had emerged. Under a decade of conservative rule during the Lee Myung-bak and Park Geun-hye administrations from 2008 to 2017, the alliance largely flourished, underpinned by the mutual embrace of a Joint Vision for the U.S.–South Korea Alliance adopted between Lee and President Barack Obama in June 2009 that broadened alliance cooperation beyond the Korean Peninsula for the first time.

South Korea again underwent a power transition to progressive political leadership under Moon Jae-in in May 2017 following the impeachment of Park Geun-hye. Moon brought back progressive leadership under circumstances much more adverse to the implementation of a progressive foreign policy platform that had remained largely unchanged since the Roh administration, with inter-Korean reconciliation, peaceful coexistence, and integration with North Korea as his top priorities. But the circumstances facing the Moon administration had changed significantly in the ten years since a progressive South Korean leader had last held power. During that time, North Korea had made significant progress in nuclear and missile testing and development, erasing doubt about the country's capabilities.

President Moon's support base included individuals within the South Korean prodemocracy movement who have been strongly associated with progressive and pro–North Korean ideology, including associations with pro–North Korean student groups from the 1980s. Many of the former "386" generation student leaders—now in their fifties and at the height of their ability to influence leadership within South Korean society—were members of radical study groups for the *juche* (self-reliance) ideology during their university days that required pledges of loyalty to the North Korean leadership. Among the most well-known and influential members of the Moon administration with past ties to student radical organizations were Moon's first chief of staff Im Jong-seok and his third minister of unification Lee In-young.

Under the Moon and Trump administrations, there was a heightened risk of a toxic and corrosive erosion of U.S.–South Korea alliance coordination and capabilities as a consequence of the interaction between North Korea–first influences within the Moon administration and the America-First rhetoric of the Trump administration. But the Moon administration faced three important structural constraints to its pursuit of greater autonomy within the structure of the alliance with the United States.

First, strong South Korean public support insulated the alliance from South Korean progressive challenges and heightened the risk of blame to President Moon in the event of any deterioration in relations with the United States. Second, Moon's ruling party controlled only a plurality of seats in South Korea's National Assembly. This circumstance made it difficult for the Moon administration to win legislative support for many initiatives and strengthened opposition voices in parliamentary hearings, including hearings to vet Moon administration cabinet appointments. But following the April 2020 National Assembly elections, the Moon administration enjoyed a substantial majority and consequently felt less constrained in pursuing progressive policy initiatives, leading to new areas of tension in the U.S.–South Korea relationship over policy toward North Korea. A third constraint on the Moon administration's freedom to aggressively pursue progressive foreign policies was the relatively unfavorable external environment for Moon's policies toward North Korea created by the North's reluctance to engage in dialogue and cooperation with South Korea. North Korea's noncooperation also had the effect of reducing friction in South Korean coordination with the United States because, even if the United States were to acquiesce to the Moon administration's initiatives in pursuit of inter-Korean economic projects, the likelihood of North Korea agreeing to cooperate remained low.

Historically, the likelihood that conservative expressions of Korean nationalism would generate tensions within the alliance has been less likely than the prospect of conflicts within the alliance under South Korean progressive leadership. The lesser likelihood of conservative-induced tensions within the alliance makes sense when one considers that the chief fears among conservatives regarding the alliance are perceptions of excessive U.S. restraint on the scope of South Korean responses to North Korean provocations or the risk of U.S. abandonment that would accompany U.S. withdrawal or failure to fulfill its security pledges to South Korea.

An example of conservative frustration with U.S. imposition of restraint on South Korea's response to North Korean provocations revealed itself in November 2009 in the aftermath of North Korea's artillery shelling of the South Korean–controlled Yeonpyeong Island located only a few miles from the North Korean mainland. The shelling resulted in four South Korean deaths, two of whom were the first South Korean civilian combat deaths since the end of the Korean War. South Korean internal debates over how to respond included recommendations by the Ministry of Defense to President Lee Myung-bak to authorize South Korean air strikes on the source of the artillery fire and on the North Korean command center that gave the instructions to fire. But these recommendations were opposed by USFK and the Obama administration out of fear that an overly aggressive South Korean response would lead to an escalatory spiral, including the possibility that North Korea might use antiaircraft artillery not only against South Korean fighters but also against civilian commercial aircraft taking off and landing at the Incheon airport.

The incident led to the review and revision of South Korean protocols for handling both the immediate response and consultative mechanisms necessary to authorize South Korea's retaliatory response and the procedures for consultation between U.S. and South Korean military authorities to ensure a fully coordinated counterprovocation response. Lee received public criticism in the South Korean media during this period for his moderate response to the North Korean shelling involving civilian casualties, revealing the possibility that nationalist-fueled responses by South Korean conservatives regarding the relative robustness or timidity of Lee's response might lead to conflicts within the alliance between the United States and South Korea. Conservatives have persistently sent low-key signals to the United States advocating for the reintroduction of tactical nuclear weapons to South Korea, underscoring their discomfort with how North Korea might try to exploit its nuclear advantage vis-à-vis the South.

During the Trump administration, South Korean conservatives found themselves perplexed by the potential impact on the alliance of Trump's summit diplomacy with Kim Jong-un, including his unilateral announcement without prior consultation with the Moon administration of the suspension of joint U.S.–South Korean military exercises following Trump's June 2018 summit with Kim. Although South Korean conservative discomfort with these developments was largely drowned out by the Moon administration's strong support for Trump-Kim summitry, Trump's actions pointed to the possibility that U.S.–North Korea summit diplomacy could lead to a compromise of U.S. commitments to South Korea's defense if U.S. security commitments were to be circumscribed or implemented prior to North Korea's denuclearization. South Korean conservatives quietly questioned the reliability of the U.S. security commitment and worried about

Trump's transactional approach to the alliance that signaled a disregard for the long-standing U.S. commitment to the protection of South Korea.

The return to power of conservatives under the Yoon Suk-yeol administration and the early focus on the need to strengthen U.S. extended deterrence commitments to South Korea in response to North Korea's continued nuclear and missile development provide evidence of both conservative priorities and concerns. But they also signal the potential risks to the alliance that might emanate from conservative concerns about the credibility of U.S. extended deterrence commitments to South Korea. Such concerns might be magnified in the face of North Korean efforts to neutralize U.S. military support for South Korea's defense by threatening a nuclear response to U.S. intervention in the event of a military crisis on the Korean Peninsula or by the return to power of a U.S. president who might renege on U.S. security commitments under the pretext of pursuing noninvolvement in a conflict on the Korean Peninsula.

STRUCTURE OF THE BOOK

This book argues that despite strengthened institutionalization of alliance coordination toward North Korea in recent years, the U.S.–South Korea alliance faces significant risks and dangers in the event that both countries were to elect nationalist America-First and Korea-first leaders. These risks and dangers have both internal and external sources, particularly South Korean nationalist ideology, American retrenchment, and domestic political polarization. Given this possibility, the book explores how the weakening or possible degradation of the alliance might influence U.S. and South Korean security strategies and the Northeast Asian regional security order. Based on this analysis, the book concludes with recommendations to the United States and South Korea on how to maintain and strengthen the alliance.

Chapter 2 looks at the impact of various leadership configurations on U.S.–South Korea alliance cooperation, with special reference to the impact of political leadership on alliance management between 2017 and 2022, to analyze the influence of political leadership on alliance cohesion and the sources of resiliency and vulnerability within the U.S.–South Korea alliance. While the expansion of common threats from China and North Korea has catalyzed enhanced institutionalization and cohesion between the United States and South Korea under pro-alliance leadership in both countries, domestic political polarization and the prioritization of self-interest over shared interests have the potential to neutralize and weaken the ability of the two countries to work together in pursuit of common objectives.

Chapter 3 analyzes the impact of South Korean domestic political polarization and progressive ideology on the alliance under the Moon administration. South Korean progressives rode to power in 2017 following a corruption and impeachment scandal that resulted in the discrediting of conservative leadership and pursued a reform drive aimed at the "eradication of past evils." Moon administration efforts to reshape the role and focus of the prosecution and press for constitutional revisions and tactical tweaks designed to gain electoral advantages contributed to a deepening of domestic political polarization. The chapter argues that political polarization remains an impediment to effective alliance coordination under the Yoon administration.

Chapter 4 explores how South Korean progressives prioritized reconciliation with North Korea and contributed to domestic political polarization around approaches to Japan, resulting in strains in the U.S.–South Korea alliance. The Moon administration's foreign policy was premised on the desirability and even inevitability of inter-Korean tension reduction leading to peaceful coexistence and economic integration. A primary assumption of South Korean progressives has been that a more powerful, independent Korean Peninsula would be able to defend itself against the perceived threat from Japan and manage China's rise without assistance or constraints imposed by the United States. But this assumption has shown itself to be impossible to achieve in practice, even if it appeals to Korean national pride and aspirations for peace. Instead, a nuclear North Korea represents a more cataclysmic and dangerous threat to South Korean security and prosperity than ever before, but conservative efforts to address these challenges together with the United States may generate new tensions that the Yoon administration will have to manage.

Chapter 5 reviews how North Korea has historically inserted itself into South Korea's domestic political struggles through influence operations intended to subvert South Korean institutions and induce division and anarchy in South Korea's democratic system. North Korea's long-standing subversion strategy has utilized propaganda and attempted to capitalize on South Korean political discontent to weaken South Korean domestic cohesion and foment tension as part of an enduring competition for legitimacy as the rightful government on the peninsula. The North's *uri minjok-kkiri* (our nation together) strategy relies on subversion and cooptation to enhance North Korean influence over South Korean domestic policies and inter-Korean relations, while the *tongnam bongmi* (communicate with the United States, ignore South Korea) strategy seeks to divide the United States and South Korea by marginalizing South Korea and emphasizing relations with the United States.

Chapter 6 assesses the challenge to the U.S.–South Korea alliance from China's rising influence and desire to replace the United States as the hegemon in Northeast Asia. The political dimension involves Chinese efforts to divide the alliance by magnifying differences in U.S. and South Korean threat perceptions of China, preferred strategies for dealing with China, and relative dependencies on China. South Korea's proximity and small geographic size compared to China make it much more vulnerable to Chinese retaliation than the United States and therefore much more willing to consider accommodation strategies for managing the bilateral relationship. The U.S. distance from China and larger size relative to South Korea make it both less vulnerable to Chinese intimidation and more willing to consider adversarial responses to China's rising influence. South Korean analysts have proposed contending strategies for buffering South Korea from the pressures to make a strategic choice between the two sides, but none of these strategies is likely to fully insulate South Korea from contending pressures between China and the United States.

Chapter 7 reviews the economic dimensions of the China challenge to the alliance, which have rested for the past decade on the tension between

South Korea's pursuit of economic opportunity through trade with China and continued reliance on the United States as its primary security guarantor. South Korea is vulnerable to economic pressure from both sides, given its deep involvement in the Chinese market in sectors such as telecommunications and its close military ties with the United States that require a secure national security infrastructure. The Biden administration's prioritization of supply chain resiliency in the semiconductor, electric battery and electric vehicle, and pharmaceutical sectors securitized technology and attempted to align South Korean private sector decisions on how to approach the Chinese and American markets, respectively, with U.S. interests. The Biden administration's strategy of securitizing high-end technologies in pursuit of closer economic alignment among like-minded nations in its technological competition with China generates new opportunities as well as risks for South Korea, which faces continued concerns about renewed Chinese economic retaliation in pursuit of its own political aims.

Chapter 8 evaluates rising doubts about the reliability of the U.S. commitment to defend South Korea during the Donald Trump administration. South Korean assumptions underpinning its dependence on a U.S. security guarantee are predicated on continued U.S. commitment to the liberal world order. However, the possibility that the United States will shed its commitment to international security, insist on prioritizing domestic issues, and abandon its leadership role in preserving the liberal international order remain a threat to the U.S.–South Korea security alliance. Thus, the alliance could come under siege from a narrowing U.S. commitment to preserving its international role and the resulting South Korean perception that U.S. security guarantees are no longer credible.

Chapter 9 imagines the hypothetical impact of the end of the U.S.–South Korea security alliance on the U.S. security strategy. The chapter argues that in the absence of the U.S. alliance with South Korea, the United States will either increase its reliance on the alliance with Japan or face a drastically weakened regional security profile resulting from U.S. retrenchment or withdrawal from the region, including from Japan. These changes in the U.S. standing and presence arising from a shift in the geopolitical orientation of the Korean Peninsula would dramatically strengthen the geostrategic role of China.

Chapter 10 offers hypothetical South Korean security options and strategies in the absence of the U.S.–South Korea security alliance. The chapter argues that absent the anchoring function of the alliance, South Korea would achieve its long-standing dream of autonomy but face higher stakes and higher-cost security choices in an effort to navigate shifting strategic rivalries among major powers including China, Japan, and the United States.

Finally, chapter 11 considers the implications of the weakening of the U.S.–South Korea alliance for the Asian regional security order and provides recommendations to the United States and South Korea for how to sustain the alliance.

2

THE INFLUENCE OF THE TRUMP
AND MOON ADMINISTRATIONS
ON U.S.–SOUTH KOREAN
ALLIANCE MANAGEMENT

T he U.S.–South Korea alliance has demonstrated a combination of durability and vulnerability as it grappled with the impact of deepening political polarization and leadership transitions on U.S. and South Korean political leadership between 2017 and 2022. During that brief period, the alliance experienced the impact of every possible ideological combination of U.S. and South Korean political leadership within the alliance. In South Korea, a conservative caretaker government served as Trump's Korean counterpart following Park Geun-hye's impeachment in early 2017, followed by the election of the progressive Moon Jae-in administration from May 2017 to the end of the Donald Trump administration in January 2021. The U.S. political transition from Trump to Joe Biden then paired liberal Democratic Party leaderships in South Korea and the United States from January 2021 to May 2022. Finally, the Biden administration worked with a conservative South Korean administration following the election of Yoon Suk-yeol as Moon's successor in May 2022.

Although the U.S.–South Korea alliance showed remarkable resiliency during this period due to the shared operational need of alliance managers to work together in response to external threats from North Korea and China, it also revealed a potential vulnerability during periods when political leaders on one side or the other were tempted to pursue perceived national interests in competition with or to the exclusion of alliance partners. For instance, advocates for an "America First" agenda such as President Trump called out the perceived deficiencies of partner contributions to alliances, accused allies of self-interested opportunism, or raised doubts about the credibility of partners to meet shared commitments. This led to the erosion of trust as alliance partners were tempted to pursue hedging. At the same time, the Moon administration's single-minded focus on establishing peace with North Korea in spite of its provocations and its pursuit of balanced relations with both the United States and China despite China's use of economic retaliation became a potential test of South Korean fidelity to U.S. interests and objectives over the interests of U.S. adversaries.

This chapter evaluates alliance management through four distinct types of political leadership. Table 2.1 illustrates the relative impact of the leadership of presidents Trump, Moon, Biden, and Yoon on alliance management outcomes, providing an opportunity to assess the various leadership combinations on the cohesion of the alliance. The chapter then considers the impact of the leadership of Donald J. Trump and Moon Jae-in on the U.S.–South Korea alliance, focusing on U.S.–South Korea summitry with North Korea under Trump and Moon. It also considers the Moon administration's efforts to manage relations with the United States under the Trump administration in comparison with leadership efforts by other U.S. alliance partners. Finally, the chapter concludes with a comparison of the leadership of Trump and Moon to the Biden administration's approaches to alliance management with the Moon and Yoon administrations.

U.S.–SOUTH KOREA RELATIONS BETWEEN TRUMP AND CONSERVATIVE ACTING PRESIDENT HWANG KYO-AHN

Revelations of the political scandal that led to the impeachment of Park Geun-hye unfolded simultaneously with the November 2016 presidential

TABLE 2.1 Impact of Partisan Political Leadership on U.S.-South Korea Alliance Management

TRUMP ADMINISTRATION AND HWANG KYO-AHN GOVERNMENT (JANUARY–MAY 2017)	TRUMP ADMINISTRATION AND MOON ADMINISTRATION (MAY 2017–JANUARY 2021)
Tensions over management of differing security and economic priorities Domestic scandal hobbles Korean political leadership Internal coordination difficulties hamper alliance management	Divergence of priorities and conflict over policy preferences Political frictions over priority and value of alliance diminish ability to respond together to peninsular and regional threats Alliance coordination eviscerated
BIDEN ADMINISTRATION AND YOON ADMINISTRATION (MAY 2022–NOVEMBER 2024)	**BIDEN ADMINISTRATION AND MOON ADMINISTRATION (JANUARY 2021–MAY 2022)**
Deepened institutional coordination within alliance and broadened scope of alliance objectives Combined approaches to deterrence and engagement toward North Korea Cooperative approach to addressing security and economic implications of China's rise	Tensions over management of differing security and economic priorities Gaps in threat perception of North Korea generate tensions in alliance management Gaps in perceptions of China generate frustration and complicate alliance coordination on regional security policy

election and inauguration of Donald J. Trump. Although Park made a congratulatory call to Trump on November 10, her political leadership was in the process of unraveling following revelations of possible corruption that led to a massive drop in public support.[1] Peaceful demonstrations in the center of Seoul mobilized the largest public participation since the 1987 prodemocracy demonstrations that brought down the authoritarian Chun Doohwan regime, and Park was impeached by the National Assembly on December 9, 2016, a little over one month prior to Trump's inauguration.[2] Unlike the successful outreach and early meeting between Trump and the Japanese prime minister Abe Shinzo at Trump Tower while Trump was president-elect, Park's impeachment paralyzed South Korean outreach to the Trump administration during the transition period between the election and Trump's inauguration.[3] South Korea was unable to clarify the intent behind Trump's campaign criticisms of the Korea–U.S. Free Trade Agreement (KORUS FTA) or his early January public response on Twitter to Kim Jong-un's statements signaling the likely testing of a North Korean intercontinental ballistic missile (ICBM) in early 2017.[4]

The ability of the U.S. and South Korean bureaucracies to interact meaningfully with each other during the Trump transition and Park's impeachment was severely circumscribed on both sides. Trump reached out to hold a phone conversation with Acting President Hwang Kyo-ahn shortly following his inauguration on January 30, 2017, but the acting government's interactions with the Trump administration faced criticisms of overreach from Democratic Party legislators who anticipated the transition of South Korean political power from conservative to progressive hands.[5] Secretary of State Rex Tillerson met with Foreign Minister Yun Byung-se on March 17, 2017, and declared that "the policy of strategic patience has ended. We are exploring a new range of diplomatic, security, and economic measures."[6] The best U.S. senior officials could do during visits to Seoul at this time was to express resolve regarding the "ironclad" alliance and to hold the line in response to North Korea's escalation of intermediate range and intercontinental ballistic missile tests.[7] While it was clear that the conservative South Korean administration and the Trump administration were on the same page regarding the necessity to punish North Korea's violations of past UN Security Council resolutions through the strengthening of sanctions, South Korea's political vacuum hampered the ability of the acting government to take meaningful actions with the Trump administration during this period.

A notable instance that underscored the cost of South Korean political paralysis during this period involved the response to North Korea's first ICBM test under the Trump administration, which occurred on February 11, 2017, simultaneously with an early summit between Trump and Abe that included a dinner at Mar-a-Lago. Trump and Abe provided a joint condemnation of North Korea's test, and Trump emphasized his support for Japan but did not mention the alliance with South Korea. Due to South

Korea's political vacuum, it was not possible to coordinate a meaningful leader-level response with South Korea to North Korea's provocations. Instead, Trump stood next to Abe and stated that "the United States of America stands behind Japan, it's great ally, 100 percent," while failing to mention South Korea.[8] It was not possible for South Korea to gain traction with the Trump administration until a presidential election on May 10, 2017, that filled South Korea's political vacuum, with Moon Jae-in winning the election held sixty days following the Constitutional Court's upholding of Park's impeachment as stipulated under the Korean constitution. The extraordinary circumstances around the election meant that Moon took office without the benefit of a transition period to prepare his administration for office.

U.S.–SOUTH KOREA RELATIONS BETWEEN TRUMP AND MOON AND IMPACT ON ALLIANCE MANAGEMENT

Despite the shortness of time available to appoint senior officials to his new administration, Moon Jae-in made an important decision early in his administration to meet with Trump at the White House only six weeks following his election. Setting the date for an early summit meant that Moon and Trump would meet prior to Moon's participation in the G20 meeting in Germany scheduled for early July. This decision signaled Moon's prioritization of the alliance and his desire to establish a close relationship with Trump despite the appointment of pro–North Korea individuals as central figures in his administration, such as Moon's first chief of staff Im Jong-seok. Although Moon had run on a propeace and proreconciliation agenda with North Korea, his early meeting with Trump sent a signal that he intended to pursue his North Korea policy by promoting close cooperation with rather than independent of the United States. It also sent a signal that Moon was confident he would be able to convince Trump to pursue dialogue with North Korea even despite the escalation of U.S.–North Korea tensions and ongoing verbal sparring between Trump and the North Korean regime.

In a *Washington Post* interview prior to his White House meeting with Trump, Moon emphasized the necessity of close cooperation between the United States and South Korea on sanctions implementation, but he also framed the need for dialogue with North Korea even prior to his first meeting with the president both as Trump's idea and as one that South Korea might support Trump in realizing. Moon presented dialogue with North Korea as "actually very similar to the engagement that President Trump is talking about. He has put resolution of the North Korean nuclear issue at the top of his priority list, and he has employed a tactic of maximum pressure and engagement, but engagement [can only occur] if the conditions are right."[9]

The U.S.–South Korea Joint Statement issued after the meeting affirmed the "shared goal of complete, verifiable, and irreversible denuclearization of the Korean peninsula in a peaceful manner," the need for UN Security Council sanctions to impose "maximum pressure" on North Korea while also emphasizing that "the door to dialogue with the DPRK remains open under the right circumstances," and that "the United States and the ROK do not maintain a hostile policy toward the DPRK and, together with the rest of the international community, stand ready to offer a brighter future for the DPRK, if it chooses the right path. The two sides will closely coordinate on a joint DPRK policy, including efforts to create conditions necessary for denuclearization talks, through a high-level strategic consultation mechanism."[10] Despite apparent skepticism within the Trump administration over the Moon administration's emphasis on dialogue with North Korea, the Moon administration succeeded in inserting language into the joint statement that highlighted Moon's efforts to serve as an intermediary between Trump and North Korea toward the realization of a U.S.–North Korea denuclearization dialogue.

While Moon's primary goal in his White House meeting with Trump was to win support for dialogue between the Trump administration and North Korea, Trump's focus in the meeting was on the need to overhaul the KORUS FTA signed under the Obama administration. During his meeting in the Oval Office with Moon, Trump derided South Korean trade practices and demanded that South Korea take actions to reduce its 2016 $27 billion trade surplus with the United States to curb alleged dumping of South Korean steel in U.S. markets. Although the stridency of Trump's criticisms of South Korean trade practices apparently took the Moon administration by surprise, the Moon administration made it a priority to take Trump's economic criticisms of South Korea off the table following the summit by working closely with the Trump administration to forge a revised FTA that both responded to Trump's criticisms and gave Trump something he could point to as a victory. In this way, the Moon administration skillfully deflected and accommodated Trump's criticisms on economic issues to preserve cooperation and focus on Moon's main objective of supporting U.S. engagement efforts with North Korea.

Following his efforts to achieve alignment with Trump on a policy toward North Korea that emphasized both sanctions and dialogue, Moon gave a speech to the Korber Foundation on the sidelines of the G20 meeting in Germany that laid out his desire that South Korea be in the "driver's seat" in promoting inter-Korean cooperation and pledged his administration's efforts to achieve peace and "denuclearization of the Korean peninsula that guarantees the security of the North Korean regime," the establishment of a permanent peace regime and a "new economic map on the Korean peninsula," and the promotion of "nonpolitical exchange and cooperation projects" between the two Koreas.[11] Moon's speech in Germany initially seemed discordant with Trump's ramping up of tensions and his pledge to pursue "fire and fury" toward the North if Pyongyang continued to escalate its missile and nuclear testing to target the United States. But through this speech and a variety of unofficial contacts in the following months, the Moon administration enticed North Korea to return to dialogue and actively utilized its role as host of the 2018 Pyeongchang Winter Olympics as a pretext for creating opportunities for inter-Korean dialogue and reconciliation.

In the months following the June 2017 summit between Trump and Moon, the most important coordination channel between the United States and South Korea occurred through frequent telephone contact and occasional unpublicized visits to Washington by National Security Advisor

Chung Eui-yong with his counterpart H. R. McMaster. McMaster describes in his memoir how he expressed concerns to Chung that an overly conciliatory "Moonshine Policy" toward the North "would not mix well" with the Trump administration's focus on "maximum pressure," but he also expressed confidence in Chung as "the right person in the leftist Moon government to help prevent the perfect storm" that might "undermine" policy coordination toward North Korea.[12] Given the sensitivity of the Moon administration's efforts to engage with North Korea and the desire to avoid publicity that might come from leaks within both governments, information regarding communications between the White House and Blue House on North Korea policy during this period was tightly held within both governments.

Rhetorical tensions ramped up between Washington and Pyongyang following Trump's August 8, 2017, statement that if North Korea continues to escalate its nuclear threat toward the United States, "they will be met with fire and fury like the world has never seen."[13] Following North Korea's sixth and most powerful nuclear test on September 3, Trump tweeted a rare public criticism of the Moon administration that "South Korea is finding, as I have told them, that their talk of appeasement with North Korea will not work, they only understand one thing."[14] This tweet was accompanied by a call between Trump and Moon during which Trump agreed to lift restrictions on payload limits for South Korean missiles in response to North Korea's nuclear test.[15] Trump used his address at the UN General Assembly on September 19 to declare that "Rocketman [Kim Jong-un] is on a suicide mission for himself" if North Korea continued to threaten the United States.[16] Following those threats, Secretary of Defense James Mattis visited South Korea for consultations in late October to further coordinate with the Moon administration.

TRUMP'S VISIT TO SOUTH KOREA, NORTH KOREA'S CHARM OFFENSIVE, AND THE PYEONGCHANG OLYMPICS

Against the backdrop of the ongoing escalation of North Korea's long-range missile testing and rising rhetorical tensions between the United States and North Korea, President Moon prepared to host President Trump during his visit to Asia that the White House characterized as intended to "strengthen international resolve to denuclearize North Korea."[17] In advance of Trump's arrival, Moon declared in a speech to the National Assembly "Our top priority is to maintain peace on the Korean Peninsula. Thus, armed conflict must be avoided under any circumstance. No military action on the Korean Peninsula shall be taken without prior consent of the Republic of Korea."[18] The following week, Moon welcomed Trump and his wife, Melania, to the Blue House with pomp and circumstance as the first state visit by an American president to South Korea in five years and as the first state visitor of the Moon administration. In his welcoming comments to Trump, Moon congratulated Trump on the one-year anniversary of his election as president of the United States, praised Trump for his international leadership on North Korea, and expressed his hope that Trump's visit to the region would mark "a turning point" in resolving the North Korean nuclear issue.[19] Trump had anticipated that he would visit the Demilitarized Zone (DMZ) by helicopter during his visit to South Korea, but those plans were canceled as a result of weather conditions.

In his address the following day at the National Assembly, Trump provided a scathing critique of North Korea's nuclear program and its human rights record, but he also addressed Kim Jong-un directly, stating that "we will offer a path to a much better future. It begins with an end to the aggression of your regime, a stop to your development of ballistic missiles, and complete, verifiable, and total denuclearization."[20] North Korea was also a centerpiece for discussion in Trump's summit meetings with other leaders during his trip, including with Abe Shinzo and Xi Jinping.

Following Trump's Asia visit, North Korea launched its longest-range missile, a Hwasong-15 type that North Korea described as equipped with a "super-large heavy warhead which is capable of striking the whole mainland of the United States."[21] Following the launch, North Korea declared that its program was complete. By claiming that the missile was the "most powerful ICBM, which meets the goal of completion of the rocket weaponry system development set by the DPRK," Kim Jong-un could claim that he was pursuing diplomacy from a position of strength. Alongside North Korea's declaration, the UN under-secretary-general for political affairs Jeffrey Feltman brought to North Korea an invitation for dialogue from the

Trump administration, and there were multiple rumored informal contacts between North and South Korean officials in advance of the Pyeongchang Olympics designed to lay the groundwork for the easing of tensions and creation of a diplomatic opening between North Korea and the United States.[22]

In his 2018 New Year's address, Kim signaled a turn toward diplomacy by declaring his country's willingness to participate in the February 2018 Pyeongchang Olympic Games in South Korea.[23] With only weeks left prior to the start of the Pyeongchang Olympics, the Moon administration rapidly opened negotiations with North Korea to secure its participation in consultation with the International Olympic Committee and the United States.[24] But those negotiations were only loosely coordinated with the Trump administration and generated some criticism that South Korea's engagement with North Korea could undermine the Trump administration's sanctions drive and emphasis on maximum pressure.

After successfully negotiating the participation of a North Korean athletic delegation and cheering squad and the fielding of a unified women's ice hockey team at the Pyeongchang Olympics, the Moon administration attempted on the sidelines of the opening and closing ceremonies to broker a high-level contact between North Korean officials including Kim Yo-jong, the sister of Kim Jong-un and a rising influence in the regime's leadership, and U.S. counterparts.[25] But senior Trump administration officials including Vice President Mike Pence purposefully avoided direct public contact with the North Korean delegation and opted for a private meeting with North Korea's head of state Kim Yong-nam and Kim Yo-jong. But the proposed meeting, which Pence stated would have had Trump's approval, was canceled, reportedly on orders from Pyongyang.[26]

A week following the closure of the Pyeongchang Olympics, Moon sent National Intelligence Service Director Suh Hoon and National Security Advisor Chung Eui-yong as special envoys to Pyongyang for a meeting with Kim, following which the pair traveled back to Seoul and onward to Washington for consultations at the White House with Trump. It was only after the two delivered Kim's message directly to the White House that Trump decided over the objections of his advisors to accept an invitation to meet directly with Kim. As the main focus of dealing with North Korea switched from pressure to engagement, alliance coordination between the U.S. and South Korean governments became more challenging.[27]

MOON/TRUMP SUMMITRY WITH KIM JONG-UN AND U.S.–SOUTH KOREA COORDINATION

The announcement of a summit between Trump and Kim Jong-un introduced a new phase of alliance-based policy coordination toward North Korea around the premise of a coordinated strategy aimed at achieving North Korea's denuclearization. The strategy and its implementation were primarily top-down, based on a shared understanding between Trump and Moon but not necessarily enjoying consensus support from the U.S. and South Korean bureaucracy and political elites.

Alongside the announcement of a Trump-Kim summit, the door to a renewal of inter-Korean summitry opened with preparatory negotiations aimed at holding an inter-Korean summit between Moon and Kim at Panmunjom. But it was not clear how successfully the two governments would be able to negotiate parallel summit tracks by the United States and South Korea respectively with North Korea. Instead, there were concerns on both sides that one side would get ahead of the other or make concessions that might disadvantage the other negotiating track, even despite affirming the shared negotiating objective of securing the complete dismantlement of North Korea's nuclear program. Those fears were allayed to some degree by a public statement by the summit preparation committee chairman Im Jong-seok that the inter-Korean and U.S.–North Korea summit preparation tracks would move forward in tandem with each other.[28]

The inter-Korean Panmunjom summit scheduled for April 27 provided Trump with an opportunity to size up Kim Jong-un and to benefit from Moon's briefings to Trump after he had hosted Kim on the southern side of the DMZ. In this respect, the inter-Korean summit placed Moon as an intermediary with Kim and as an interlocutor committed to paving the way for Kim's successful interaction with Trump. The inter-Korean summit focused primarily on the cessation of inter-Korean hostilities, the resumption of exchanges toward the objectives of "co-prosperity and independent reunification," and the building of a peace regime on the peninsula. However, given North Korea's historical preference for negotiating nuclear issues with the United States rather than with South Korea, an unusual topic of the summit declaration involved denuclearization pledges related to "the common goal of realizing through complete denuclearization, a nuclear-free Korean peninsula." In this respect, the Panmunjom summit language as well as language contained in a summit document between Xi and Kim only weeks prior to the inter-Korean summit provided a precedent for the Trump administration's efforts in Singapore to secure Kim's pledge of "complete denuclearization."[29] Following the inter-Korean summit Trump tweeted "After a furious year of missile launches and Nuclear testing, a historic meeting between North and South Korea is now taking place. Good things are happening, but only time will tell!" and "KOREAN WAR TO END! The United States, and all of its GREAT people, should be very proud of what is now taking place in Korea!"[30]

The main challenge and difficulty of coordinating a top-down approach between Trump and Moon for summitry with Kim became apparent in preparations for the Singapore summit. Moon, flushed with the success of the Panmunjom summit and encouraged by his extensive direct conversations with Kim, met Trump at the White House to debrief him on the summit results in early May. But Trump had been having misgivings regarding the planned summit in Singapore based on working-level coordination difficulties that had cropped up in negotiations between U.S. and North Korean working-level officials in Panmunjom and the failure of North Korean officials to participate in consultations in Singapore.

Worried that Kim might embarrass Trump and become a no-show in Singapore, Trump announced shortly following his meetings with Moon in the Oval Office his intention to cancel the summit with Kim.[31] This announcement set off an anxious scramble by Moon and his closest advisors to put the pieces of the summit back together through secret consultations with Kim. Revelations of a secret second Panmunjom summit held on May 25 devoted to rescuing the Trump-Kim meeting were not revealed until after Moon had secured and conveyed pledges by Kim that he was committed to meeting with Trump in Singapore.[32] Advance delegations successfully met with each other and the summit proceeded as scheduled, but the fragility of the U.S.–North Korea interactions and the thinness of personal trust between Trump and Moon in managing a process not under-girded by consensus within the U.S. and South Korean bureaucracies were revealed.

The main substantive negotiations between U.S. and North Korean working-level officials were held at Panmunjom, but those talks made lit-tle substantive progress. The task of managing negotiations over logistical issues between the two sides, the relative lack of time available for substan-tive negotiations, and the absence of authorization or overlap between the fundamental positions of the two sides prior to the summit made the pur-suit of conventional negotiations impossible. Given the top-down nature of preparations for the meeting, the ability of the United States and North Korea to forge a substantive agreement would depend on Trump and Kim rather than their subordinates. Beyond the mention of "complete denucle-arization" at the inter-Korean summit and efforts to keep the meeting on track, there was little else that Moon could contribute in advance of the Singapore summit.

Trump and Kim successfully staged an international diplomatic media spectacle in Singapore, but the joint declaration forged between the two leaders contained only four points: the establishment of new relations between the United States and North Korea, the desire to establish peace on the Korean Peninsula, North Korea's pledge to work toward "complete denuclearization," and North Korea's pledge to return the remains of POW/MIAs from the Korean War.[33] In addition, Trump caught the Moon administration by surprise with a unilateral pledge to Kim, which was only revealed to the Moon administration at Trump's press conference follow-ing the summit, to suspend joint U.S.–South Korean "war games" on the Korean Peninsula.[34]

Following the Singapore summit, the Moon administration sought to persuade the Trump administration to pursue an end-of-war declaration with North Korea as a means by which to draw North Korea into denucle-arization talks. But North Korea quickly rejected Secretary Pompeo's explo-ration of possible North Korean steps toward denuclearization in his visit to Pyongyang following the Singapore summit, accusing Pompeo and the

United States of "brigandish" behavior.[35] The Trump administration appointed Stephen Biegun as a special negotiator for North Korea and Pompeo visited Seoul and Pyongyang to introduce Biegun the following fall, but substantive high-level negotiations between Washington and Pyongyang never materialized.

In the meantime, the Moon administration sought to build momentum through inter-Korean channels as a means by which to catalyze progress between the United States and North Korea, but those efforts generated under-the-surface tensions between Washington and Seoul. Despite the lack of responsiveness in Pyongyang to U.S. efforts to move forward with working-level negotiations on denuclearization, the Moon administration actively continued to prepare for a third inter-Korean summit to be held between Moon and Kim in Pyongyang.[36]

In his Liberation Day address that year, Moon suggested that inter-Korean relations might be a catalyst for improvements in U.S.–North Korea relations.[37] His administration pursued negotiations on a range of symbolic inter-Korean military confidence-building measures including the creation of an inter-Korean liaison office designed to ease military tensions and build an atmosphere of peace between the two Koreas. Additional measures, negotiated in inter-Korean working-level talks at the DMZ in advance of the September summit in Pyongyang, were briefed to senior U.S. Forces Korea (USFK) military officials including Commander Vincent Brooks, but broader South Korean consultations with the UN Command and senior Pentagon officials were insufficient.[38]

Through the agreement that became known as the Comprehensive Military Agreement (CMA), the Moon administration sought to set a tone of conciliation and peace building with both North Korean and American counterparts. The agreement included concrete military confidence-building steps including restrictions on land, sea, and air exercises in the vicinity of the DMZ, pledges to transform the DMZ into a peace zone, the reestablishment of transport and communications lines, and the establishment of an inter-Korean joint military committee to mediate disputes between the two sides. The Pyongyang Declaration acknowledged these concrete confidence-building measures designed to transition the inter-

Korean relationship from war to peace and contained additional North Korean pledges including the dismantlement of a missile testing site at Dongchang-ri and the dismantlement of nuclear facilities at Yongbyon in return for U.S. "corresponding measures," widely interpreted as the relaxation of UN economic sanctions on North Korea.[39] In light of these agreements, North Korea anticipated the resumption of inter-Korean economic exchanges and South Korea anticipated the possibility of a fourth inter-Korean summit to be held in Seoul by the end of the year.

The contents of the Pyongyang Declaration and the CMA were greeted with concern among those in Washington who worried that Moon was too eager to accept North Korean pledges of denuclearization without ensuring the rigorous implementation of those pledges. Such fears were fanned by the tone of Moon's statements at the UN General Assembly in New York and in his subsequent visit to Europe the month after the inter-Korean summit in Pyongyang.[40] Moon's public hints that the Pyongyang Declaration marked the beginning of the denuclearization process and that soon economic restrictions on North Korea might be relaxed were wildly out of step with the expectations of Trump administration officials, and there is little evidence to suggest that the pathway forged by the Moon administration represented the thoughts of Trump himself. Indeed, the subsequent efforts to forge a U.S.–North Korea agreement prior to the Hanoi summit and the failure of the summit itself suggest that Moon had reached the limits of his ability to influence Trump and seriously misjudged Trump's willingness to support a possible pathway to denuclearization and the easing of tension offered in the Pyongyang Declaration.

In part due to the gap between Pyongyang's pledges to Seoul and its unwillingness to engage in working-level negotiations with Washington, implementation of the Pyongyang Declaration stalled. A U.S.–South Korea working group on policy toward North Korea was established to ensure a coordinated U.S.–South Korea response to North Korea, but far from being a venue by which to coordinate the relaxation of restrictions in line with the Moon administration's promises to North Korea, the working group served as a mechanism that restrained South Korea from prematurely relaxing economic sanctions on the North.[41] The Moon administration quietly sought in vain to convince the Trump administration to relax restrictions on transportation links and economic sanctions in line with the Pyongyang Declaration pledges.[42]

Following a delay in the dispatch of the North Korean senior official Kim Yong-chol to the United States that was anticipated to occur following the inter-Korean Pyongyang summit, arrangements were made for Kim to visit Washington in January 2019 together with Kim Hyuk-chol, a North Korean senior foreign ministry official selected to serve as a negotiating counterpart to Stephen Biegun.[43] The purpose of Kim's visit was to explore the possibility of a second Trump-Kim summit meeting that would move the implementation of the Singapore agreement forward. Public evidence of South Korea's role in facilitating the Kim Yong-chol meeting remains murky, but anticipation swirled in South Korea that a second summit might catalyze the resumption of U.S.–North Korea negotiations necessary to achieve a breakthrough in the peace and denuclearization agenda along the lines foreshadowed in the Pyongyang Declaration.[44] Much speculation revolved around the possibility that the United States and North Korea might negotiate a "small deal" in which partial relaxation of economic sanctions would occur in tandem with the dismantlement of North Korea's nuclear facilities at Yongbyon.

At the White House meeting between Trump and Kim Yong-chol, Trump agreed to move forward with a second Trump-Kim summit that was eventually scheduled for February in Hanoi. Anticipation of a second summit led to a flurry of negotiations between Biegun and his North Korean counterparts in Stockholm and Pyongyang. While those negotiations led to greater understanding on improving U.S.–North Korea relations and easing tensions between the two countries, it became clear that the North Korean negotiators were not empowered to negotiate on the nuclear issue.[45]

The Trump-Kim summit in Hanoi dramatically revealed the extent of the expectations gap between the United States and North Korea as Trump first negotiated with Kim on the outlines of an agreement, then walked out on the negotiations. Clearly, Kim had brought to Hanoi different expectations for a summit outcome and for what the United States would be willing to accept in the name of denuclearization. But Moon administration officials watching the Hanoi summit coverage from Seoul were equally disappointed, revealing a chasm in the positions of Trump and Kim following the Pyongyang summit that Moon had failed to close.

Trump's third summit with Kim at the DMZ on June 30, 2019, provided an ironic if fitting picture of the evolution of U.S.–South Korean coordination on policy toward North Korea. The North Koreans responded positively on short notice to Trump's tweet from Japan, and the U.S. and South Korean bureaucracies coordinated closely to negotiate an encounter with Kim at the DMZ in a scene that approximated a reprise of the inter-Korean Panmunjom summit in April of the previous year. Trump finally got the DMZ visit that was denied during his previous visit to South Korea in November 2017, a final photo opportunity with Kim, and the distinction of being the first sitting U.S. president to set foot on North Korean soil at the military demarcation line dividing North and South Korea. But Moon was reduced from intermediary to bystander on the outside of an hourlong bilateral meeting between Trump and Kim that ultimately produced no meaningful resumption of diplomatic negotiations to implement the Singapore Agreement.

The above review of North Korea policy coordination under the Trump and Moon administrations suggests that despite the extensive institutionalization of bureaucratic coordination between Washington and Seoul, the Trump and Moon administrations dealt with the most important aspects of North Korea policy in a highly centralized and top-down fashion. Moon and his administration took the most important and sensitive issues involving North Korea and efforts to establish dialogue with Kim Jong-un directly to the White House and if possible, directly to Donald Trump. This approach had the effect of diminishing the effectiveness of institutionalized bureaucratic coordination on the North Korea issue. The Moon administration utilized the top-down approach effectively to get Trump on board with the idea of summitry with Kim, but in the end, Moon was unable to persuade Trump or deliver the concessions Kim most desired to achieve a breakthrough in U.S.–North Korea relations and denuclearization. On issues not directly related to summitry with North Korea, the United States effectively used stronger institutionalization of bureaucratic coordination on North Korea policy as a brake and a means by which to ensure that the Moon administration did not improvise or deviate substantially from the main U.S. policy framework of maximum pressure alongside dialogue with North Korea.

OTHER ALLIANCE MANAGEMENT COORDINATION ISSUES UNDER TRUMP AND MOON

Beyond policy coordination on North Korea, Trump showed a personal interest and had a direct impact on two additional issues as part of U.S.–South Korea alliance management. These issues involved Trump's handling of economic relations, and specifically his desire to reset the U.S.–South Korea trade relationship by replacing the Obama-era KORUS FTA with his administration's own agreement, and Trump's desire to dramatically increase South Korea's financial contribution toward the cost of the U.S. troop presence on the Korean Peninsula. In both cases, Trump pursued his own desires despite bureaucratic resistance from within his own administration, while the Moon administration pursued a strategy of accommodation on trade and a strategy of obdurate resistance toward the renegotiation of South Korean support for costs related to the U.S. troop presence.

Aside from the specific issues on which Trump took a personal interest, other issues were managed primarily by alliance managers who took policy direction from the White House and Blue House, but did not have to contend with direct, sustained personal interest and/or intervention from Trump or Moon themselves. Significant issues left mainly to alliance managers to resolve within the contours of the respective policies of each administration include regional policy coordination toward China, Japan, and Southeast Asia.

RENEGOTIATION OF THE KORUS FTA

President Moon appeared to have been caught by surprise in his June 2017 White House summit meeting regarding Trump's personal vehemence toward the KORUS FTA and the perceived imbalances in the U.S.–South Korea trade relationship. Since Moon had placed his top priority on securing Trump's cooperation on North Korea policy, he directed his administration to pursue an accommodative approach to addressing the Trump administration's grievances on trade. This proved to be a wise policy given that Trump almost unilaterally abrogated the KORUS FTA if it had not been for Gary Cohn's decision to remove the legislation prepared for Trump's signature from his desk in the Oval Office.[46] Moon's accommodative approach included both efforts to proactively reduce South Korea's bilateral merchandise trade surplus by increasing purchases of U.S. goods and defensive efforts to dissuade the Trump administration from applying tariffs on imports of South Korean steel to the U.S. market.

As a result, the Moon administration did not seek to draw out KORUS FTA negotiations and in fact handed Trump the first major trade agreement revision of his administration. This strategy of accommodation not only helped remove South Korea as a target of Trump's public criticisms on trade but turned the KORUS FTA into a positive talking point for Trump that he repeatedly used as evidence of his administration's accomplishments, as discussed in chapter 8.

The revised KORUS FTA included some major pledges to ease import restrictions on U.S.-made automobiles for sale in South Korea and accepted tariff restrictions likely to delay South Korean companies from entering the U.S. light truck market as well as pledges, under the shadow of U.S. threats to impose tariffs on South Korean steel exports, to voluntarily limit shipments of Korean steel to the United States. The agreement also pledged to address unfair South Korean currency practices and to expand U.S. access to the South Korean pharmaceutical market.[47]

COST RECOVERY FOR U.S. TROOPS
STATIONED IN SOUTH KOREA

Alongside grievances regarding the bilateral U.S.–South Korea trade relationship, Trump paid close attention to the financial contributions of U.S. allies in return for U.S. defense and troop commitments abroad. Trump's initial attention on this issue focused on NATO, where he forcefully demanded that NATO members live up to their pledges to commit 2 percent of GDP to defense and threatened to pull out of the alliance. South Korean defense expenditures exceeded NATO levels at around 3 percent of GDP, but that did not stop Trump from taking issue with the Special Measures Agreement (SMA) negotiations by demanding a substantial increase in the scope of South Korea's contribution from past levels.

Historically, the amount of South Korea's contribution in support of the U.S. presence, which constituted the traditional scope of the SMA negotiations, was restricted to contributions covering specific U.S. operational costs on the peninsula and the salaries of local Korean employees who worked on U.S. bases. Trump sought to expand the scope of South Korean contributions to cover the costs of U.S. deployments to the region and exercises on the Korean Peninsula, among other costs. But Trump's demands were not easily translated into the traditional framework, so the Trump administration settled on a one-year extension of the SMA in 2017 rather than the traditional three-year time span. The one-year extension allowed the Trump administration to introduce a new global framework for determining cost sharing for countries hosting U.S. forces while also continuing negotiations to expand the scope of South Korea's contribution.[48] By revising the cost-sharing framework with South Korea in such a manner as to double South Korea's contribution from under $1 billion per year to around $5 billion annually, Trump hoped to use the conclusion of a revised framework with South Korea as leverage in upcoming cost-sharing negotiations with Japan in which the Trump administration would demand an even larger increase in Japan's financial contribution from $2.5 billion to $8 billion to support U.S. troops stationed there.[49]

Trump's transactional approach to assessing the contributions of allies in support of U.S. defense pledges encountered opposition from both allies and congressional critics who judged the approach to be overly mercenary and heavy-handed, as discussed in further detail in chapter 8. In addition, Trump's proposals faced significant resistance from the Korean public, which valued the U.S. presence but rejected the idea that South Korea's ongoing contributions were insufficient, especially considering South Korea's financial support for the construction of a new $10 billion base at

Camp Humphreys for which South Korea had paid over 90 percent of the costs. In light of South Korean public resistance, the Moon administration offered a double-digit increase in its contributions to the U.S. presence in South Korea while rejecting Trump's proposal for the revised framework for assessing South Korean costs. U.S.–South Korean cost-sharing negotiations dragged on into 2020 as the Moon administration simply waited out the result of the U.S. presidential election. With the return of the Biden administration, SMA negotiations on South Korea's contribution were rapidly concluded with the acceptance of South Korea's best offer as a means by which to clear impediments to cooperation in the name of reinvigorating the alliance.

COORDINATION OF POLICIES TOWARD CHINA

The Moon administration sought to stabilize South Korea's relationship with China following its economic retaliation for South Korea's decision to allow the deployment of the Terminal High Altitude Air Defense (THAAD) in South Korea. As a presidential candidate, Moon criticized the process by which the Park administration had decided on the deployment and its location, but he did not block the deployment. Once Moon became president, Moon's foreign minister Kang Kyung-hwa sought to restore the relationship with China by announcing a "three no's" policy (no deployment of additional THAAD units, no trilateral missile defense cooperation with Japan and the United States, and no trilateral U.S.–Japan–South Korea security alliance) based on consultations with China. The THAAD deployment continued to be a low-level source of irritation between the Moon and Trump administrations due to the Moon administration's failure to clear protesters from the road supplying the THAAD battery site, which remained accessible only by helicopter as a result of the continued presence of protesters at the THAAD site in Seongju.

As discussed further in chapter 6, the Moon administration maintained an expectant and respectful posture toward China in hopes of securing Xi Jinping's cooperation and support for inter-Korean reconciliation, exchanges, and cooperation. Moon's insistence on maintaining this posture led his administration to pursue policies of choice avoidance in hopes of maintaining both bilateral economic opportunities with China and a close security relationship with the United States. Following the announcement of the Trump administration's 2017 National Security Strategy that identified China as a potential adversary and as the rivalry between the United States and China mounted, South Korea found itself under increasing pressure to align with the United States given South Korea's shared values and the security alliance. While the Moon administration was willing to pursue security cooperation with the United States below the surface, senior Moon administration officials avoided direct public criticisms of Chinese actions even as U.S.–China tensions mounted and the importance of policy coordination toward China became a more important priority within the alliance. The South Korean ambassador to the United States Lee Soo-hyuk suggested that South Korea might benefit from the U.S.–China rivalry by avoiding choosing one side or another, and Foreign Minister Chung Eui-yong actively sought to balance South Korea's foreign policy orientation between Washington and Beijing.[50]

Meanwhile, the Trump administration took a sharply critical turn in its policies toward China including rhetorical blasts from Secretary of State Pompeo and Vice President Pence. In this environment, the Moon administration actively avoided being called out by the United States, brushing off questions about whether South Korea might join the Quadrilateral Security Dialogue (Quad) or other economic cooperation regimes proposed by senior administration officials in the waning days of the Trump administration.[51] Although China did not emerge as a major issue of public discussion between Trump and Moon, there remained a palpable distance between the two administrations in their approaches toward China.

COORDINATION OF POLICIES TOWARD JAPAN

The Trump administration did not support Asian regionalism, preferring to handle relations with each of its allies bilaterally. Thus, Trump neither had a personal interest in promoting coordinated policies between Japan and South Korea nor did he prioritize the establishment and maintenance of a bureaucratic framework capable of managing frictions between Japan and South Korea. In the absence of such a coordinating framework, it should not be surprising that Japan–South Korea relations deteriorated under a progressive South Korean president and a conservative Japanese administration. But against the backdrop of Trump's preference for bilateral management of relations and his suspicion of allies, there was no safety net readily available to prevent the deterioration of relations between Japan and South Korea.

As discussed in detail in chapter 3, relations between the progressive Moon administration and the conservative Abe administration began to deteriorate when the Moon administration conducted an internal review of the steps leading to the 2015 comfort woman agreement during the Park Geun-hye administration. An October 2018 South Korean Supreme Court decision holding Japanese private firms financially accountable for forced labor practices under the management of wartime predecessor companies seven decades earlier led the Abe administration to question whether the Moon administration was seeking to revise the 1965 Japan–South Korea normalization treaty and claims agreement, which Japan interpreted as settling all outstanding claims.

The Japan–South Korea relationship entered a cycle of deterioration involving a June 2019 Japanese announcement of economic restrictions on precursor chemicals and processes essential to the manufacture of semiconductors, and South Korea retaliated weeks later by threatening to withdraw from a bilateral information-sharing agreement that had strong support from the United States. The Trump administration found itself powerless to halt the deterioration. Although National Security Advisor John Bolton requested both U.S. allies to adhere to a "standstill agreement" aimed at halting the deterioration in ties, the main focus of his July 2019 visit to both countries was to win support for Trump's burden-sharing scheme in which both countries would face exorbitant increases in the amount of their contribution for the U.S. troop presence in Asia.[52] Having abandoned regular vice-minister-level trilateral consultations with Japan and South Korea that had been established under the Obama administration in 2015, Trump administration senior officials struggled to generate sufficient leverage to overcome the intransigence of South Korean and Japanese diplomatic counterparts.

COORDINATION OF THE U.S. INDO-PACIFIC AND SOUTH KOREAN NEW SOUTHERN POLICIES

As part of the rollout of its policy toward the Indo-Pacific, the Trump administration sought to promote the alignment of infrastructure and investment policies toward Southeast Asia with Japanese and South Korean allies. The Moon administration initially responded coolly to U.S. overtures, but Moon finally authorized bilateral efforts to coordinate the U.S. Indo-Pacific policy with South Korea's New Southern Policy on the sidelines of the Kyoto G20 meeting held in June 2019. Following that meeting, the United States and South Korea negotiated a bilateral joint fact sheet issued on the sidelines of the November 2019 East Asia Summit, but Trump's failure to attend the summit ensured that the statement would largely be overlooked.

The November 2019 U.S.–South Korea Joint Fact Sheet drew parallel lines between U.S. and South Korean infrastructure investment, development, and capacity-building policies in the region.[53] However, the document represented a statement of intent that defined areas of overlap in approaches toward Southeast Asia rather than a tangible combined action plan. The Moon administration referred to the coordination of policies toward Southeast Asia in bilateral meetings with the United States but rarely publicly mentioned the alignment of its New Southern Policy with U.S. policies in dialogue with Southeast Asian leaders.

ASSESSMENT OF ALLIANCE MANAGEMENT UNDER TRUMP AND MOON

Depending on one's perspective on the history and contributions of alliance cooperation between the United States and South Korea, the story of the alliance under Trump and Moon is either a tale of vulnerability or a tale of durability. The United States and South Korea maintained close coordination and deepened cooperation in a shifting threat environment, in spite of rather than because of a leadership combination in which an American president sought to tip the scales in favor of exclusive American interests over traditional alliance commitments to South Korea while a South Korean progressive president pursued inter-Korean peace and reconciliation while minimizing the significance of North Korea's nuclear program as an issue requiring coordination with the United States and the intransigence and global instability that Kim Jong-un has sought to export.

The impact of the leaderships of Trump and Moon on alliance management is the story of individual leadership and the impact of leadership chemistry on the U.S.–South Korea relationship; it is the story of how the two leaders interacted with their respective bureaucracies; and it is the story of how two political leaders navigated both their personal interests and their respective national interests against the backdrop of growing domestic political polarization in both countries. The Trump-Moon era of alliance management provides a historical case study that intertwines personal dynamics at the leader level, bureaucratic dysfunctions between the respective leaders, and the bureaucracies that they managed.

Under Trump and Moon, the U.S.–South Korea alliance faced and survived both an unconventional top-down leadership style under both presidents and divergent positions resulting from differing ideological predispositions and outlooks between the two administrations. Management of the particular ideological leadership combination between American conservative and South Korean progressive administrations was not a new challenge for alliance managers (given the experience of the George W. Bush and Roh Moo-hyun administrations from 2003 to 2008), but it has proven to be the most challenging leadership combination within the alliance. The added difficulty of managing Trump's America-First inclinations revealed new vulnerabilities that, paired with Moon's peace-first approach to the alliance, heightened tensions between Seoul and Washington. Fortunately, Moon continued to treat the alliance as a means by which to achieve his main objective of peace and reconciliation with North

Korea despite the North Korea–first inclinations of some senior members of his administration.

One of the most significant difficulties the alliance faced under Trump and Moon was the fact that the top-down leadership approach by Trump and Moon to coordinating policy toward North Korea marginalized the caution and resistance built into the process of bureaucratic coordination. Rather than trying to win over and utilize the bureaucracy as an instrument by which to achieve policy aims, Trump and Moon sidestepped and marginalized their respective bureaucracies. This approach naturally created tension for alliance managers who either received insufficient direction on alliance matters or resisted the direction they did receive based on conventional and long-standing views of their respective countries' national interests. If Trump or Moon had used the top-down approach to directly challenge the alliance in favor of exclusive America-First or Korea-first objectives, they might have faced bureaucratic and political resistance, but they might also have ultimately succeeded in severely damaging the alliance or opening up the possibility of alliance degradation.

The second factor contributing to friction between Trump and Moon was ideological. Progressive Moon supporters and conservative Trump supporters held vastly different views of how to deal with North Korea, which required them to exercise patience toward the unconventional means each leader used to pursue their objectives. Moon's pursuit of close U.S.–South Korea coordination and his efforts to win over the United States in support of an end-of-war declaration and the renewal of inter-Korean exchanges generated frustration among South Korean progressives who saw the United States as a malevolent impediment to inter-Korean reconciliation. American conservatives had long condemned North Korea's socialist dictatorship but tolerated Trump's unconventional pursuit of summitry with Kim because it was Trump who claimed that he was on the way to solving the North Korea problem.

The pursuit of unconventional means by which to achieve their policy goals generated some measure of consternation in both publics. Trump gained popularity among South Korean progressives for his willingness to meet with Kim despite the concerns of South Korean conservatives, while American support for the defense of South Korea grew steadily (despite alliance management frictions) due to North Korea's threats and growing American public appreciation for South Korean pop culture during the Trump and Moon administrations.[54]

STRATEGIES OF ALLIANCE PARTNERS IN MANAGING TRUMP

American alliance partners faced a common dilemma in dealing with Trump and his America-First approach. U.S. alliance partners were dependent on a good relationship with the United States as a security guarantor, yet Trump leveraged the security dependency of allies for his own purposes by belittling the contributions of alliance partners, accusing allies of taking advantage of the United States, and seeking to maximize the benefits of the relationship to the United States at the expense of allies. Thus, the political calculation of foreign leaders in managing their relationships with Trump revolved around what mix of flattery and confrontation would yield the most desirable political outcome. At the bureaucratic level, counterpart institutions generally sought binding relationships intended to preserve existing forms of alliance cooperation as a hedge against the unpredictability of dealing with Trump.

On the spectrum of political strategies between flattery and confrontation for managing Trump, most leaders chose flattery, but some found themselves on the wrong end of confrontation, often dictated by Trump's own personal and political agenda. The Japanese prime minister Abe Shinzo clearly employed a strategy that relied primarily on flattery rather than confrontation with Trump. Abe's strategy involved the gift of a $3,775 gold-plated golf club and a letter nominating Trump for the Nobel Peace Prize, which won him thirty-seven phone calls and fourteen direct meetings but little apparent influence on Trump's policies.[55] Abe's approach appears to have served as a model for Moon's approach to Trump, which generated initial success through the achievement of Trump-Kim summitry but ultimately failed to deliver on Moon's goal of bringing peace to the Korean Peninsula. European allies such as Germany's Angela Merkel pursued strategies that stressed U.S. historical contributions to Germany as the foundation for traditional shared alliance interests and roles, but the task of managing public interactions with Trump proved challenging.[56] The Canadian prime minister Justin Trudeau and the Australian prime minister Malcolm Turnbull found themselves on the wrong end of confrontations over political issues with Trump.[57] The Israeli prime minister Benjamin Netanyahu was a rare friend of the United States who benefited from a strong personal relationship with Trump that translated into shared policy approaches, but one effect of stronger U.S.–Israeli cooperation during the Trump administration was the deepening of American political polarization around central issues in U.S.–Israeli relations.[58]

Despite the personalization of foreign policy relationships under the Trump administration, bureaucratic management of alliance relationships primarily involved efforts to strengthen institutional cooperation as a buffer against White House unpredictability. For instance, Mark Beeson and Alan Bloomfield point to the strength of institutional ties and deep Australian public support for the U.S. alliance along with a lack of strategic alternatives as factors.[59] Despite concerns about the defection of the United States from its traditional international leadership, Canadian leaders managed Trump's desire to rip up the North American Free Trade Agreement (NAFTA) together with Mexican counterparts while cooperating with the United States by resisting Chinese demands for the extradition of Huawei CFO Meng Wanzhou.[60] Washington-based senior envoys such as the British ambassador Kim Darroch sought input from U.S. counterparts on how to manage Trump and provided frank assessments of dysfunctionality within the Trump administration.[61] European allies responded to Trump's threats and exhortations by gradually raising defense spending targets within NATO closer to the recommended 2 percent of GDP, and even Japan eventually abandoned its long-standing 1 percent cap on defense spending in favor of a 2 percent target during the Biden administration.

THE MOON STRATEGY IN DEALING WITH TRUMP

Prior to Moon's first meeting with Trump, there was speculation regarding what type of relationship would be possible between a progressive political leader such as Moon Jae-in and the egocentric America-First approach of Donald Trump. As a counterpart whose election occurred following that of Trump rather than as a sitting leader, Moon had the opportunity to benefit from the experience gained in watching Trump deal with other sitting leaders in advance of his own direct encounter with Trump. Among the lessons that might have been drawn by Moon from watching Trump's initial interactions with leaders of other countries, one could imagine Moon might have developed a conscious or unconscious strategy of not directly challenging or confronting Trump on issues, regardless of whether they were fact-based or imagined, accommodating Trump on secondary priorities within the bilateral relationship that were of importance to Trump himself, and proposing opportunities likely to place Trump at the center of global attention.

Moon's own personality may have been particularly well-suited to the task of getting along with Trump. In his own political career, Moon had not been predisposed to seek the limelight but rather sought to shape the environment from offstage and to make decisions that would win support by alienating the least number of constituents. In this respect, Moon was not known as a strong leader but rather as a savvy political operator capable of leading a consensus in favor of a given course of action. Moon would not be a leader who would compete with Trump to be in the spotlight, but he might be one who could convince Trump to move in the direction he desired if he could present to Trump a payoff that would provide a maximum role for Trump on center stage. Moon was a tactical politician but one who was motivated by the clear strategic goal of creating a channel of dialogue between Trump and Kim Jong-un. Regardless of whether it was Moon or someone else who first pitched Trump the idea that a Trump-Kim summit might enable Trump to be not only a historic peace broker but also a possible Nobel Prize recipient,

Moon would have been fully prepared to encourage Trump to take such an opportunity.

To feed Trump's ego and prevent such a course of action from being blocked by lower-level bureaucrats within the Trump administration, Moon and his advisors would have realized at an early stage that the best strategy for convincing Trump to pursue summitry with Kim would be to pursue a top-down approach that would eliminate bureaucratic obstacles to such a path. That approach mirrored the type of approach that would be necessary for the Moon administration to convince Kim Jong-un, the only decision maker in North Korea, to take the risk of pursuing summitry with Trump.

Alongside a strategy of flattering Trump and appealing to his ego, the Moon administration appeased Trump in its approach to his economic grievances regarding the perceived unfairness of the KORUS FTA. While avoiding public confrontation with Trump, Moon attempted to bring U.S.–South Korea bilateral trade into balance by surrendering South Korea's merchandise trade surplus and authorized an early revision of the FTA in an effort to appease Trump rather than antagonizing him unnecessarily by stretching out negotiations. However, when it came to Trump's demands for South Korea to exorbitantly increase its contributions in support of the U.S. troop presence in South Korea, the Moon administration decided to stretch out negotiations in hopes that the clock would wind down on the Trump administration. This strategy proved correct, but it was premised on the possibility that new American leadership would take a more reasonable approach to the issue of burden sharing within the U.S.–South Korea alliance.

U.S.–SOUTH KOREA RELATIONS BETWEEN BIDEN AND MOON

The U.S. political transition from President Trump to President Biden marked the return to a more conventional American foreign policy in which the strengthening of alliances was identified as an essential means to achieve the broader U.S. strategy of competition with China to preserve a rules-based liberal international order. The Biden administration retained the adversarial view of China adopted in the Trump administration's 2017 National Security Strategy but pursued it through a strategy that attempted to capitalize on the role and capabilities of like-minded allies rather than antagonizing or bullying allies into lining up with the United States in opposition to China.[62]

The shift in approach to alliances from Trump to Biden yielded immediate improvements in the trajectory and public management of the U.S.–South Korea alliance under Biden and Moon. The Biden approach obscured but did not remove the differences between a U.S. approach focused on deterrence of North Korea and expanded strategic competition with China and the Moon administration objectives of accommodating China and opening a pathway to peace with North Korea. Moreover, the transition revitalized the importance of bureaucratic processes as the main mechanism by which the governments coordinated policies based on directions from the respective leaderships of the two countries.

Having identified the reinvigoration of alliances as a central pillar of U.S. strategy, the Biden administration made early moves to take the Trump administration's America-First approach to the U.S.–South Korea alliance off the table. Specifically, the Biden administration quickly concluded the SMA that defined South Korea's financial contributions in support of the alliance by accepting the offer that South Korea had already tabled during negotiations with the Trump administration. In addition, the Biden administration signaled the importance of alliances as components of its foreign policy strategy by scheduling in-person "two-plus-two" meetings with the foreign and defense ministers of Japan and South Korea as the new administration's first high-level diplomatic exchanges.

The March 2021 visit of Secretary of State Antony Blinken and Secretary of Defense Lloyd Austin to Tokyo and Seoul and subsequent White House hosting of the Japanese prime minister Suga Yoshihide in April and President Moon in May clearly demonstrated the Biden administration's commitment to strengthening the alliances with Japan and South Korea.[63]

But the Moon administration's handling of the two-plus-two visit, especially in direct comparison with the outcome of the U.S.–Japan meeting, revealed notable differences despite the Biden administration's use of nearly identical framing for its diplomacy with both allies. For instance, the U.S.–Japan two-plus-two statement explicitly called out China's challenges to the rule of law and international order while the South Korean statement avoided mentioning China altogether.[64]

The U.S.–South Korea Joint Statement issued following the first Biden-Moon summit in May 2021 was surprisingly robust, reflecting the potential breadth and depth of U.S.–South Korean policy coordination on a wide range of functional issues.[65] The summit coincided with the conclusion of the administration's North Korea policy review, following which the administration announced that it would take a "calibrated, practical approach" by pursuing a combination of "diplomacy and stern deterrence." The Biden-Moon Joint Statement was surprisingly forward leaning in the extent of functional cooperation the Moon administration was willing to sign on to, including the establishment of major consultation mechanisms to address supply chain resiliency, technology cooperation, energy security, space cooperation, and joint vaccine production as well as joint support for peace and stability across the Taiwan Straits. It also contained language emphasizing U.S. openness to establishing negotiations with North Korea, and the summit was accompanied by South Korean corporate pledges of significant inward investment in the United States and the naming of Sung Kim as the U.S. envoy for negotiations with North Korea.[66]

In behind-the-scenes consultations regarding policy toward North Korea, the Moon administration continuously pressed the United States to send conciliatory signals to North Korea and join South Korean efforts to press for an end-of-war declaration, even during the Moon administration's final months, despite the Biden administration's efforts to strengthen sanctions on North Korea while keeping the door open for diplomacy. Although the Biden administration attempted to downplay differences with South Korea over North Korea policy so as to project an image of alliance solidarity, South Korean advocacy of U.S. support for a gesture in support of the end-of-war declaration finally drew a public statement from National

Security Advisor Jake Sullivan indicating tactfully that such an approach was a nonstarter.[67]

Thus, the U.S. political transition from Trump to Biden marked a transition away from America-First policies that had generated tension with the Moon administration, restoring and enhancing traditional government-to-government coordination based on shared interests, and a conventional bottom-up approach to alliance management. Ideological differences between the Biden and Moon administrations over how to deal with China and North Korea remained, but they were managed in a fashion that emphasized public solidarity despite behind-the-scenes differences.

U.S.–SOUTH KOREA RELATIONS BETWEEN BIDEN AND YOON

The transition from the Moon to the Yoon Suk-yeol administration following Yoon's election as South Korea's president in March 2022 marked a return to a South Korean foreign policy that viewed the "comprehensive strategic alliance" with the United States as the centerpiece of South Korea's foreign policy.[68] As a result, the major impact of South Korea's transition to the Yoon administration was to bring South Korea into alignment with the United States around shared strategic objectives, including the upholding of freedom and rule of law as shared principles of international governance and Yoon's declaration of willingness to "step up" its international leadership as a "global pivotal state."[69] In practical terms, Yoon pursued a closer alignment with the United States, including on China-related policies, and shifted South Korea's North Korea policy toward deterrence in response to North Korea's focus on nuclear and military development. Notably, Yoon emphasized that South Korea's alignment with the United States based on shared values did not mean an antagonistic or zero-sum relationship with China as long as the relationship was based on "mutual respect."[70] Given North Korea's historical animosity toward South Korean conservative leadership, the election of Yoon has led North Korea to pursue even more antagonistic and provocative policies even as the South has restored military exercises and emphasized readiness to deter the undiminished threat from the North. As was the case during the Obama and Lee Myung-bak administrations, the combination of American Democratic Party leadership and South Korean conservative leadership under Biden and Yoon has provided a solid basis for close cooperation between the United States and South Korea.

The Biden administration wasted no time in welcoming and affirming the outlines of the Yoon administration's approach to foreign policy, as Biden met with Yoon in Seoul in advance of an already-planned visit to Japan less than two weeks following Yoon's inauguration. The Biden-Yoon Joint Statement reaffirmed and expanded on many elements of the Biden-Moon Joint Statement issued the previous year but replaced the prior administration's emphasis on diplomacy with North Korea with an emphasis on the credibility of extended deterrence in response to North Korea's stepped-up missile tests and military development goals and refusal to respond to the Biden administration's offers of dialogue.[71] During his visit to Seoul, President Biden also met with Hyundai's chairman Chung Eui-sun, who pledged over $10 billion of investment in electric vehicle–related factories to be built in Georgia.[72] The Yoon administration opted to participate in the Biden administration's Indo-Pacific Economic Framework and Chips-4 dialogue with the United States, Japan, and Taiwan, despite Chinese objections, and carefully navigated Chinese efforts to place limits on aspects of the U.S.–South Korea alliance perceived as impinging on Chinese interests.

A more challenging task for the Yoon administration has been the management of the South Korean backlash against the U.S. Inflation Reduction Act, which excluded Hyundai-made electric vehicles from consideration for a major U.S. tax credit despite Hyundai's pledges of investment in the United States. The Yoon administration has also faced new U.S. restrictions on exports of semiconductors to China, where SK Hynix and Samsung have sought exceptions in recognition of their significant sunk investments in the production of legacy semiconductors.

Under the Yoon administration, the looming threat to the alliance stems not from efforts to promote peace with North Korea but rather from conservative Korean nationalist desires to gain parity with North Korea's nuclear development, either through the reintroduction of U.S. tactical nuclear weapons to the peninsula or by gaining U.S. acquiescence for South Korea's development of an indigenous nuclear capability to match that of the North.[73] The full-fledged version of such a policy might even bridge Korean ideological lines between conservatives and progressives in the form of pressure to develop South Korea's own nuclear weapons for its own defense in spite of U.S. security guarantees provided through the alliance. This version of a Korea-first approach to alliance planning and coordination, if pursued over U.S. objections, would potentially be as destructive to the U.S.–South Korea alliance as an America-First policy that focuses exclusively on U.S. needs without the consideration of South Korean prerogatives. Such internal risks require attention and effective management even despite the high level of cooperation and institutionalized coordination that characterizes alliance management between the Biden and Yoon administrations.

IDEOLOGY, POLITICAL TRANSITION, AND THE CHALLENGE OF U.S.–SOUTH KOREA ALLIANCE MANAGEMENT

The U.S.–South Korea alliance has shown resilience and has accommodated a wide range of political transitions and shifts in policy preferences over the decades. Alliance cooperation has endured despite ideological differences between American and South Korean leaders, but alliance management under Trump and Moon revealed potential vulnerabilities to sustained cooperation in the context of preferences for top-down alliance management. In addition, there is the prospect that either or both an America-First or Korea-first political leadership might challenge the sustainability and raison d'être for the relationship in spite of rising common threats. Under ideological leadership combinations in which both sides maintain the centrality of the U.S.–South Korea alliance as part of their respective and convergent national security strategies, the internal challenge to the alliance is manageable in the context of efforts to respond to shared external threats.

But the risk that the alliance might again face challenges from a leadership combination that includes an America-First or a Korea-first agenda is no longer inconsequential. The reason for this emerging vulnerability lies with the increase in domestic political polarization and the fragmentation of domestic consensus around specific hot-button foreign policy issues in both countries. The impact of internal shifts, including political polarization and fragmentation of domestic consensus and efforts by external actors to exploit domestic political divisions, will be further discussed in the following chapters.

3

POLITICAL POLARIZATION UNDER THE MOON JAE-IN ADMINISTRATION

South Korea's domestic political polarization has distracted or prevented political leaders in the country from making the decisions necessary to forward shared strategic objectives by generating domestic political preoccupations that have distracted from alliance goals. The danger to effective alliance coordination comes to the extent that South Korea's capacity to overcome domestic political divisions and respond effectively to alliance issues may be weakened. For instance, wrangling over high-stakes domestic issues such as judicial reform became so politicized under the Moon administration that there were dueling public demonstrations held in different parts of Seoul. Political polarization is an enabler for ideologies that appeal to exclusive forms of nationalism rather than alliance cooperation to the extent that it creates an environment of paralysis in the absence of agreement between the two governments. In this respect, South Korean political polarization became a factor during the Moon administration that, together with ideology, influenced the degree of effective alliance coordination, even when it was based on shared values.

In South Korea, political polarization deepened under the Moon administration following burgeoning candlelight demonstrations involving millions of peaceful South Korean protestors in response to allegations of bribery and political influence peddling in late 2016 that led to the impeachment of President Park Geun-hye. The impeachment was affirmed by South Korea's Constitutional Court in March 2017, resulting in a new presidential election won by the Democratic Party candidate Moon Jae-in in May 2017. In his presidential inaugural address held the day after his election, Moon pledged "I will become an honest president who keeps promises. . . . Genuine political progress will be possible only when the president takes the initiative in engaging in trustworthy politics. I will not talk big about doing the impossible. I will admit to the wrong I did. I will not cover up unfavorable public opinion with lies. I will be a fair president."[1]

As the president who came into office having led candlelight demonstrations that resulted in his predecessor's impeachment on charges of corruption, Moon espoused high ideals and pledged to pursue a welcome path of reform. Given that most South Korean presidents since the 1980s have been investigated or indicted for various forms of corruption following their terms in office, South Koreans welcomed Moon's aspiration to govern fairly as a breath of fresh air. But instead, the Moon administration too often exacerbated rather than ameliorated domestic political polarization by promising political reforms tinged with an element of revenge, and by exploiting populist nationalist sentiments as a cudgel for attacking political opponents. In so doing, Moon fell into the same trap as his predecessors, utilizing the perquisites of power to reward members of his in-group rather than maximizing his administration's ability to achieve the public good.

The Moon administration's campaign to eradicate "deep-rooted evil perpetrated by those in authority" as the main purpose behind its pursuit of institutional reforms deepened political divisions within South Korea.[2] As touted in his inaugural address, Moon came into office as a reformer both determined and well-positioned to overcome a history of presidential corruption. But the candlelight president's administration was too quick to forfeit the moral high ground and proved just as willing to apply double standards as his predecessors. The main targets of Moon's domestic reform that catalyzed political polarization within South Korea were reforming the judicial sector, disputes over election maneuvering, and tactical use of the constitutional reform issue for electoral purposes. Actions intended to achieve needed judicial and political reforms of Korean institutions contributed to deepening domestic political polarization and were perceived by the opposition as self-dealing efforts to lock in structural political advantages and achieve perpetual political power.

One of the biggest impacts of the Moon administration's campaigns for institutional reform was its contribution to domestic political polarization within South Korean society. The common, if plainspoken, critique of Moon's Democratic Party leadership that "if I do it, it is a romance, but if you do it, it is a scandal" hits the mark. Political polarization deepened to the degree that, in 2019, progressives and conservatives carved out different sections of Seoul as gathering points for competing shows of support and opposition to Moon's nominee for justice minister. Progressives gathered to demonstrate in support of Moon's appointment near the Supreme Court in southern Seoul, while Korean and American flag-waving conservatives protested the nomination at Gwanghwamun in central Seoul.

The Stanford sociologist Shin Gi-wook characterized the content and implementation of the Moon administration's policy agenda as contributing to "democratic backsliding," arguing that rather than pursuing democratic consolidation, South Korea under the Moon administration "has instead gone the other way, exacerbating polarization, eroding democratic norms, and appealing to chauvinistic nationalism."[3] The nub of Shin's criticism addresses the question of whether Moon's self-imposed mandate to eradicate "deep-rooted evil" from Korean society—by improving Blue House communication with the people and by pursuing institutional reforms of the prosecution, police, and intelligence services—constitutes a healthy step toward reform or a pursuit of political revenge masquerading as reform. This chapter will illustrate how the Moon administration's pursuit of judicial reforms and tactical maneuvering around the issues of constitutional reform and revision of election rules contributed to domestic political polarization, which in turn limited South Korea's political will to pursue effective cooperation within the U.S.–South Korea alliance.

MOON'S JUDICIAL REFORMS AND THEIR IMPACT ON KOREAN DOMESTIC POLITICAL POLARIZATION

The Moon administration's reorganization of the role and functions of the prosecution was the most sensitive initiative that the administration took under the mantle of reform. Critics perceived Moon's efforts as an instrument of revenge against political enemies and as an effort to control administration of the law. Despite introducing some necessary changes intended to enhance fairness and curb potential abuses of prosecutorial power, Moon's judicial reforms became a lightning rod for criticism that the reorganization and establishment of a commission for investigating high-level political officials might be used as a means for attacking challengers and preserving political power, rather than as a democracy-buttressing reform of the current system.

The progressive Minbyun (Lawyers for a Democratic Society) was the most influential supporter of Moon's proposals for prosecutorial reform. Minbyun's arguments for the limitation and distribution of prosecutorial power away from the Korean Prosecutors' Service (KPS) asserted that such reforms were necessary to safeguard democracy and to prevent unchecked prosecutorial power from threatening the health of Korean democracy. Minbyun's recommendation to distribute most subpoena and investigatory powers to the police and establish a separate investigation agency to handle corruption by high-ranking public officials represented the main prosecutorial reforms pursued under the Moon administration.[4]

But Moon's critics claimed his mandate of reform for the sake of public good and social progress cloaked an antidemocratic effort to tilt the electoral playing field decisively in favor of the ruling progressive party. Conservatives expressed concerns about antidemocratic tendencies within the Moon administration, and Moon's actions and conservative critiques of perceived overreach contributed to South Korea's polarized political environment. These concerns stemmed in part from the fact that conservatives who had grown accustomed to privileges, power, and protection under authoritarian governments were suspicious that progressives would follow past precedent and take their own measures to lock in power. Now that conservatives have returned to power with a former prosecutor at the helm, that past record suggests a continued need for watchfulness around the independence and transparency of judicial institutions and prosecutorial powers in their new forms.

HISTORICAL CONTEXT FOR THE PURSUIT OF PROSECUTORIAL REFORM AND SEPARATION OF EXECUTIVE-JUDICIAL RELATIONS

Progressive political leaders, many of whom had been victimized as prodemocracy activists in the 1980s by the long-standing close relationship among the executive branch, the National Intelligence Service (NIS), and the KPS have consistently sought NIS and KPS reforms.[5] Historically, South Korea's authoritarian leaders used executive-prosecutorial cooperation backed by South Korea's national intelligence agency to suppress dissent and punish opposition challengers, so it is natural that progressive leaders would see the need for institutional reform of the Korean prosecution.

Previous progressive governments had sought to reform the KPS's prosecutorial functions but never fully succeeded. Former President Kim Dae-jung exercised self-restraint in Blue House dealings with the KPS, instead calling on the KPS to initiate self-reform to eradicate corruption and abuse of power.[6] His successor Roh Moo-hyun took a more active role in calling for prosecutorial reform, initiating a high-profile "Conversation with Prosecutors" live TV debate that shined a spotlight on institutional bias within the KPS. But as a consequence of his reform efforts, Roh found himself targeted by the KPS as part of a corruption investigation that continued after his presidency.[7] Prosecution attacks on Roh—a possible source of mental stress following Roh's presidency that may have contributed to his suicide—are reported to have left a deep impression on Moon. As Roh's chief of staff, Moon had worked with Roh to initiate the KPS's self-reform.[8] However, Moon later called the idea of self-reform a "naïve plan" and emphasized the need for a higher authority to oversee the prosecution's extensive power.[9] When he first ran for president in 2012, Moon had expressed his firm determination to reform the KPS.[10] These experiences contributed to Moon's resolve in pursuing the institutionalization of reforms that fundamentally challenge the power and role of the KPS.[11]

The impeachment of Park Geun-hye created an opportunity for Moon not only to be elected president but also to pursue prosecutorial reforms. During his presidential campaign in 2017, Moon's reform goal aligned with citizen demands for prosecution reform. The role of the KPS was a major agenda item among activists who led the protests against the Park administration and became the core of the "candlelight movement" in 2016 following revelations by the media company JTBC of corruption, extortion, and embezzlement by Park's close friend Choi Soon-sil.[12] Preexisting frustrations among Park's critics centered around the KPS's failure to more actively investigate the institutional corruption that led to the *Sewol* ferry sinking in 2014, a major political scandal under Park that cost the lives of hundreds of people including many youths on a high school field trip to Jeju Island. The investigation following the sinking showed that the accident would have been preventable if not for a cascading series of incidents of institutional corruption and regulatory failures. The KPS investigated the incident for six months and arrested 154 people. But South Korean activists criticized the KPS for focusing only on lower-level Coast Guard officials, for excluding high-level government officials from the investigation, and then for failing to respond to public questions around responsibility for the incident.[13]

Given instances under authoritarian leaders of collusion between the KPS and other agencies to persecute political enemies, there has long been a widespread recognition of the need to reform the KPS, but neither the government nor the KPS have been well-positioned to lead such reforms. The public has long suspected that the inertia stemmed from collusion between high-level government officials and the prosecutors.[14] Park's scandal only served to ignite South Koreans' preexisting anger toward the KPS. The key to successful KPS reform would be to achieve the twin objectives of holding the KPS accountable while also promoting judicial independence from executive influence, not replication of overly close judicial-executive ties and certainly not on terms that favored the installation of new progressive elite powerholders to replace the former conservative privileged elite class. The goal of reforming the prosecution may have been worthy, but the manner in which it was pursued and the alternative structures created by the reforms appear to have created at least as many problems as they resolved.

MOON ADMINISTRATION PURSUIT OF PROSECUTORIAL REFORM

Despite Moon's prioritization of prosecution reform, it took time for the proposed legislation to work its way through the National Assembly. An impediment was the ruling party's plurality of votes in the National Assembly, as a result of which Moon needed acquiescence from other parties to secure the legislative foundations necessary for the judicial reform initiatives.[15] But a politically polarizing fight over the justice minister appointment of Cho Kuk, a close Moon confidante and progressive movement darling, intersected with unfolding allegations that Cho had pursued personal gains through the same exertions of social privilege and connections that had sparked scandals that brought down the Park administration.[16] As a result, Moon's agenda of judicial reform became deeply polarized and personalized as his own chief prosecutor Yoon Suk-yeol resisted Moon administration measures to weaken the power and role of the KPS. The initiative deepened political polarization within Korean society over the intent and likely impact of progressive reform of the prosecutorial role within the Korean judicial structure. In an ironic twist, it also propelled Yoon's entry into politics and contributed to his election as Moon's successor.

Weeks following Moon's 2017 inauguration, his administration launched a Police Reform Committee (경찰개혁위원) within the government with subcommittees on human rights protection, municipal policy, and investigation reforms chaired by the former UN human rights ambassador Park Gyeong-seo.[17] To spearhead implementation of these reforms, on July 19, 2017, the government released a five-year plan and its one hundred top goals, including the goal of adjusting the roles and responsibilities of the prosecution and police.[18] By December the Police Reform Committee recommended the separation of the investigation and indictment roles within South Korea's judicial system through a transfer of some KPS authorities to the police.[19]

The then senior presidential secretary for civil affairs Cho Kuk's January 2018 announcement of a proposed reform to adjust the roles of the prosecution and police stimulated a divided reaction between progressives and conservatives. Progressives welcomed the proposed redistribution of power between the police and KPS.[20] But conservatives expressed concerns that the redistribution might provide executive power holders with additional means to unduly influence the judicial process and outcome of police investigations.[21] The minister of interior and safety Kim Boo-gyum and the minister of justice Park Sang-ki signed the Agreement on the Adjustment of the Rights of the Prosecution and Police (검.경수사권 조정합의문), expressing the formal intent by the executive to pursue these reform measures, on June 21, 2018.[22] Naturally, the KPS announced its opposition to measures in the agreement that would take away aspects of the prosecution's authority and power. Based on the agreement, a new Special Committee on Judicial Reform was launched on July 26, 2018, to further develop the proposed reforms.

By April 2019, the Moon administration had secured partial legislative support for the Adjustment of the Rights of the Prosecution and Police as well as the establishment of a Corruption Investigation Office for High-Ranking Officials, but the main opposition Liberty Korea Party (LKP) refused to participate.[23] The LKP's boycott of the legislation ensnared the proposed institutional reforms in Korea's polarized politics. Moon appointed the senior prosecutor Yoon Suk-yeol as the new KPS prosecutor general on July 16, 2019, amid the administration's reform effort. Thus, Yoon came to the leadership of the KPS as Moon's appointee during an ongoing transition and reform effort through which the KPS faced a diminished role and curtailed responsibilities.

Moon then announced the appointment of Cho Kuk as justice minister to shepherd the adoption and supervision of the reform plan on August 9, 2019.[24] Moon's appointment of Cho personalized the reform fight and generated significant pushback from conservatives as both sides rallied to demonstrate their respective support for the KPS on the one hand and Cho's nomination as justice minister on the other.

Moon administration supporters held pro–Cho Kuk rallies, while right-wing groups and university students held rallies calling for Cho's resignation.[25] Right-wing groups opposed the reform plan in general, and university students opposed Cho's leadership of the plan due to allegations that Cho and his wife had used their influence to secure their daughter's admission to Korea University and subsequently to medical school.[26] Following a contentious National Assembly hearing that exposed many questions about the Cho family's efforts to enrich themselves and enhance their daughter's prospects for university admission, the prosecution issued search warrants and seized relevant records on August 27 as part of an investigation into allegations surrounding Cho's family.[27] Moon opted to appoint Cho as justice minister absent a National Assembly endorsement on September 9, 2019. The Cho Kuk scandal split South Korean public opinion on the KPS reform plan. A poll conducted at the time of Cho's appointment showed that, while 51 percent of Koreans surveyed objected to Cho's appointment and 38 percent supported the appointment, 57 percent supported Moon's prosecutorial reform initiative compared to 37 percent opposed.[28]

On September 17, 2019, one week following his appointment as justice minister, Cho announced a Prosecutor Reform Support Group within the ministry designed to set reform tasks, support the enactment of prosecution reform, provide proposals on who would control prosecutorial functions, and devise measures to strengthen the Ministry of Justice's monitoring of prosecutors.[29] Meanwhile, investigations led by the prosecution into the new justice minister's family ramped up based on revelations of Cho's personal life generated by his National Assembly hearing. These allegations deepened political divisions within South Korean society, with progressives viewing the right-wing media as exaggerating Cho's flaws and conservatives viewing Cho's shortcomings as evidence of both Cho's personal hypocrisy and progressive double standards.[30]

Faced with the inevitability of an institutional restructuring, Prosecutor General Yoon announced the KPS's own reform plan on October 1,

2019.[31] First, the KPS stated that it would reduce the number of Special Investigation Departments (특수부) from seven to three and return all fifty-seven prosecutors dispatched to outside agencies to its criminal and public trial departments.[32] Second, the KPS abolished public summons—the release of the time and place of suspects' appearance to the media during KPS investigations involving public figures, high-level government officials, and businessmen. This practice had been criticized as a form of extrajudicial public shaming since the media widely covered public figures summoned to appear at investigatory hearings. The major prosecution reform plan earlier presented by Cho Kuk encompassed both initiatives, but Yoon sought to protect the KPS's independent authority by preempting Cho's reform plan with his own.

Cho Kuk responded to the KPS's independent reform plan by pointing out that the government should propose reform measures after listening to the opinions of the prosecution and other related agencies.[33] He emphasized the hierarchical relationship between the Ministry of Justice and the prosecution by stating that the prosecution should deliver its opinion to the Ministry of Justice before pursuing its own reform plan. Cho sought to use the executive oversight power vested in the Ministry of Justice to erode the independence of the KPS by insisting on the Ministry of Justice's right to control and forcefully restructure the KPS according to its own preferences.

On October 14, 2019, Cho stepped down as justice minister after serving only thirty-five days in office, and Moon nominated his replacement Choo Mi-ae in December 2019.[34] After her National Assembly confirmation hearing, Choo was appointed as justice minister on January 2, 2020.

The feud between the Ministry of Justice and the KPS intensified following Cho Kuk's resignation. Based on a legislative agreement among the major parties, the Special Committee on Judicial Reform (사법개혁특별위원회) called for the revision of two bills, the Criminal Procedure Act and Prosecutors' Office Act, to redistribute investigation authority between the prosecution and police.[35] The National Assembly passed the Act on the Establishment and Operation of Criminal Investigation Department for High-Level Public Officials on December 30, 2019.[36] This bill established the Anti-Corruption Agency to investigate corruption by high-level government officials.[37] The National Assembly passed the revised Criminal Procedure Act and Prosecutors' Office Act on January 13, 2020, only three months prior to the end of the National Assembly term and the holding of new National Assembly elections.[38]

Amid tensions between the Moon administration and the KPS, the prosecution also experienced great internal turmoil. Two prosecutors resigned a day after the National Assembly passed the Prosecution and Police Rights Adjustment Act (검·경 수사권 조정 법안), and the Ministry of Justice announced plans to reduce the number of the special-direct investigation departments.[39] Kim Woong, one of the two prosecutors who resigned, posted a message on the prosecution's internal network that criticized the bill, writing "I'm resigning to protest this massive fraud. . . . These bills are not reform. They are the most abhorrent plot and regression since democratization."[40]

In January 2020, Choo ordered Yoon to restructure the prosecution in a move generally perceived as an effort to force the KPS to bow to the Moon administration's political will. Although Yoon initially resisted Choo's instructions, he acquiesced to Ministry of Justice orders, including orders to drop high-profile cases involving alleged misdeeds by the Moon administration in the Ulsan local elections. This case and its handling raised questions about whether the Moon administration was primarily interested in prosecutorial reform or gaining influence over prosecutorial instruments to protect their own and attack their political enemies. For only the second time since its establishment, Choo invoked the Ministry of Justice's investigation command right to take over an ongoing investigation on the so-called prosecution collusion scandal between a senior prosecutor and a reporter on July 2, 2020.[41] Choo again ordered the KPS to stop their investigation into an apparent investment scam on October 19.[42] The battle between Choo and Yoon further escalated on November 24, with Choo's order to suspend Yoon from his duties as prosecutor general. But the judiciary stepped in to invalidate the order and preserve its independence from Ministry of Justice overreach. The Seoul Administrative Court, which is under the judicial jurisdiction of the Seoul High Court and in turn the

Supreme Court, invalidated the order a week later and Yoon resumed his duties as prosecutor general. The Ministry of Justice's own Inspection Committee also found that Choo's order was inappropriate.

In December 2020, the Ministry of Justice disciplinary committee held meetings on Yoon's behavior and ordered him to face a two-month suspension, which was once again overturned by the Seoul Administrative Court within a week of the Ministry of Justice's announcement in a second move to preserve prosecutorial independence from the executive branch.[43] Meanwhile, the National Assembly passed the Revised Police Officials Act, the Revised Act on the Establishment and Operation of the Corruption Investigation Office for High-Ranking Officials, and the revised NIS Act in December 2020, completing the Moon administration's structural overhaul of judicial and prosecutorial responsibilities.[44]

Having taken the first steps to implement judicial reform on behalf of Moon, Choo submitted her resignation as justice minister on December 16, 2020. Moon accepted Choo's resignation on December 27 and announced Park Beom-kye as her successor on December 30. Having failed to resist Moon administration prosecutorial reforms, Yoon also resigned prior to the completion of his two-year term on March 4, 2021, and began to prepare for his run for president. Due to his steps to resist Moon administration reform efforts, Yoon had become a leading presidential candidate in South Korean public opinion polls by the time of his resignation.[45]

EVALUATION OF MOON ADMINISTRATION JUDICIAL REFORM EFFORTS

Given long-held South Korean skepticism of the relationship between the prosecution and executive power holders, prosecution reform was a logical political priority for Moon and an initiative that had substantial public support. In fact, there was a consensus on the need for some level of prosecutorial reform among all five major candidates during the 2017 presidential election.[46] According to a survey conducted by the Korean Broadcasting System (KBS) in September 2019, 52 percent of South Koreans supported the Moon administration's reform plan.[47] Despite growing political polarization, South Koreans continued to express their desire for prosecutorial reform. According to a 2019 Gallup report on the public's evaluation of Moon's performance, among the people who evaluated the president's performance positively, 15 percent referenced his prosecution reform plan efforts as their reason for doing so.[48] Moon's reform plans foundered not because South Koreans opposed the reforms themselves but rather because the way the reforms were pursued and implemented became politicized and because of the personal shortcomings of the designated agents of reform themselves.

The main objectives of Moon's prosecutorial reform plan involved the following: separation of the right to conduct investigations from the right to issue indictments and investigate crimes independent of the prosecution by creating a National Office of Investigation (NOI) within the NPA; the establishment of an Anti-Corruption Agency (subsequently known as the CIO) to investigate high-level political corruption; the transfer of domestic investigative authority for counterintelligence cases from the KPS to the NOI; and the protection of the basic rights of defendants during the investigation process.[49]

To separate investigatory responsibilities from the issuance of indictments, the Moon administration proposed the transfer of prosecutorial functions from the KPS to the NPA. But the NPA is not likely to exercise greater independence than the KPS and has less experience and capacity to professionally handle legal aspects surrounding indictment and investigation. Likewise, the establishment of the CIO to investigate high-level corruption is also intended to distribute power away from a single all-powerful KPS. To be effective, the CIO would require independence from the executive branch, yet the executive branch and ruling party would likely maintain influence over the agency through its powers to appoint the leadership of the agency. Although legislation to establish the CIO provides the opposition with the right to appoint two members of a seven-person commission, the main institutional power will lie with the ruling party and executive branch. Using the NPA rather than the KPS for investigatorial purposes may protect defendant rights by ensuring a more equal division of power and reduce corruption in the judicial process, but this is only if NPA independence from executive interference can be assured.

The distribution of the indictment and investigation roles between the NPA and prosecution and the establishment of the Anti-Corruption Agency constitute the main reforms implemented under the Moon administration. If these reforms make South Korea's judicial system fairer and more resistant to manipulation by the executive branch, then they can be regarded as a success. But if undue executive influence persists, either through executive branch manipulation of the CIO or through pressure on the NPA, then the reforms will clearly have failed.

Following Yoon's election as president, the National Assembly, at the behest of the outgoing Moon administration, took an additional step to narrow the authority of the prosecution with the passage of amendments to the Prosecutor's Office Act (검찰청법 개정안) and the Criminal Procedure Act (형사소송법 개정안).[50] These amendments further narrowed the powers of the Prosecutor's Office to initiate investigations only on economic-related crimes, eliminating powers to investigate crimes by public officials, election-related crimes, defense industry–related crime, and major catastrophes, and to only investigate crimes forwarded by the police narrowly on charges related to the original case. The People Power Party initially engaged in negotiations on the scope and language of the bill but pulled out of discussions following criticisms from party members and then President-elect Yoon. The National Assembly passed both amendments in the waning weeks of Moon's presidency and were officially announced by Moon on his last day in office. Evaluation of the efficacy of the reforms implemented under the Moon administration has been further complicated by the fact that responsibility for effective implementation of the reforms fell to the administration of President Yoon, who had vocally opposed and resisted implementation of the reform plans under the Moon administration.

OTHER RISKS OF POLITICAL POLARIZATION DURING THE MOON ADMINISTRATION

Judicial reforms were the most significant and polarizing reform issue taken up by the Moon administration. In addition, the Moon administration pursued reforms in a number of other areas including constitutional and electoral reforms. These reforms either contributed to political polarization or were subject to claims that the Moon administration tried to influence the playing field to lock in political advantages. In this respect, the Moon administration, despite its candlelight origins as a mass protest mobilized against revelations of corruption and bribery by close associates of Park Geun-hye, utilized strategies and tactics that reflected long-standing efforts by elites within South Korea's electoral system to restrict and control participation in politics.[51]

CONSTITUTIONAL REFORM

Constitutional reform is perhaps the most consequential long-term reform issue affecting the health of South Korea's democracy that could become a victim or cause of deepening political polarization. South Korea's current constitution was passed in the waning days of Chun Doo-hwan's authoritarian rule as a compromise document that would help pave the way for South Korea's democratic transition. Although there are well-recognized flaws and limitations inherent in South Korea's current constitution, the issue of constitutional reform touches a nerve that brings to the surface deep divisions between conservative and progressive factions. Rather than being an instrument for unifying the population around a common set of values and ideas, constitutional reform proposals have reflected existing political divisions.

For instance, during his 2017 campaign, Moon pledged to include the spirit of the May 18 Prodemocracy Movement in the preamble to the constitution. But the framing of constitutional revision around this issue was divisive because it implicitly repudiated conservatives perceived to have past associations with authoritarian governments and implied that prodemocracy activists have a special claim to legitimacy as national leaders. Moon's proposed inclusion of references to the Prodemocracy Movement in the constitution stoked conservative fears that progressive administrations intended to use their political power to tilt the political playing field permanently in their favor.

The need for constitutional reform itself was not controversial at the time of Moon's campaign. A survey of 241 lawmakers conducted by *JoongAng Ilbo* in the fall of 2017 revealed that 94.2 percent supported constitutional revision.[52] Support among conservatives was high in part because they hoped that the powers of the presidency would be redistributed to curb the concentration of power in the hands of one leader. But conservatives doubted the sincerity of the Moon-led constitutional reform. *Dong-A Ilbo* observed that "this administration seems to have lost interest in revising the Constitution and is instead preoccupied with rooting out the evils of Lee Myung-bak and Park Geun-hye."[53]

Despite conservative doubts about the sincerity of the proposed reforms, Moon submitted a constitutional revision bill to the National Assembly on March 22, 2018.[54] The bill contained three main points. First, it expanded popular sovereignty and basic rights to include foreigners living in South Korea and to reinforce workers' rights.[55] Second, it expanded the sovereignty of local governments to form a horizontal relationship between the central and local governments.[56] Third, it redesigned the government's power structure to engage more citizens in politics, to decrease the president's power, and to replace the one five-year term limit for the presidency with a four-year term that has a limit of two terms.[57] However, the bill failed to gain support from a more than two-thirds majority of the National Assembly (greater than or equal to 200 out of 300 members) due to an opposition boycott of the vote, and Moon's first attempt to revise the constitution failed.[58]

Moon's 2018 constitutional revision proposal was in many ways symbolic given that the ruling party held only a plurality of seats in the National Assembly at the time and the possibility of building a multiparty coalition in favor of constitutional revision would have required more quid pro quos and special favors than Moon could offer. Instead, the proposal ignited debate over reforms, including whether the proposed revisions went far enough in diluting executive power. Conservative critics noted that the proposed revisions did not provide for a legislative role in the appointment of the prime minister and asserted that "the revision announced by the Blue House does not embody the values of the whole nation but only those of the current administration."[59]

Since previous presidents—such as Rhee Syngman, Park Chung-hee, and Chun Doo-hwan—have used changes to the constitution to maintain power, South Koreans tend to be hesitant in their support for constitutional revision bills.[60] Nevertheless, 55 percent of South Koreans supported Moon's first constitution revision bill according to a March 2018 survey.[61] The survey results seem to convey that citizens want their presidents to have the opportunity to serve two consecutive terms.

On March 11, 2020, Moon submitted a new constitutional revision bill.[62] This constitutional revision proposal came just over a month prior to new National Assembly elections and was designed to mobilize reformist votes as part of a national campaign to increase legislative support for the ruling party in the National Assembly. Moon called the bill the One Point Constitutional Revision (원포인트 개헌) because it only focused on one point: allowing the public to directly propose a constitutional amendment.[63] The existing clause for amending the constitution stipulates that "the amendment to the Constitution has to be proposed by a majority of the National Assembly's members or by the president." The One Point Constitutional Revision added the phrase "more than 1 million electors," empowering the public to directly propose constitutional amendments. The Moon administration planned to put the constitutional revision bill to a referendum during the general elections on April 15, 2020. However, the bill once again failed, in part because the initiative appeared to be a tactical campaign measure intended to stoke populism rather than a serious effort to achieve constitutional reforms. Money Today concluded that "both progressives and conservatives are concerned about the referendum's impact on the local election. . . . Nowhere is discussion on the people's rights or values to be seen."[64]

Though Moon's plan for a referendum failed, he continued to advocate to the public for a constitutional revision bill. For example, in his commemorative speech at the 40th anniversary of the May 18 Gwangju Democratization Movement on May 18, 2020, Moon expressed the need to include the movement in the preamble to the constitution.[65] This speech served as a subtle reminder to the public of the need to revise the constitution, but it also fanned the worst fears of conservatives who found themselves on the defensive following the April 15 landslide election that gave the ruling party and its allies three-fifths of all National Assembly seats, enough to enact legislation without significant hindrance from the opposition but still insufficient to amend the constitution without support from beyond the ruling party.

ELECTORAL REFORM

The Democratic Party's impressive showing in the April 2020 National Assembly elections touched on other troubling factors that increased political polarization, including the Moon administration's tactical approach toward adjusting the rules of the electoral game in 2020.

Shortly before the election, the Democratic Party proposed to divide the allocation of the forty-seven proportional representation seats into two groups. Seventeen seats would be allocated on the basis of nationwide votes for a specific party, while thirty seats would be allocated based on a formula designed to promote representation from smaller parties that might not otherwise win district races. The purpose of this proposal was to enhance the influence of smaller parties in the National Assembly by permitting them to take a greater share of seats allotted to proportional representation. The formula would allow greater representation for small parties that gained a plurality of votes across a wide number of districts but fell behind in first-past-the-post district voting. The new system was pushed through the National Assembly days prior to the start of the National Assembly electoral campaign.

But both the ruling and opposition parties immediately subverted the intent behind the electoral reform by establishing satellite parties to run candidates in districts where main party candidates were likely to come in second, enabling the satellite parties to capture seats through the new formula. In the end, tactical manipulations by both parties yielded the consolidation of a two-sided system in which large parties and satellite parties combined to take almost all the seats intended under the new rules to enhance representation by smaller parties. The ruling Democratic Party proved more successful than the opposition at capturing seats through the new system, both on the strength of a surprising district-by-district show-ing and through performance by the Democratic Party's satellite party. As Shin Gi-wook argued, this sort of tactical electioneering eroded the moral high ground of the ruling Democratic Party, suggesting that they were motivated more by the desire to perpetuate their own power than by the goal of achieving more representative electoral reforms.[66]

THE PROGRESSIVE AGENDA, POLITICAL POLARIZATION, AND BACKLASH

Despite President Moon's inaugural pledge to be a fair president for all and a force for unity, many of his main reform initiatives sparked political polar-ization and division. Moon's critics interpreted these major reform initia-tives aimed at "uprooting deep-rooted evils within society" as instruments really intended to punish political enemies and permanently lock in politi-cal power for the progressive party. In fact, the Moon administration's pur-suit of these initiatives revealed double standards among those charged to implement the reforms and caused them to lose the moral high ground, underscoring the long-standing aphorism that "power corrupts, and abso-lute power corrupts absolutely." Moon's reform efforts became a lightning rod for deepening political polarization within South Korea. Moreover, leg-islative maneuvering by the Democratic Party in the waning days of the Moon administration drove the wedge of political polarization even deeper on the issue of prosecutorial reforms. Far from upholding the candlelight spirit that enabled his election, Moon's casting of his reform campaign as an effort to uproot institutional evils disappointed reformists, polarized the public, and demonized opponents rather than expanding a level democratic playing field and overcoming South Korea's institutional flaws.

The political transition from Moon to Yoon marked a new opportunity for South Korea's political leadership to escape the deeply ingrained poli-tics of political revenge by judiciously implementing existing rules without continuing the practice of generating in-group rewards and out-group punishments of former political powerholders. The greatest pressures and the earliest temptation the Yoon administration faced in this regard were related to the power of appointments and the question of how much political pressure would be used to force Moon administration appointees holding fixed terms at government-controlled institutions to depart their posts early.[67]

Likewise, a challenge for the Yoon administration, in the context of a reformed and redistributed prosecutorial system, was the investigation of perceived wrongdoing within the Moon administration, or whether prosecutorial reforms initiated under the Moon administration would indeed contribute to the breaking of the vicious cycle in Korean politics whereby former presidents and senior powerholders spend time in jail. The Yoon administration missed an opportunity to strengthen both Korean democracy and the alliance to the extent that it has perpetuated political polarization rather than seeking to heal and overcome the deep political divisions that constrain the South Korean government from more effective governance, including more efficient management of priorities and objectives within the U.S.–South Korea alliance.

4

SOUTH KOREAN PROGRESSIVE FOREIGN POLICY AND TENSIONS IN THE U.S.–SOUTH KOREA ALLIANCE

S outh Korean political polarization not only engenders domestic political conflict but has also generated frictions within South Korea and within the U.S.–South Korea alliance. South Korean progressives have historically sought to exercise greater autonomy than conservatives both in shaping the future of the Korean Peninsula and in exercising an independent foreign policy orientation within Northeast Asia in ways that have required redoubled efforts between U.S. and South Korean alliance managers.[1] In a nutshell, South Korean progressives are more likely to fear entrapment in U.S. priorities and interests, while conservatives are more likely to fear the prospect of U.S. abandonment of the alliance. As discussed in chapter 2, the alliance has shown resiliency regardless of the type of political party leadership in both countries but has faced fewer tensions under South Korean conservatives than progressives.

Progressive leaders such as the South Korean presidents Moon Jae-in and Roh Moo-hyun have as a practical matter accepted the value of the alliance as a tool for assuring near-term national security needs but have also challenged the alliance through efforts to expand South Korean autonomy and reduce U.S. influence on South Korean foreign policy.[2] Tensions in the U.S.–South Korea alliance during progressive administrations will be inevitable so long as progressives perceive the alliance as a source of potential entrapment in regional conflicts and a factor that constrains or denies South Korea the ability to fully achieve its foreign policy aspirations. These tensions often do not play out as direct conflicts between the two allies but rather emerge as differences in progressive and conservative priorities in the context of managing policies toward North Korea and Japan.

Progressive influence on South Korean foreign policy has historically generated tensions within the alliance to the extent that progressives view the United States as preventing South Korea from reconciling with North Korea. This view stems in part from the idea that while the United States has been a security ally, it has also made decisions as a great power that have had negative consequences for the Korean Peninsula. This list includes the Taft-Katsura Memorandum that ceded the Korean Peninsula to Japanese imperial influence, the agreement in the waning days of World War II to temporarily divide the peninsula into American and Soviet spheres of occupation at the 38th parallel, and Cold War preoccupations with the deterrence of North Korea that led the United States to support authoritarian regimes in South Korea from the 1960s through the 1980s rather than weighing in decisively to support prodemocracy forces.

In contrast, conservatives have generally prioritized the issues of defense and deterrence at the center of the U.S.–South Korea alliance, with occasional frictions occurring over U.S. direct diplomatic engagement with North Korea at the perceived expense of South Korea in the 1990s and the U.S. emphasis on stability and management of conflict escalation during tensions with North Korea between 2009 and 2010.[3] This distinction leads progressives to seek unification through the pursuit of economic interdependence, trust building, and integration, while conservatives continue to expect unification to occur as a consequence of North Korea's regime failure and the expansion of South Korean values of freedom and democracy—a Korean version of the German model of unification.

Progressives see inter-Korean reconciliation and autonomy as two sides of the same coin. A South Korea in the driver's seat of policy toward North Korea is most likely to lead to progress in inter-Korean relations. At the same time, rapprochement with North Korea will enable South Korea to gain autonomy and eventually free itself from perceived overreliance on the United States, both by eliminating the necessity of U.S. troop presence on the Korean Peninsula and by strengthening the ability of South Korea or the two Koreas together to influence or create distance from the rising security competition between the United States and China.

South Korean progressives have tended to believe that the United States perceives continued Korean division as being in its interest because it provides a pretext for maintaining U.S. forces on the Korean Peninsula. Thus, they blame the United States for its perceived reluctance to achieve the peaceful denuclearization of North Korea and for the constraints that U.S. deterrence and security-focused policies have imposed on South Korea's pursuit of reconciliation with the North. Furthermore, progressives perceive the United States as committed to broader strategic objectives of maintaining global hegemony and restraining China from surpassing the United States and believe that the U.S. pursuit of those objectives will ensnare South Korea in a new cold war in Northeast Asia, denying full inter-Korean reconciliation and reinforcing the likelihood of continued division.

At the same time, though they regard North Korea's denuclearization as a distinctly less important and less feasible foreign policy objective, progressives desire a U.S. policy that supports South Korea's leadership role in achieving reconciliation with North Korea.[4] In other words, progressives see the United States as a necessary partner for South Korea in achieving its goals but fear that the United States ultimately will act according to its own hegemonic interests that interfere with South Korean aspirations of inter-Korean reconciliation and unification.

Progressives also believe that the United States failed following World War II to hold Japan fully accountable for its past atrocities due to its own strategic interests in maintaining stability and resisting the spread of the communist ideology. As a result, progressives believe that the United States did not require Japan to take sufficient responsibility for and repudiate its imperialist past. South Korean progressives prioritize holding Japan to account for historical wrongs more so than their conservative counterparts. Conservatives, who have a legacy of accommodation toward Japan including responsibility for negotiating what progressives have viewed as a flawed treaty on diplomatic normalization in 1965, see a stable relationship with Japan as both a pragmatic necessity and desirable in the context of the U.S. strategy of building a coalition to deter and pressure North Korea.[5] Progressive efforts to hold Japan accountable generate tensions in relations with the United States because such approaches do not prioritize security issues over historical ones, but the nature of the U.S. alliances with Japan and South Korea prioritizes security.

In sum, South Korean progressives seek to promote harmony with North Korea, justice against Japan, and the establishment of a more autonomous role for South Korea to reduce great power interference or constraints on South Korean interests and objectives.[6] The United States is not opposed to better inter-Korean relations but retains a commitment to ensuring that improvements in the inter-Korean relationship do not come at the expense of South Korea's security. The United States likewise desires to see a stable and amicable relationship between Japan and South Korea that builds on and reinforces rather than challenges the foundations of its own security alliances with both countries. However, to the extent that South Korean progressives pursue grievance politics with Japan at the expense of normalized bilateral relations, policy coordination on North Korea and Japan will remain a source of domestic political polarization and a source of friction in alliance management with the United States.

PROGRESSIVE VIEWS OF NORTH KOREA AND TENSIONS IN THE U.S.–SOUTH KOREA ALLIANCE

Progressive views of South Korea's relationship with North Korea and the country's role in the world were primarily formed in opposition to views reflected in authoritarian and postauthoritarian conservative administrations that made the U.S.–South Korea alliance the centerpiece of the fight against communism. These views were further developed through progressive experiences in power under the Kim Dae-jung, Roh Moo-hyun, and Moon Jae-in administrations. Many progressive thought leaders on foreign policy have served in previous progressive administrations and retained close ties with senior officials in the Moon administration.[7]

South Korean progressives emphasize reconciliation with North Korea as a national objective that is ideally independent from and a higher priority than a coordinated approach to North Korean denuclearization within the U.S.–South Korea alliance. The progressive emphasis on a South Korea–led inter-Korean reconciliation process generates friction at several levels within the U.S–South Korea alliance. First, it places inter-Korean reconciliation as a higher priority than the shared benefits to be gained from effective alliance coordination. Second, it plays into North Korean nationalist *uri minjok-kkiri* (우리 민족끼리) strategies designed to split the United States from South Korea (to be discussed in greater detail in chapter 5). Third, it reaps security benefits from the alliance while casting the United States as a constraint on the idealistic goal of achieving a unified Korean state. The former South Korean National Unification Advisory Committee chairman and former minister of unification in the Kim Dae-jung administration Jeong Se-hyun views the historical mismatch in U.S. and South Korean policies toward North Korea as resulting from the U.S. tendency to constrain developments in inter-Korean relations. Jeong sees the denuclearization issue as primarily the responsibility of the U.S.–North Korea track but believes that efforts to strengthen inter-Korean relations should serve to enhance North Korea's dependence on South Korea, thereby generating a source of leverage that can improve prospects for denuclearization.

The progressive desire for greater autonomy from the alliance is often presented as a goal best achieved via inter-Korean reconciliation, which itself many progressives believe can only be achieved by shedding the alliance as a constraint on South Korea's diplomatic freedom of action. Jeong has written that strengthening the inter-Korean relationship should be South Korea's top priority because it strengthens South Korea's hand amid a complex regional security situation. Moreover, inter-Korean reconciliation can reduce the possibility that the Korean Peninsula, a historical flashpoint for major power rivalry, would be drawn into renewed cold warlike tensions between China and Russia on one side and the United States and Japan on the other.[8]

Progressives perceive the U.S.–South Korea alliance as constraining and entrapping South Korea in the pursuit of policies ultimately counterproductive to South Korean national interests. Lee Jong-seok, Roh Moo-hyun's former national security advisor, has argued that South Korea should blunt U.S. policies in areas such as sanctions implementation and military exercises that he sees as deepening North Korean mistrust, perpetuating U.S.–North Korea tensions, and preventing the growth of inter-Korean relations. While Lee has not argued for the abandonment of the U.S.–South Korea alliance, he did urge the Moon administration to take the initiative in areas that conflict directly with preferred U.S. policy approaches to North Korean denuclearization.

Similarly, Jeong Se-hyun has expressed his concern that the installation of the Terminal High Altitude Area Defense (THAAD) system in South Korea will entangle the nation in a regional arms race that will generate new economic, political, and military pressures on South Korea. Jeong has called for South Korea to instead strengthen its diplomatic leverage by playing the role of mediator and facilitator between the United States and North Korea. Furthermore, Jeong has asserted that excessive focus on the United States will not serve South Korea's interests in light of China's growing international influence.

Lee Jeong-seok also views sanctions as an insufficient tool for inducing North Korean denuclearization and instead advocates for a step-by-step cooperative approach. Moon Chung-in, former special advisor to Moon Jae-in, echoes this view, stating that "engagement, dialogue, and negotiations with North Korea are still the most credible way of handling Pyongyang."[9] As part of this strategy, Moon advocates for South Korea to take the lead in driving negotiations and dialogue with North Korea, a recurring theme that surfaced in President Moon Jae-in's speeches on North Korea. Moon sees tension reduction as obviating the need for a U.S. troop presence in South Korea as well as South Korea's need for extended nuclear deterrence commitments from the United States.

In contrast, South Korean conservatives hold a traditional view of the importance of the alliance with the United States as a primary instrument by which to both preserve South Korea's security and enhance its diplomatic standing internationally as a close partner of the United States. Korean conservatives prioritize the importance of the alliance as an instrument of deterrence against North Korea and hold a guarded approach toward inter-Korean reconciliation. For this reason, conservative South Korean media were particularly poised to pounce on any perceived missteps the Moon administration might make in its relations with Washington and often looked to Washington as a source of leverage to magnify possible differences with Moon and other progressives, particularly on issues related to North Korea and Japan.

South Korean conservatives worried that the Moon administration was too idealistic and naive in its approach to reconciliation with North Korea. They also worried that the Moon administration would make security compromises that allowed North Korea to benefit by introducing needless tension and divisions into U.S.–South Korea alliance management. Conservatives have prioritized harmony with the United States based on shared values and have remained skeptical of the Moon administration's prioritization of both inter-Korean relations and efforts to restore harmony with China, especially in the context of the U.S. shift to values-based arguments for taking a harder line toward China.[10] Korean conservatives have been much more open to U.S. encouragement to join the Quadrilateral Security Dialogue (Quad) than progressives.[11] Even when progressives took positive steps to improve alliance coordination with the United States, conservatives remained skeptical that the Moon administration was simply making empty pledges with no intention to follow through fully to expand the scope and breadth of U.S.–South Korea alliance coordination.[12]

THE MOON ADMINISTRATION AND CHALLENGES IN U.S.–SOUTH KOREA ALLIANCE COORDINATION TOWARD NORTH KOREA

The U.S. and South Korean government bureaucracies under Presidents Moon and Trump initially coordinated well to align policies toward North

Korea despite the emergence of dramatically differing rhetorical policies during 2017. These differences in approach at the presidential level reflected serious gaps in priorities and values.

Prospects for close personal coordination between Trump and Moon initially appeared dim due to ideological differences between Korean progressives and American conservatives. As discussed in chapter 2, Trump seemed to be on a trajectory toward escalation with Kim Jong-un following his August 2017 comments that he would unleash "fire and fury" on North Korea, threats to destroy North Korea in his September 2017 speech to the UN General Assembly (UNGA), and November 2017 speech detailing North Korea's grim human rights record delivered at the South Korean National Assembly. But with Kim's declared success in missile development and shift to a diplomatic offensive in January 2018, Trump and Moon both placed a premium on developing a personal relationship with Kim and saw political benefits and shared interests in the pursuit of summitry.

With Kim's 2018 opening of summit diplomacy, the main debate reflecting progressive influence on Moon's policy toward North Korea was over the pace of developing inter-Korean relations and the extent to which progress in those relations should be linked with progress in U.S.–North Korea relations. Behind this debate loomed the question of whether complete denuclearization is essential for or an obstacle to peace on the Korean Peninsula. For progressives, inter-Korean reconciliation is primary and North Korea's denuclearization secondary. But for conservatives, leaving nuclear weapons in North Korean hands means remaining vulnerable to extortion and blackmail.

Moon's initial push for peaceful coexistence on the Korean Peninsula was criticized as idealistic, but it also gained South Korean public support due to growing anxieties in 2017 about the risks of U.S.–North Korea conflict and due to Moon's success following the Pyeongchang Olympics in reengaging in summit diplomacy with North Korea. Support for Moon's North Korea policy skyrocketed from 45 percent at the end of October 2017 following Trump's harsh speech at the UNGA to 83 percent in May 2018 following the first inter-Korean summit at Panmunjom and prior to the anticipated Trump-Kim summit held the following June in Singapore.[13]

Moon's July 2017 Berlin speech signaled his desire for mutual restraint on the part of the United States and North Korea. His quiet exploration of overtures to the North appeared worth pursuing in light of the paucity of alternative paths to conflict de-escalation.[14] But Trump escalated his rhetoric in response to North Korean missile and nuclear tests in his September 19 speech at the UNGA that called Kim Jong-un "Rocket Man" and included a threat that "if [the United States] is forced to defend itself or its allies, we will have no choice but to totally destroy North Korea."[15]

When Kim offered an olive branch to South Korea in the form of willingness to support the maintenance of a peaceful environment for the 2018 Pyeongchang Olympics in return for North Korea's participation, Moon appeared eager to accept. In fact, South Korea accepted North Korea's offer with minimal consultation with the United States. Moon's efforts to catalyze U.S.–North Korea communication around the opening and closing Olympic ceremonies were well-intentioned but not always welcomed from a U.S. perspective. The gaps in tone and posture between the allies were apparent as the U.S. delegation refused to meet with the North Koreans around the welcoming ceremonies and the U.S. vice president Mike Pence studiously avoided interactions with Kim Jong-un's sister Kim Yo-jong or the vice chairman of the Korean Workers' Party Kim Yong-chul at the closing ceremonies. It was not until Moon's special envoys Suh Hoon and Chung Eui-yong brought an invitation from Kim for a summit meeting directly to Trump that tensions around South Korea's intermediating efforts began to evaporate.

As summit diplomacy started to gain momentum, Moon's chief of staff Lim Jong-seok remarked at a briefing of the planning committee for the inter-Korean Panmunjom summit that a lesson of past engagement with North Korea was that the inter-Korean and U.S.–North Korea relationships needed to move in sync with each other.[16] Lim's statement signaled that the Moon administration would not get carried away with inter-Korean summitry at the expense of progress on denuclearization via U.S.–North Korea talks. Such coordination persisted in preparations for the inter-Korean Panmunjom summit and U.S.–North Korea Singapore summit. The inter-

Korean declaration reached at Panmunjom referenced Kim's pledge to work toward complete denuclearization as a major area of progress tied to inter-Korean exchanges and conventional tension reduction.

During the period between the Panmunjom and Singapore summits, the Moon administration played the critical roles of intermediary and catalyst in an effort to bring Trump and Kim together. Despite the alliance, however, Moon could not fully gain the trust of Trump or other high officials in his administration, hampering South Korean efforts as a go-between. The Panmunjom summit put on the record a direct commitment from Kim to work toward "complete denuclearization," providing a foothold for Trump to build on at the Singapore summit. But Trump did not mention his decision to break off planning for the Singapore summit during an Oval Office meeting with Moon in early May, instead he publicly announced his intention not to go to Singapore shortly after Moon returned to Seoul. Moon in turn held a secret second summit meeting with Kim in Panmunjom in late May as a last-ditch effort to put preparations for the Trump-Kim Singapore summit back on track.

Moon's efforts to mediate between Trump and Kim marked a high point for Moon as he engaged with Kim to put the Singapore summit back together, but Moon does not appear to have played a substantive role forwarding negotiations between the United States and North Korea. The Singapore Summit Declaration benefited from the Panmunjom Declaration forged weeks prior to the Trump-Kim summit, but the brevity of the Singapore Declaration highlights a relative lack of coordination between the two processes rather than evidence of extensive coordination. Although the declaration was thin, the single commonality between Panmunjom and Singapore was Kim's repeated willingness to work toward "complete denuclearization" along with commitments to the normalization of relations and pursuit of a permanent peace.

Over the summer of 2018, the United States had difficulty pinning North Korea down to concrete actions on denuclearization, while momentum was gathering as part of inter-Korean preparations for the September 2018 Pyongyang Summit. As the United States struggled to schedule working-level negotiations with North Korea, Moon leaned forward, pushing for the establishment of an inter-Korean liaison office at Kaesong and arguing that the inter-Korean relationship could have a catalytic role in jumpstarting U.S.–North Korea relations. Moon publicly argued in his August 15, 2018, Liberation Day speech that "developments in inter-Korean relations are not the by-effects of progress in the relationship between the North and the United States. Rather, advancement in inter-Korean relations is the driving force behind denuclearization of the Korean Peninsula."[17]

The South Korean government continued to push forward in late August and early September through working-level negotiations between the Blue House and the North Koreans to draft the Comprehensive Military Agreement (CMA), an inter-Korean tension reduction agreement that aspired to demilitarize the demilitarized zone (DMZ) through the removal of guard posts and small arms from the Joint Security Area (JSA) of Panmunjom.[18] In addition, Moon's short address to 150,000 North Korean citizens at the May Day stadium in Pyongyang and a joint trip to Paekdu Mountain (the mythological site of the origin of the Korean people) with Kim generated euphoria within the Blue House. The Pyongyang Declaration pledged cessation of military hostilities, resumption of inter-Korean economic and humanitarian cooperation, and tangible steps toward military dismantlement at Dongchang-ri and Yongbyun. But tangible steps toward implementing the declaration evaporated within weeks of Moon's return to Seoul.[19]

South Korean consultations with USFK were cursory, advice from the USFK commander Vincent Brooks was sidelined or ignored, and South Korea informed more than consulted, leaving the Trump administration to deal with a fait accompli. Senior Pentagon officials were caught off guard by aspects of the agreement, while the USFK was disappointed in their South Korean counterparts' failure to fully reflect U.S. concerns despite their efforts to constructively support the agreement. The Pyongyang summit agreements were more sweeping and concrete than U.S. officials had been led to expect, generating concerns that Moon cared more about peace and inter-Korean relations than denuclearization.[20] In retrospect, the euphoria of the Pyongyang summit may have carried the seeds of South Korean miscalculation, as Moon appears to have led Kim to expect more from

Trump on a deal involving sanctions relaxation in exchange for partial denuclearization than Trump was willing to deliver.

Perhaps more concerning following the euphoria of the Pyongyang agreement was Moon's attempt to water down the threshold for denuclearization in his comments at UNGA and in his tour of Europe in early October 2018. South Korea leaned forward on promoting inter-Korean cooperation absent commensurate progress in U.S.–North Korea denuclearization negotiations. Moon declared that North Korea's pledges were tantamount to a commitment to denuclearization, generating alarm within the Trump administration that Moon might move too fast on sanctions lifting and/or send signals to European counterparts to ease pressure on North Korea prematurely. Moon expressed his optimism during a summit with the French president Emmanuel Macron that Kim would "halt nuclear and missile tests and dismantle their production facilities but also destroy all nuclear weapons and materials stockpiled should the United States take corresponding measures" and that "if North Korea's denuclearization is judged to enter an irreversible phase, its denuclearization should be further facilitated by easing UN sanctions."[21] But Moon's expectations for North Korean actions did not materialize, nor did U.S. willingness to offer relief from UN sanctions as a unilateral gesture aimed at inducing North Korea's denuclearization. Moon's optimism and statements seeming to urge relaxation of sanctions prior to concrete actions by Pyongyang generated concerns in Washington among analysts who were much more skeptical of Kim's intentions and willingness to advance unilateral concessions.

Moon and his progressive supporters were moving in a direction that threatened to cause significant tension in the U.S.–South Korea relationship unless closer policy coordination was restored. In response, the U.S. and South Korean governments decided in November 2018 to establish a U.S.–ROK working group involving the South Korean Ministry of Foreign Affairs and the U.S. Department of State.[22] The working group, designed to strengthen bureaucratic coordination of major aspects of U.S. and South Korean policies toward North Korea, proved somewhat successful in addressing these emerging conflicts. The mechanism provided a de facto focal point for interagency consultation on the South Korean side with U.S. counterparts and ensured that neither side was caught off guard by the other, a particularly challenging feat to accomplish in the Trump administration.

The first indicator of slowing prospects for progress through summitry with North Korea came with the North's unexplained decision to call off a planned visit to the United States by Kim Yong-chul to meet with the U.S. secretary of state Mike Pompeo in early November. Second, expectations for an early summit visit by Kim to South Korea by the end of the year went unfulfilled. As 2018 wound to a close, momentum in joint implementation of the CMA faded and no discernible progress emerged from the Pyongyang Declaration.

With the advent of 2019 came a signal of possible new momentum as Kim visited Beijing for his third summit with President Xi Jinping. On this occasion, fulsome greetings underpinned pledges of closer cooperation and North Korean state media effusively praised the strength of China–North Korea relations. Shortly thereafter, North Korea made new overtures for a rescheduled visit by Kim Yong-chul to Washington to lay the groundwork for a second Trump-Kim summit. But despite progress toward a second summit meeting, U.S. bureaucrats struggled to secure North Korea's participation in the sustained working-level dialogue necessary to build on implementation of the Singapore Declaration. The U.S. special representative for North Korea Stephen Biegun met a new counterpart at a January 2019 meeting, the senior North Korean diplomat Kim Hyuk-chul. Subsequently, Biegun and his team traveled to Pyongyang for a week of negotiations on every aspect of the Singapore Declaration but denuclearization. With major questions on denuclearization outstanding days prior to the Trump-Kim summit in Hanoi, Biegun connected with Kim Hyuk-chul and Kim Yong-chul in Hanoi only hours prior to Trump's and Kim's arrivals but was still unable to have a productive exchange on denuclearization. Once again, denuclearization-related issues could only be addressed at the summit itself through leader-to-leader talks between Trump and Kim.

Moon and his team watched expectantly from Seoul as the drama in Hanoi played itself out, anticipating the announcement of a "small deal" between the United States and North Korea. The Moon administration appeared hopeful that, although such a deal would not pin down Kim to concessions sufficient to achieve "complete denuclearization," the start of a diplomatic process would be sufficient to put the United States and North Korea onto a track in which sanctions-easing measures might be exchanged for steps in the direction of denuclearization. The then U.S. national security advisor John Bolton later publicly detailed his efforts to persuade Trump not to accept such a deal, but the lack of adequate working-level negotiations also made any possible agreement premature and would clearly not have put the United States and North Korea on a pathway to the desired goal of "complete denuclearization."

The Hanoi summit's failure had multiple repercussions, most notably for inter-Korean relations and for Moon's efforts to promote a sustainable and productive U.S.–North Korea negotiation process. Kim responded to his perceived humiliation in Hanoi with a strong degree of vituperation toward Moon, suggesting that Kim somehow held Moon responsible for the summit's failure either by leading Kim to believe that Trump would deliver or by failing to convince Trump to ease sanctions on North Korea. As Kim regrouped in Pyongyang, rumors swirled about repercussions for the North Korean negotiating team. Kim took steps to erase his diplomatic failure by holding a summit with the Russian leader Vladimir Putin, demanding concessions from the United States with an end-of-year deadline and threatening to go in a different direction if the United States failed to return to the negotiating table on Kim's terms.

The breakdown of summit diplomacy revealed progressive discontent and frustration with the United States as an obstacle to progress in inter-Korean relations. These frustrations were magnified by North Korea's vituperation and South Korea's marginalization amid the stalemate between the United States and North Korea following the failed Hanoi summit.

Progressives blamed the United States for taking the overly demanding stance of requiring denuclearization first before providing North Korea with sanctions relief, and Moon received constant pressure from his progressive supporters to break the stalemate with North Korea. Despite North

Korea's poor treatment of Moon and public criticisms of the South, progressives blamed the United States for not showing more flexibility toward North Korea. They blamed Trump for not taking a small deal and advocated for the United States to reengage with the North, even as North Korea's position toward both the United States and South Korea became more intransigent.

Progressive frustrations targeted the U.S.–ROK working group, which increasingly came to be perceived as an instrument by which the United States could control South Korea and keep the inter-Korean relationship from moving forward without progress on denuclearization. Such views completely absolved North Korea of responsibility for the impasse, ignoring the role of Kim's apparent frustrations with Moon's inability or unwillingness to deliver the economic benefits Kim expected would accompany inter-Korean reconciliation. Progressives even attributed North Korea's physical destruction of a South Korean–built inter-Korean liaison office at the Kaesong Industrial Complex to U.S. failures to accommodate progress in inter-Korean relations rather than recognizing the act as North Korean retaliation for promises from Moon that went beyond his capacity to deliver.

PROGRESSIVE INFLUENCE ON MOON'S NORTH KOREA POLICY AND FRICTION IN THE U.S.–SOUTH KOREA ALLIANCE

Following the Democratic Party's April 2020 landslide victory in the National Assembly elections, progressive frustrations grew over the breakdown in U.S.–North Korea negotiations and ongoing tensions in inter-Korean relations. The election removed a domestic constraint on Moon's freedom of action as his party secured a substantial majority over the threshold that required consultations with the opposition, taking control of all National Assembly committee chairmanships and gaining greater influence over North Korea policy.

Having received a decisive electoral mandate, Moon moved to jumpstart inter-Korean relations by installing a more North Korea–first foreign policy team. Moon appointed Park Ji-won, a career politician and former cabinet member under Kim Dae-jung, as director of the NIS. As Kim's minister of culture and tourism, Park had taken part in brokering and making payment arrangements for the historic first summit between Kim Dae-jung and Kim Jong-il in June 2000. In that role, Park had negotiated a secret agreement with North Korean counterparts pledging the transfer of $500 million to arrange the summit that was concealed from the public at the time. A copy of the agreement with his signature was produced at Park's confirmation hearing, reminding the public of his involvement in this scandal.[23]

Park replaced the North Korea expert Suh Hoon, who took the helm as South Korea's national security advisor, and Suh replaced Chung Eui-yong, who subsequently became foreign minister. As Moon's special envoy, Suh had met Kim in March 2018 along with then National Security Advisor Chung, and played an instrumental role in facilitating Kim's summits with both Moon and Trump.

The individual on Moon's new foreign policy team who most embodied North Korea-first impulses was the minister of unification Lee In-young, a former pro–North Korea student activist at Korea University during the 1980s, founder of the National Council for Student Representatives (전국 대학생대표자협의회, or 전대협), former member of the Anti-American Youth Association (반미청년회), and long-time Democratic Party national assemblyman. Following a contentious hearing in which Lee deflected questions from conservative national assembly members about his former ideological beliefs and associations and whether he still held those views, Lee was appointed minister of unification on July 27, 2020.

TENSIONS OVER MECHANISMS OF ALLIANCE COORDINATION

As minister of unification, Lee publicly challenged the authority of the U.S.–ROK working group and sought to circumvent it. Lee proposed to then U.S. ambassador to South Korea Harry Harris that the working group be reformed to enable South Korea's independent pursuit of inter-Korean projects regardless of developments on the issue of denuclearization. Lee publicly floated assertions that the Ministry of Unification should not be bound by working group consultations and sought to minimize the scope of the group's influence as an alliance coordination mechanism.

Lee's challenges made the U.S.–ROK working group a lightning rod for debate and criticism from progressives on the basis that the working group constituted an obstacle to expanded inter-Korean cooperation. The working group has received criticism for blocking efforts to resume tourism at North Korea's Kumgang Mountain, work at the Kaesong Industrial Complex, build an inter-Korean railway and road system, deliver medical supplies to North Korea, build a video facility in North Korea for family reunification purposes, and conduct a joint waterway study of the Han River. Progressives have insinuated that the working group's veto of these projects serves as evidence that the United States is preventing implementation of the Pyongyang Declaration, despite the steady stream of public vituperation of Moon and South Korea by North Korean state media and propaganda outlets following the 2019 Hanoi summit failure.

The U.S. use of sanctions through the policy of "maximum pressure" to induce North Korean denuclearization also received criticism from progressives following the April 2020 National Assembly elections. Progressive critics of the United States view economic sanctions as an obstacle to inter-Korean economic cooperation and reconciliation. The expansion of UN sanctions after 2017 has particularly frustrated progressives who sought to use improved inter-Korean economic relations as an incentive to induce closer inter-Korean relations. Moon himself had advocated for a vision of a unified Korean economy contingent on the relaxation of UN Security Council (UNSC) sanctions on North Korea. Although the use of sanctions assumes relaxation as an incentive for denuclearization, progressives also see sanctions relaxation as a mechanism by which to induce North Korean economic dependence that would in turn lessen the North Korean military threat.

VALUE CONFLICTS OVER NORTH KOREA'S
HUMAN RIGHTS POLICIES

The influx of progressive influence on the Moon administration also generated tensions with the United States over North Korean human rights issues. To pave the way for inter-Korean reconciliation, the Moon administration assiduously avoided taking a stance on North Korean human rights issues at the UN and opted not to support or sponsor UN resolutions critical of North Korea's human rights record. The Moon administration failed to establish a human rights commission as mandated under South Korea's 2016 Human Rights Act and opted not to appoint an ambassador for North Korean human rights to succeed South Korea's inaugural ambassador Lee Jung-hoon, who had served under the Park Geun-hye administration. For its part, the Trump administration failed to appoint an envoy for North Korean human rights despite the U.S. congressional renewal of the North Korean Human Rights Act, and Trump downplayed human rights issues at the UN following the Trump-Kim summits in June 2018 and in 2019. But U.S. reengagement in discussions on North Korean human rights at the UN Human Rights Council and at the UNSC in 2020 drew attention to the Moon administration's inaction and to the gap in U.S. and South Korean approaches to addressing human rights in North Korea.

A major lightning rod for tensions around human rights and freedom of expression between the United States and South Korea was the National Assembly's December 2020 passage of the Inter-Korean Relations Development Act. This ambiguously written legislation banned North Korean refugee and human rights groups from launching leaflets into North Korea, a practice that had been normalized in the Lee and Park administrations.[24] The law banned the distribution of propaganda materials, goods, and money in the area near the DMZ and imposed criminal penalties of up to three years in prison or thirty million won in fines. The act's initial draft was written so broadly that it could have applied to the spread of any materials offensive to North Korea from any location, including third-party countries. The National Assembly passed a final, pared-down version of the law on December 14, 2020.

The Moon administration characterized the decision to ban leaflet drops as a national security issue and pointed to concerns from local residents close to the DMZ that such actions could cause tensions to spike and put them at risk of North Korean retaliation. The Ministry of Unification circulated a backgrounder about the new provisions that cast the law as a necessary step in implementing pledges not to slander North Korea made in the 2018 Pyongyang Declaration, and noted that those pledges extended as far back as the July 4, 1972, South–North Joint Communique and 1992 Inter-Korean Agreement on Reconciliation, Nonaggression, Exchanges, and Coopera-tion (also known as the Basic Agreement).[25] The ministry asserted that the possibility of North Korean military retaliation for the leaflets puts at risk the lives and safety of over one million South Korean residents living in the border area and cited a 2016 South Korean Supreme Court ruling that leaflet dissemination should be stopped in response to this "obvious and existing danger."[26] The author of the legislation—Song Young-gil, a mem-ber of the South Korean National Assembly—claimed that the passage of the legislation was the culmination of a twelve-year legislative process.[27] Following criticisms regarding the scope of and ambiguities within the leg-islation, the Ministry of Unification took up a revision process following passage of the law.

The new law drew international media attention and criticism on the grounds that it arbitrarily limited freedom of expression within South Korea in a fashion contrary to the nation's democratic values. It also generated the perception that the Moon administration had fallen into the trap of look-ing like it was taking orders from North Korea following Kim Yo-jong's June 2019 public criticism of the leaflets and their dissemination. More-over, the passage of the law became a point of political contention in the United States. The law drew criticism from Representative Chris Smith (R-NJ) at a hearing of the Tom Lantos Human Rights Commission as a sig-nificant breach in the shared alliance commitment to the democratic value of freedom of expression.[28]

The conflict over the leaflets revealed a deeper challenge than that of balancing the safety of the South Korean citizenry, a reasonable priority, against the ability of North Korean defectors and other concerned parties to freely send information across the border. As South Korean lawmakers sought to defuse inter-Korean conflict and accommodate North Korea for the sake of inter-Korean reconciliation, they were creating a conflict with U.S. legislative priorities codified in the 2004 North Korean Human Rights Act, which authorized funding to support North Korean refugees and other organizations in disseminating information into North Korea through a wide range of means, including leaflets.[29] This conflict between South Korean leaflet laws and the U.S. North Korean Human Rights Act added fuel to the arguments of progressives who believed that the United States was once again generating obstacles to inter-Korean reconciliation and recklessly endangering South Korean lives. In contrast, the U.S. Congress saw the North Korean Human Rights Act as a foundational step toward providing North Koreans with information independent from regime propaganda about the reality of conditions inside and beyond North Korea and viewed South Korea's leaflet law both as an improper restriction on freedom of expression and as an obstacle to the necessary dissemination of truth to the people of North Korea.

PEACE AND DENUCLEARIZATION

A final area of tension within the alliance that resulted from growing progressive influences within the Moon administration related to the question of the relationship between peace and denuclearization. The Moon administration's peace-centered approach to North Korea emphasized up-front gestures designed to reassure North Korea, such as an end-of-war declaration. The progressive camp viewed these gestures as declaratory shifts in policy that could sufficiently assure North Korea to induce greater engagement and cooperation. Progressives view the establishment of peace as the primary goal and as more realistic than denuclearization, which may or may not even be necessary if North Korea commits to peaceful cooperation.

In contrast, the United States takes the view of such declarations as useless in the absence of an underlying process and set of quid pro quos through which trust is built based on concrete actions that justify the development of a better relationship. The central question is whether peace can be achieved by top-level assertions and declarations not backed by institutional progress toward peace building, or whether it is necessary for both sides to demonstrate through small, concrete actions that there is a basis on which to extend trust and reduce hostility. Past experiences with arms control agreements with the former Soviet Union have shaped the U.S. viewpoint, while the Korean progressive viewpoint appears to be shaped by the belief that an ideal outcome would be achieved through mutual trust and by hopes that all sides will take necessary actions in good faith to achieve that ideal.

The Moon administration periodically advertised its interest in achieving an end-of-war declaration. Discussion of the prospects for such a declaration took place in 2018 in the aftermath of the Singapore Declaration. South Korean progressives saw an end-of-war declaration as a tangible step forward in peace building that both Washington and Pyongyang could take that might result in a more favorable environment for denuclearization. Trump administration probing of the issue, however, seemed to confirm that North Korea itself did not see much benefit in pursuing such a declaration. Trump briefly seemed enamored of the idea of a peace declaration with North Korea as a possible accomplishment he could sell alongside the summit as worthy of Nobel Peace Prize consideration, an idea Moon encouraged, but Trump's inability to achieve tangible progress beyond the Singapore Declaration imposed major constraints on his ability to pursue such ideas absent commensurate progress on denuclearization.

The Moon administration subsequently tried to draw attention to the concept of an end-of-war declaration through engagement with and funding of American peace groups willing to advocate for permanent peace without regard to denuclearization. In concert with the Moon administration, groups such as Women Crossing DMZ and Korea Peace Now stepped up lobbying of progressive U.S. congressional representatives in an attempt to build political support and generate pressure on the U.S. government to consider establishing a peace treaty with North Korea as part of efforts to pare down international commitments and shift attention to domestic priorities.[30] These efforts did not gain traction with the Trump administration and similarly failed to gain traction with the Biden administration, which remained committed to denuclearization rather than an end-of-war declaration as the primary U.S. objective and economic sanctions as an essential instrument by which to maintain pressure on North Korea toward that goal.

In fact, the Biden administration reverted from Trump's America-First approach to a more conventional bottom-up approach to foreign policy based on traditional post–World War II U.S. values and a worldview that emphasized alliance restoration as a major administration priority. Ironically, while the Biden administration's more conventional approach removed some sources of tension in the U.S.–South Korea alliance by replacing trans-actional demands with cooperative efforts to forge partnerships, it also revived tensions with progressives on issues such as the relative priority of policy toward North Korea versus policy toward China (to be discussed in chapters 6 and 7) and conditions under which it would be possible to resume inter-Korean economic cooperation. These developments in the United States brought the influence of progressives within the Moon administration and their North Korea–first inclinations into focus and revealed significant cleavages in U.S. and South Korean views on how to coordinate policy toward North Korea.

PROGRESSIVE VIEWS OF JAPAN

In addition to tensions with South Korean progressives over how to deal with North Korea, the United States also found itself in disagreement with progressives over issues related to Japan. The progressive-conservative divide within South Korean politics stems from differences over how to deal with the legacy of Japanese imperial rule, with conservative elites more likely to have pursued forms of collaboration and passive resistance under Japanese colonial rule and progressives more likely to have actively resisted and faced severe punishments by colonial authorities. In the view of South Korean progressives, the United States took an overly accommodating approach to Japan in pursuit of a postwar settlement. Progressives felt that the United

States had failed to insist on sufficient reckoning within Japanese society for atrocities committed under imperial rule. Progressives were also resentful that the United States, during its post–World War II occupation of Korea, had supported conservatives such as Syngman Rhee, who pursued strongman tactics in suppressing progressive political opponents, and cultivated relationships with elite conservative holders of power, money, and land who had collaborated with the Japanese imperial government.

The backdrop of ideological and class polarization left a legacy of relative support for Japan within South Korea's conservative elite and relative hostility toward Japan among progressive Korean nationalists. These longstanding political divisions over attitudes toward Japan persist within South Korea. Polarization over how to deal with Japan has grown prominent especially under progressive South Korean leaders, who have harbored grievances both regarding conservative approaches toward Japan perceived as overly accommodationist and toward the Japanese government for concluding a settlement with South Korea under the authoritarian rule of Park Chung-hee that was seen as unfair and was both politically contested and domestically opposed.

THE MOON ADMINISTRATION AND UNRAVELING OF RELATIONS WITH JAPAN

The Moon administration came into office intending to manage relations with Japan through a dual-track policy in which South Korea would pragmatically pursue cooperation on future-oriented issues while separately addressing historical issues by directly appealing to the Japanese government to take a more forthright approach in taking historical responsibility for past wrongs. But the circumstances surrounding his predecessor Park Geun-hye's impeachment had led to repudiation of Park's other presidential accomplishments, including the 2015 comfort women agreement with Japan that had been met with mixed reviews when it was originally announced.

The 2015 agreement sought to address the suffering of Korean women and girls pressed into sexual slavery in service of Japanese soldiers during World War II.[31] Already under fire following allegations that the Park administration had inadequately consulted with the surviving victims themselves, the agreement lost public support as her administration's corruption scandal and impeachment unfolded in late 2016. The 2015 agreement consisted of a formal statement of apology from the Japanese government and the provision of one billion yen to be administered by a Korean government–established foundation in support of comfort women and their families. The agreement also included language declaring the settlement "final and irreversible," and the Korean government pledged not to continue raising the issue in international forums. At the time of the agreement's announcement, the progressive *Hankyoreh* reflected long-standing progressive critiques of the South Korean government for failing to secure the Japanese government's legal responsibility for the comfort woman issue, arguing that "it is a humiliating diplomacy almost comparable to the Korea–Japan agreement in 1965, but the government does not even seem ashamed."[32]

Moon's progressive support base throughout his election campaign included many critics of the past accommodations conservative governments had made with Japan, going back as far as the initial forging of the 1965 Japan–South Korea Diplomatic Normalization Treaty and Claims Agreement. Korean progressives have long viewed Japan's annexation of Korea in the early twentieth century as illegal and have been frustrated by South Korea's failure to win compensation or official apologies that reflect this view. The Japanese government has consistently rejected these demands, and Japan has used the omission of such language in the normalization treaty to deflect progressive demands for decades. The Moon administration initially sought to maintain good relations with Japan, but a dominant view among Moon's progressive support base included demands and expectations that went well beyond the contents of Park's comfort women agreement.

Therefore, it was unsurprising that, shortly following his election in May 2017, Moon announced an internal review of the comfort women agreement, the results of which were announced in January 2018. Ultimately, the agreement was left in place, but Moon declared it "defective" and urged Japan to "accept the truth and apologize with a sincere heart."[33]

Due to long-standing progressive opposition to Japan–South Korea normalization on the grounds that the Japanese government had failed to acknowledge the illegality of its occupation of Korea under international law, the Abe administration was concerned that the Moon administration intended to challenge and demand renegotiation of the 1965 treaty between the two countries. The Abe administration accordingly maintained a rigid approach to any political or legal challenge from South Korea under progressive political leaders that could serve as a pretext for challenging the treaty.

Events during 2018 and early 2019 further entangled the Japan–South Korea relationship in an increasingly polarized South Korean domestic political environment. The most significant of those developments involved the charging and trial of the former Supreme Court justice Yang Sung-tae as part of the Moon administration's campaign to reform the executive-judicial relationship and redress "past accumulated evils." Yang was accused of a variety of misdeeds regarding bias in internal appointments and administrative management of the Supreme Court, including improperly consulting with senior Park administration officials on the court's handling of World War II–era forced labor cases brought against the successor corporations of imperial Japanese corporate entities.[34] The Yang case played out against the backdrop of controversial Moon administration reform efforts that targeted the role and perceived unaccountability of the Korean prosecution discussed in chapter 3.

With a new Moon-appointed Supreme Court chief justice in place and Yang imprisoned in part for deciding that the forced labor case should not be taken up based on consultations with the Ministry of Foreign Affairs, a primary obstacle to the court's hearing of the forced labor case was removed. The court finally accepted appeals of the forced labor case from lower courts and announced a judgment on October 30, 2018, that Nippon Steel and Sumitomo Metal Corporation were liable for 100 million won to each of the four plaintiffs. In contrast to prior Japanese court judgments, the Korean court unprecedentedly ruled that the Claims Agreement accompanying the

1965 Normalization Treaty did not exclude consideration of individual damage claims, and that successor corporations to Japanese wartime corporate entities should be held liable for compensation based on those claims. Unsurprisingly, the Japanese government rejected the South Korean Supreme Court ruling as contrary to the Claims Agreement and Normalization Treaty. In the Japanese view, the ruling constituted a breach of the treaty and should be addressed through independent arbitration, possibly through referral of the case to the International Court of Justice.

Following the announcement of the judgment in the forced labor case, the Moon administration took a concrete steps toward unraveling the 2015 comfort women agreement on November 21, 2018, when it announced that it would dissolve the Reconciliation and Healing Foundation, the Korean government–founded organization tasked with supporting comfort women and funded by the Japanese government under the agreement. Abe expressed disappointment that the agreement he had signed with Park was not being honored by the Moon administration, stating that "relations between states don't work when international agreements aren't kept."[35] On November 29, the South Korean Supreme Court upheld additional lower court rulings against Mitsubishi Heavy Industries, ordering compensation to the families of forced laborers in cases filed in Korean court in 2012 that were dismissed by Japanese courts in 2008.

The Supreme Court judgments contributed to a negative spiral in Japan–South Korea relations that quickly spread to other spheres of the relationship. The December 20, 2018, "fire-lock incident" involving an encounter in Japan's Exclusive Economic Zone off the Ishikawa prefecture between a South Korean destroyer engaged in a humanitarian operation and a Japanese Maritime Self-Defense Forces P-1 patrol aircraft caused further tension in the relationship.[36] Conflicting narratives regarding the incident between the Japanese Self-Defense Forces and South Korean Ministry of National Defense eventually led to the public release of video footage by both nations designed to support their respective points of view. Japan's Ministry of Defense argued that the South Korean patrol irradiated the P-1 aircraft with its fire-control radar, while South Korea's Ministry of National Defense released its own video of the incident and argued that it did not direct its radar at the Japanese patrol plane. The nature of the incident and the competing claims generated internal political pressures on both defense ministries to defend their positions and blame the other side.

The deterioration of the Japan–South Korea relationship led the Japanese government to impose restrictions on the export of three chemicals critical to the manufacture of South Korean semiconductors and to remove South Korea from its White List of closest trading partners.[37] These measures generated strong public backlash in South Korea, including boycotts of some Japanese consumer products popular in South Korea and boycotts against Japanese firms such as the clothing brand Uniqlo. Japanese exports to South Korea dropped from over $54.6 billion in 2018 to $47.5 billion in 2019, an almost 15 percent year-over-year decline.[38] The dispute resulted in an approximately 25 percent decline in South Korean tourism to Japan between 2018 and 2019.[39] Moon urged South Korean firms to pursue self-sufficiency in the production of chemicals provided by Japan and claimed at a cabinet meeting that "we won't be defeated by Japan again."[40] South Korea pursued arguments against Japan's export restrictions at the World Trade Organization (WTO) and threatened to withdraw from the bilateral General Security of Military Information Agreement (GSOMIA) with Japan that entered into force in 2016. But South Korea's GSOMIA withdrawal threat drew substantial public pressure from the Trump administration, which viewed the withdrawal as a step that would set back South Korea's security and indirectly weaken U.S. alliances with Japan and South Korea.

The South Korean government decided at the end of 2019 to "suspend its withdrawal" from GSOMIA. Japan's removal of South Korea from its White List and imposition of export controls did not cause significant damage or even a halt in supply, as the Japanese government did not in practice block exports of these chemicals but rather imposed additional procedures on their exports. Japan's export controls were primarily symbolic, but they had a disproportionate political effect.

South Korean media collectively urged cautious handling of the downturn in relations with Japan. For instance, in response to the initial Moon administration decision to set aside the comfort women agreement, the conservative *JoongAng Ilbo* wrote that "the government wants the comfort women issue to be handled separately from other issues, but this is only our hope. As emotions worsen due to controversy over the comfort women agreement, it is unreasonable to expect Japan to come out cooperatively as another matter."[41] Similarly, the left-leaning *Kyunghyang Shinmun* responded that "the government's announcement is in line with the 'two-track' stance that the comfort women issue should be treated as a long-term task in a victim-centered manner, but this issue should not affect other Korea–Japan relations."[42]

South Korean progressive and conservative media both responded with caution and calls for prudence following the "fire-lock incident" and the resulting propaganda competition between the South Korean and Japanese defense ministries. The South Korean media was unified in its response to Japan's decision to impose export controls on required materials for the manufacture of semiconductors on South Korean companies. And both progressive and conservative South Korean media outlets expressed caution regarding the Moon administration's possible withdrawal from GSOMIA.

But the South Korean progressive-conservative divide grew more pronounced when the United States entered the picture by urging South Korea not to retaliate against Japan's export control restrictions by abandoning the GSOMIA agreement. The progressive *Hankyoreh* sharply complained that the U.S. State Department spokesperson had "not mentioned Japan's unjust retaliatory measures that caused the situation. In this way, the U.S. argument that Korea and Japan should talk is not persuasive, and it only raises the Korean people's resentment to the pressure from the U.S. The U.S. should stop taking side of Japan and do the job as an ally."[43] In contrast, the conservative newspaper *Dong-A Ilbo* acknowledged U.S. pressure while attempting to shift the blame for any breach in the U.S.–South Korea alliance to the Moon administration, stating "The U.S is taking the upcoming expiry of the GSOMIA very seriously. Once the GSOMIA comes to an end, South Korea may be held responsible for its expiry as tensions in the alliance between South Korea and the U.S. are building resulting from the negotiations on the sharing of defense costs, the transfer of wartime operational control, etc."[44]

WEAPONIZING RELATIONS WITH JAPAN AS A SOURCE OF DEEPENING POLITICAL POLARIZATION

Worsening Japan–South Korea relations further magnified political differences between South Korean progressives and conservatives. The main driver for rising tensions with Japan involved efforts by South Korean progressives within the Moon administration to capitalize politically on tensions with Japan.

Cho Kuk—whose tenure as Moon's senior presidential secretary for civil affairs and short and controversial term as minister of justice were discussed in chapter 3—contributed in particular to an atmosphere of political polarization on how to respond to Japan. In response to Japan's July 2019 announcement of export control measures, Cho posted inflammatory opinions aimed at Korean conservatives on his personal Facebook page.[45] Cho suggested that opposition to Moon's policies toward Japan evidenced pro-Japan sympathies, evoking Korean historical analogies to play on Korean emotions in opposition to Japan.

Cho's social media posts received extensive coverage in both conservative and progressive media outlets, with the conservative scholar Ko Seong-guk arguing on TV Chosun that Cho's posts aimed to paint conservatives as pro-Japan. Cho's comments and postings referring to past Korean confrontations with Japan were particularly controversial because they appeared as fanning the flames of the Korean public response. In a series of posts, Cho shared a student demonstration song, accused the conservative media of promoting heightened anti-Korea feelings in Japan, defended Moon's response to Japan as patriotic, and asserted that Korean people who do not support their government and the Supreme Court ruling on forced labor were pro-Japanese. Conservatives suspected that Cho's postings reflected a broader campaign strategy, as his social media received support from other prominent progressives such as the assemblyman Lee In-young ("If we criticize our players and even praise Japanese players, it is a new pro-Japanese") and the progressive blogger Ryu Si-min ("It is natural and constitutional to boycott Japanese products as an expression of anger").[46] All three had prior associations with each other through participation in radical student groups during their college days.[47]

Progressive media responded to conservative coverage of Cho's social media messaging by critiquing the conservative focus on Cho rather than on Japan's economic retaliation against South Korea.[48] The *Hankook Ilbo* daily newspaper observed that, "even though it is on his social media account, Cho calling Japan as an enemy and the current situation as a war is a very careless behavior for a key public figure of the government."[49] The *Hankyoreh* reporter Seong Han-yong further stated that "it is true that the remarks of Cho Kuk went too far. . . . But I believe that as long as the LKP cannot abandon its identity as a pawn for vested interests and the security establishment, they cannot get out of the pro-Japanese frame."[50]

THE U.S. RESPONSE TO RISING TENSIONS IN JAPAN–SOUTH KOREA RELATIONS

The Trump administration largely viewed the Moon administration's backtracking from the 2015 comfort women agreement and the South Korean Supreme Court judgment on forced labor as the catalysts for the deterioration of Japan–South Korea relations. The entanglement of Japan–South Korea relations in South Korean domestic political considerations generated tensions in the U.S.–South Korea alliance as it became an issue requiring management in the alliance context. Unfortunately, a vacuum in leadership under the Trump administration left the United States ill-positioned to play a constructive role in halting the negative spiral in Japan–South Korea tensions.

In his memoir of his time as Trump's national security advisor, John Bolton provides a revealing glimpse into U.S. perspectives of the Japan–South Korea dispute through his visit to Tokyo and Seoul in the summer of 2019. Bolton accurately reports the positions of the two governments as shared by their respective national security advisors, but his sympathies clearly lay with Prime Minister Abe, who Bolton describes as "as shrewd and tough as they come" in his invocation of export laws in response to the perceived South Korean infringement of the 1965 Normalization Treaty and Claims Agreement.[51] In contrast, Bolton describes Moon's secret meeting with Kim in an effort to get the Singapore summit back on track as going behind the back of the United States. Bolton's mistrust of Moon is evident in his self-professed desire to "get Moon out of the business of negotiating" denuclearization with North Korea.[52]

Bolton's brief description of the Japan–South Korea dispute and his talks with his counterparts from both nations reveal his wariness that any direct efforts by Trump to facilitate a better Japan–Korea relationship might backfire. The best Bolton felt he could achieve was a temporary "standstill" agreement in which Japan and South Korea agreed to refrain from actions that would further harm their bilateral relationship. Bolton apparently could not envision positive actions the Trump administration might take to help stabilize the Japan–South Korea relationship. Bolton's account reveals that the main purpose of his visit to both countries was to advance an integral feature of Trump's America-First agenda: mercenary demands for billions of dollars in defense cost-sharing contributions from both Seoul and Tokyo. This objective impeded the Trump administration's ability to secure meaningful steps by either country to reverse the negative downward spiral in their relationship. But Bolton claims success in at least inducing Japan and South Korea to pursue a "standstill" approach by which both sides pledged not to make the situation worse than it had already become.[53] An environment in which all parties placed their respective domestic interests above combined security needs and failed to understand the positions of the other, if sustained, would be toxic to the security needs of all three countries.

The Biden administration took early steps to fill the vacuum in U.S. leadership vis-à-vis its Japanese and South Korean allies by encouraging a stable Japan–South Korea relationship almost from the beginning of the administration and by dropping the exorbitant burden-sharing demands. The U.S. secretary of state Antony Blinken and the secretary of defense Lloyd Austin made the administration's first overseas diplomatic visit to Tokyo and Seoul in March 2021 for two-plus-two meetings with both allies, and Prime Minister Suga and President Moon were the first two foreign leaders to meet Biden at the White House in April and May 2021. The revitalization of the two alliances was not only motivated by a U.S. desire to arrest the downturn in Japan–South Korea relations but also by the emergence of the U.S. strategic rivalry with China as a top strategic concern of the Biden administration, pitting authoritarianism against democracy in a values contest in which Biden expected to call on like-minded allies for support and partnership.

This framing of U.S. strategy toward Asia prioritized alliance coordination as well as cooperation between allies, creating expectations for Japan and South Korea to show greater bilateral cooperation and join an active set of trilateral consultations on foreign policy, intelligence, and defense matters. Wherever opportunities for trilateral coordination have emerged, from North Korea policy to the holding of trilateral meetings on the sidelines of significant multilateral gatherings such as the G7 Foreign and Development Ministers Meeting and Leaders' Summit in the United Kingdom in April and May 2021, the Biden administration pushed for coordination among Seoul, Tokyo, and Washington.

The Moon administration received the message that efforts should be made to improve the Japan–South Korea relationship immediately following Biden's election in November 2020. The Moon administration sought to improve relations with Japan in hopes of replicating summitry involving North Korea around the Tokyo Olympics set for July 2021, but North Korea's withdrawal from the games in the spring of 2021 squelched that opportunity. Moreover, despite Moon's rhetorical change in tone toward Japan, the Moon administration failed to implement the reassurance measures Japan had insisted on as a prerequisite for the resumption of leader-level meetings, which included blocking judicial implementation of the Supreme Court's judgment in the forced labor case. Due to Suga's unwillingness to move forward despite Moon's change in tone, plans for bilateral meetings around the G7 meetings and the Tokyo Olympics repeatedly failed to materialize, revealing that many pitfalls remained despite the Biden administration's efforts to bring Japan and South Korea together both to coordinate policy toward North Korea and to strengthen alignment among alliance partners in their respective approaches to China.

The Biden administration's overall emphasis on alliance restoration created constraints and opportunities for progressive influences within the Moon administration. Strong domestic support for the alliance and favorability toward the United States within South Korea constrained Moon's ability to take actions that might generate frictions with the United States and opened the Moon administration up to additional public critique in its final year in office. The looming presidential election in South Korea reinforced the potential costs and risks that would accompany friction with the Biden administration's strategic focus on rivalry with China, yet Moon retained a personal commitment to the revival of U.S.–North Korea diplomacy and to maintaining stability with China to ensure its cooperation on North Korea–related issues.

CONSERVATIVE FOREIGN POLICY PRIORITIES AND ALLIANCE MANAGEMENT

South Korea's early 2022 presidential election campaign manifested polarized views of relations with Japan that were reflected in the platforms of the main progressive and conservative presidential candidates, Lee Jae-myung and Yoon Suk-yeol. The Democratic Party presidential candidate Lee hewed to a cautious and critical line toward Japan, indicating that he would pursue continuity with the Moon administration's dual-track policies in his approach to Japan. Yoon, the People Power Party candidate, in contrast, boldly expressed his intent to improve South Korea's relationship with Japan to its highest level since normalization, explicitly referencing the 1998 Kim-Obuchi Joint Declaration that announced a new partnership for the twenty-first century. Yoon's public embrace of an improved relationship with Japan seemed to be grounded in a perception that South Korean views of the importance of a good relationship with Japan had shifted in the context of rising South Korean anxieties and concerns regarding China and rising Chinese tensions with the United States. Yoon's intent to improve relations with Japan further reinforced his focus on developing a "comprehensive strategic alliance" with the United States as the centerpiece of South Korea's foreign policy, especially given the Biden administration's strong emphasis on enhancing trilateral policy coordination among the United States, Japan, and South Korea.

Upon coming into office, President Yoon showed early enthusiasm for a rapid improvement of relations with Japan, but his efforts faced two main obstacles. First, while the Yoon administration's desire to improve the relationship with Japan was welcomed, it was necessary for the Kishida administration to recover a base of support from both political elites and the Japanese public before it would be possible for the Japanese government to respond to the Yoon administration's overtures. Second, the Yoon administration faced a National Assembly controlled by the opposition Democratic Party that could easily oppose Yoon's efforts to improve relations with Japan by capitalizing on any missteps that might cost Yoon support among the South Korean public for a better Japan–South Korea relationship.

The most likely pathway to success for the Yoon administration would be to show political leadership by building a public consensus in South Korea in support of its effort to improve relations with Japan and by avoiding political missteps that might provide opportunities for the opposition to criticize the administration's handling of the issue. To successfully achieve this objective and to avoid missteps that had resulted in South Korean public criticism of the Park administration's handling of the 2015 comfort women agreement, the Yoon administration needed to both find a way to uphold the validity of South Korean court judgments on the comfort woman and forced labor issues while managing those issues with the Japanese government and induce the Japanese government to engage in a political process by which engagement on outstanding historical issues would build on rather than challenge the 1965 diplomatic normalization treaty and claims agreement. Such an approach would not completely overcome South Korean progressive calls for a Japanese governmental reckoning over Japan's imperial past on the Korean Peninsula, but it might provide a strategic rationale and approach sufficient to win South Korean public consensus in favor of a stable and productive relationship with Japan.

PART II

EXTERNAL THREATS TO THE ALLIANCE

5

NORTH KOREAN INFILTRATION AND INFLUENCE OPERATIONS

North Korea has consistently pursued policies of confrontation, subversion, and cooptation vis-à-vis South Korea in pursuit of its goal of unification of the peninsula on North Korean terms. North Korean efforts to exploit South Korean domestic political divisions are similarly long-standing. Kim Il-sung pursued this strategy during his military invasion of South Korea in 1950, with the expectation that thousands of sympathetic South Korean leftists opposed to Rhee Syngman's corrupt and oppressive rule would rise up to support Kim's effort to liberate South Korea from cronyism and imperialist foreign influences. Subsequently, North Korea has sought to work with dissidents inside South Korea to discredit South Korea's leadership, assert the superiority of the North's system, and sow dissent and chaos within South Korea.

Historically, North Korea has pursued extensive efforts to infiltrate South Korea under authoritarian rule and launched influence operations targeting South Korean prodemocracy protesters in the 1970s and 1980s. North Korean efforts to influence South Korea's domestic environment aimed to exploit and stir up dissent against South Korean ruling authorities. North Koreans reached out to South Korean compatriots through state-run United Front Department organizations and other covert operations designed to establish pro–North Korean groups in South Korea, extend North Korean influence, and incite South Korean opposition attacks on the legitimacy of South Korean dictatorships.[1] During this time, authoritarian South Korean leaders often used the draconian National Security Act (NSA) to brand and punish all dissidents as pawns of North Korean efforts to infiltrate and overthrow South Korea. Indiscriminate application of the NSA blurred the line between real North Korean influence operations and authoritarian pretexts for the suppression of opposition voices. Successive progressive administrations have attempted to revise and/or repeal the law, which still remains on the books.

In the context of South Korea's democratization, the distinction between North Korean influence and South Korean freedom of thought can be blurry: in an open society, pro–North Korean thoughts should not be subject to prosecution unless they cross the line into action and incitement, yet the South Korean state has also used pro–North Korean sympathies to broadly tar critics and dissidents under authoritarian regimes with the NSA. As a result, the ongoing debate within South Korea over the legitimacy of the NSA has pitted South Korean rights to freedom of expression and action against national security concerns deriving from North Korean sympathies that could lead to unpatriotic or treasonous actions.

As a main component of its foreign policy strategy, North Korea has sought to weaken and ultimately sever alliance ties between the United States and South Korea. To this end, North Korea has historically used wedge-driving strategies designed to increase pressure on the alliance and generate separation between the United States and South Korea. To maximize pressure, North Korea has alternated between strategies designed to engage with the United States while marginalizing South Korea and strategies designed to bind Koreans together in national unity while eschewing foreign involvement in inter-Korean affairs. As reflected in table 2.1, North Korea has sought to take advantage of favorable ideological inclinations of progressive South Korean administrations by pursuing cooperation and seeking material benefits from South Korea while taking a more confrontational approach toward South Korean conservative administrations. North Korea pursues these political strategies alongside infiltration and influence operations within South Korea to encourage anti-U.S.

sentiment and to incite resentment against the U.S. military presence in South Korea. The susceptibility of the South Korean public to this strategy has fluctuated in accordance with varying levels of South Korean public support for the U.S.–South Korea security alliance.

NORTH KOREAN INFILTRATION OPERATIONS

North Korean infiltration operations into South Korea have historically aimed to damage and weaken South Korean leadership or institutions, conduct espionage for the purpose of exploiting South Korean weaknesses or engage in reconnaissance in preparation for possible military conflict, exact revenge against North Korean defectors who have betrayed the motherland, and disrupt South Korean essential activities and raise funds for the North Korean regime through cyberattacks on South Korean government and business institutions. Over time, North Korean infiltration operations have gravitated from assassination attempts on South Korea's leadership to cyber operations conducted for disruption, intelligence-gathering, and fundraising purposes.

Even following Kim Il-sung's failure to take over the South and unify the Korean Peninsula under his rule, North Korea pursued military provocations designed to measure South Korean readiness as well as infiltration and influence operations with the purpose of subverting South Korean rule and weakening its political leadership. North Korea's most brazen infiltration occurred during the Park Chung-hee era, when North Korea was economically and militarily more powerful than South Korea and the United States was preoccupied with the Vietnam War. On January 18, 1968, thirty-one armed commandos from North Korea Special Operations Forces Unit 124 infiltrated South Korea and came within a kilometer of the Blue House before being driven back by the South Korean police. Twenty-nine of these commandos were killed in South Korea, one was captured, and one escaped back to North Korea.[2] The captured North Korean operative later revealed Unit 124's plan to assassinate President Park to drive a wedge in the U.S.–South Korea alliance. The assassination attempt greatly concerned

Park, who demanded increased U.S. assistance in preventing future infiltration efforts by North Korea.[3] North Korean infiltration operations during the Cold War peaked in 1967 with over 184 known North Korean operations across the DMZ into South Korean territory at the height of the U.S. involvement in Vietnam, but such operations declined steadily through the 1970s.[4]

The largest post–Cold War North Korean infiltration operation occurred in 1996 and involved a North Korean submarine carrying twenty-six armed soldiers and three special forces operatives who conducted surveillance and intelligence-gathering on South Korean military bases around Gangneung, a city on South Korea's east coast. The submarine ran aground offshore and was discovered by a local taxi driver, triggering a forty-nine day nationwide manhunt for North Korean soldiers.[5] Twenty-four of the North Korean soldiers were killed, one soldier was reported missing, and the submarine helmsman Lee Kwang-su was captured.[6] The Ministry of Unification identified the operatives as members of the 22nd fleet of North Korea's Reconnaissance General Bureau, North Korea's primary arm for pursuing intelligence collection and clandestine operations, and characterized the mission as an attempt to increase North Korea's negotiating power with the United States related to implementation of the Geneva Agreed Framework.[7]

North Korean infiltration efforts have focused on achieving specific intelligence collection goals. In 2006 South Korea's National Intelligence Service (NIS) arrested Jeong Gyeoung-hak, an agent from the Korean Workers' Party Unit 35.[8] The NIS caught Jeong traveling with a Thai passport on his way out of South Korea following attempts to gather intelligence on the Uljin nuclear power plant, the Cheonan air force radar base, and the U.S. military base at Yongsan.[9] He had entered South Korea three times in total and had also attempted to photograph the Blue House twice but failed due to the high level of security in the area.[10] North Korea allegedly sought to use intelligence from Jeong to make precision strikes on major South Korean facilities, including the nuclear plant.[11] Jeong was arrested and tried under the Roh administration, and his case was kept quiet to minimize the impact on South Korean public support for engagement with the North. In

December 2022, the North Koreans flew drones into South Korea in an effort to surveil and collect intelligence on South Korean military facilities.[12]

Other North Korean infiltration operations in South Korea have focused on assassinating North Korean defectors. In October 2008, Won Jeong-hwa, an agent affiliated with North Korea's National Security Agency, entered South Korea with a Chinese passport and posed as a North Korean defector.[13] She was ordered to find Hwang Jang-yop, a vocal critic of the North Korean regime who had defected to South Korea in 2000, locate key facilities in South Korea, and kill two South Korean intelligence officers responsible for collecting information on North Korea. After her arrest, Won was convicted of violating the National Security Act by stealing classified material, maintaining communication with North Korea, and publicly showing banned material glorifying North Korean leaders.[14] In addition, two North Korean agents arrived in South Korea in July 2010 with orders from the head of North Korea's Reconnaissance General Bureau (RGB), General Kim Yong-chol, to pose as defectors and assassinate North Korea's highest-level defector Hwang Jang-yop.[15]

There is not yet a direct link between highly public statements issued in the name of Kim Yo-jong and the RGB or other intelligence institutions within North Korea, but Kim's direct attacks on North Korean defectors as the main source and catalyst behind laws banning the dissemination of leaflets by balloon from areas in South Korea adjacent to the DMZ contain the hallmarks of a North Korean propaganda operation designed to achieve the objective of punishing or silencing North Korean defectors. Kim's use of strongly derogatory language to describe the defectors as "human scum little short of wild animals who betrayed their own home-land" generated political pressure on President Moon at the time. The clear intent of the statements to induce the Moon administration to silence and punish these defectors strongly suggests that the effort may have originated with the RGB.[16]

North Korea has also invested in cyberattacks on South Korean targets. The first major North Korean cyberattacks on South Korean institutions took place in the form of denial-of-service attacks in July 2009 and affected thirty-five major organizations and government agencies. The initial aim of North Korean cyberattacks appears to have been targeted at generating social disruption more than financial gains.[17] The attacks started with U.S. government websites and expanded to commercial U.S. websites and commercial and government websites in South Korea.[18] A second wave of attacks followed on July 7, with major targets including the websites of South Korea's Ministry of National Defense and National Assembly.[19] On July 15, a third wave targeted sixteen South Korean government agencies. The attacks were traced to the North Korean Ministry of Post and Telecommunications office in China. The South Korean government responded by establishing a National Information Service System responsible for policy coordination within the government under the Ministry of Interior and Safety and by creating an upgraded Presidential Committee on National Information Strategy, including upgraded capabilities to respond to distributed denial of service (DDoS) attacks.[20]

March 2013 marked the start of a wave of North Korean cyberattacks designed to disrupt essential institutions and infrastructure and to steal cybercurrency.[21] North Korea planted "DarkSeoul" malware that damaged around 32,000 servers, leading to mass outages and damaging South Korea's computer infrastructure.[22] The attack was traced to a Chinese IP address used in a previous North Korean cyberattack and further spurred South Korean efforts to strengthen cybersecurity, including the announcement of plans to introduce a national cybersecurity plan.[23]

In June 2013, a wave of cyberattacks targeted 131 servers of sixty-nine South Korean organizations, including the Blue House and the Office for Government Policy Coordination, causing websites to display messages such as "The Great Kim Jong-un" and "Praise to the Unification President Kim Jong-un."[24] These attacks were launched from the same Chinese IP address that the attack in March originated from.[25] In response to these attacks, the South Korean government released a National Cybersecurity Plan that strengthened the ability of the government to lead an effective response to attacks on communication and information infrastructure.[26] The plan reduced the anticipated response time for an attack from six hours to thirty minutes, promoted phishing blocking apps on newly released smartphones, and incentivized private companies to strengthen their cybersecurity systems.[27]

In March 2016, it was revealed that North Korea had hacked 25,000 phones in South Korea, including the mobile phones of a dozen top government officials.[28] North Korea has also been suspected of having stolen 235 gigabytes of classified military documents, including sensitive operational war plans for North Korea.[29] There have also been reports of North Korean cyberattacks on South Korea's nuclear infrastructure but no reports of North Korean success in penetrating critical systems responsible for controlling nuclear plants.

North Korean cyberattacks have been prominently mentioned in connection with theft of cybercurrencies, especially from South Korean–run cybercurrency exchanges. The global profile of North Korean cyberattacks has increasingly become associated with financial motives following operations targeting the Bank of Bangladesh and cash distribution systems in Hong Kong, Chile, and other countries. But the aim of North Korean cyberattacks in South Korea have historically not been confined to financial gains and have continued to pursue both information collection and societal disruption as central aims. It is likely that the cyber cat-and-mouse game that has arisen between North Korean offensive cyber operations and South Korean lines of defense will continue to evolve as new technologies proliferate and new vulnerabilities associated with technological development continue to emerge. Through these efforts, North Korea gains the capital necessary to survive and probes for weaknesses in South Korean defenses using asymmetrical means that benefit to some degree from the ambiguity of immediate attribution.

NORTH KOREAN INFLUENCE OPERATIONS AND THE JUDGMENT OF SOUTH KOREA'S CONSTITUTIONAL COURT

The deliberations of a single case involving a South Korean Constitutional Court decision to disband the United Progressive Party (UPP) and the parallel Supreme Court decision to convict the UPP's leader Lee Seok-ki and several UPP colleagues provide perhaps the clearest legal window into the history and modus operandi of North Korean influence operations.[30] Therefore, this examination will rely on the court's decision as the primary basis for examining North Korean influence operations in detail. A review of the UPP case also reveals how the court interpreted the constitutional balance between freedom of expression and treasonous or antistate actions in modern democratic South Korea. This is an issue that has become increasingly relevant to efforts to safeguard democracy from foreign misinformation in other countries, including the United States.

The reasoning and evidence provided in the 340-page 8-1 opinion of the December 19, 2014, Constitutional Court decision mandating the dissolution of the UPP provides legal documentation concerning North Korean influence efforts within South Korea. The Constitutional Court decision and accompanying Supreme Court judgments concluded that Lee Seok-ki committed treasonous acts while stopping short of concluding that Lee acted under the direction of North Korea. The case marked the first time that the Constitutional Court had ordered the dissolution of a South Korean political party since 1958. But the decision remains controversial as part of an ongoing debate over whether the UPP's dissolution served to safeguard or erode democratic practices.

THE CREATION AND OPERATION OF THE UNITED PROGRESSIVE PARTY AND EVENTS LEADING TO ITS DISSOLUTION

The United Progressive Party (UPP) was established on December 13, 2011, in a merger of three parties that sought to create a broad coalition among progressives in the run-up to the April 2012 South Korean National Assembly elections. The merger itself, alleged by the conservative assemblyman Ha Tae-kyung to have been conducted on orders from North Korea, brought together the labor-focused Democratic Labor Party, the liberal-led Participation Party, and the radical New Progressive Party, but internal conflicts in the respective policy positions of the merged party leadership proved difficult to reconcile.[31] The former Participation Party and the Democratic Labor Party focused on trade and national social welfare and labor rights issues, respectively, while representatives of the former New Progressive Party took stances in defense of North Korea and critical of the United States.

But in the course of the merger, the official stances and representation of the party moved radically toward a pro–North Korean orientation. For instance, the party refused to criticize North Korean missile launches and the UPP leader Lee Jeong-hee put forward a pledge to abolish the U.S.–South Korea military alliance, withdraw U.S. forces from the Korean Peninsula, achieve peaceful Korean unification, and abolish the National Security Act at an event commemorating the twenty-first anniversary of the establishment of Beomminryon (Pan-Korean Alliance for Reunification) held at Chosun University in Gwangju on December 18, 2011.[32]

The coalition performed well enough in the April 2012 National Assembly election to secure thirteen seats, seven from districts and six awarded by proportional representation based on party popularity among 6 percent of Korean voters. However, it became known after the election that the internal selection of proportional representation list representatives during the March 14–18 party conference had been manipulated through vote-rigging in favor of the former New Progressive Party members Lee Seok-ki and Kim Chae-yon.[33] In response to allegations that internal party voting processes had been manipulated, the party fractured the August following the elections and the social progressive cochairs Shim Sang-jung, Ryu Si-min, and Cho Joon-ho left the party.[34] Shim established the Democratic Justice Party the following October and was joined by four other National Assembly representatives. The UPP maintained control over three seats, including the proportional representation seats held by Lee Seok-ki and Kim Chae-yon.

Within the National Assembly, Lee and Kim held positions that either aligned with or refrained from criticizing North Korean views and actions. These positions were consistent with the UPP's party platform. The primary catalyst for Lee's National Assembly expulsion and investigation was a secret speech he gave to members of the Revolutionary Organization on May 12, 2013, advocating for a domestic rebellion and the destruction of South Korean infrastructure.[35] Lee stated "We can create and realize an autonomous world, a reunified world, a new stage of autonomous society after driving out the Americans, and the dream of the Korean nation, which is an era with no exploitation and suppression. . . . Let us do or die in the final, decisive battle to build a new future throughout the nation, by forming one physical force, not just with talks or determination of a few people. . . . Are you ready to prepare yourselves for combat immediately when you receive an order?"[36]

In response, the Park Geun-hye administration petitioned for Lee's arrest, but Park's motives for pursuing the arrest were viewed by some critics as thinly veiled revenge for the UPP's attacks on Park, including the UPP candidate Lee Jeong-hee's use of the Japanese pronunciation of Park's name during the presidential debates. Nonetheless, the National Assembly voted to revoke Lee's immunity as a member of the National Assembly by a vote of 255 to 2, with seven abstentions. Then assemblymen Moon Jae-in and Lee In-young, along with five other Democratic Party members, abstained from the vote. Lee and three colleagues faced criminal charges for plotting an insurgency to take up a violent revolution in March 2013 and for violating the National Security Act by possessing a wide range of materials produced in North Korea that supported North Korea and by leading pro–North Korea rallies.

CONSTITUTIONAL COURT FINDINGS AND THE DISSOLUTION OF THE UPP

The South Korean Constitution contains an amendment, put in place in 1960 following the government's effort to dissolve an opposition political party, that established a judicial role for the dissolution of parties.[37] This amendment was put into place following the Syngman Rhee administration's closure of a leftist Progressive Party on grounds of collaboration with North Korean agents and communist sympathizers. (A 2010 Supreme Court judgment ruled the closure unjustified on grounds that the evidence for the party's closure was based on a coerced, false confession.)[38] The Constitutional Court judgment weighed the balance between the "foundational belief that a citizenry's autonomous decision-making process will ultimately lead to the right decision" and the power vested in the Korean constitution to dissolve a political party if its objectives or activities constitute a threat to "basic democratic order."[39] The decision reviewed the exceptional situation created by Korea's division and the ongoing threat to the "basic democratic order" posed by North Korean efforts to subvert South Korea's political system.

It then reviewed the history of the development of progressive political parties since South Korea's 1988 democratic transition and the ideological divisions that emerged between the People's Democracy (PD) and National Liberation (NL) wings of the progressive movement. The PD wing, or "Equality Faction," viewed South Korea's social order—based on "monopoly capitalism" and "class dominance"—as the core problem to be overcome and focused on progressive policies inspired by classical Marxist-Leninist thought that emphasized labor rights and social welfare. The NL agenda hewed much closer to North Korea's guiding ideology of *Juche*, or "self-reliance."[40] The NL wing, including the hard-core pro–North Korea *Jusapa* faction, worked toward a national liberation revolution aligned with North Korean ideology that would achieve "anti-American autonomy, anti-fascist democratization, and unification of the South and the North, which would overthrow Korean capitalism tied to imperialism."[41]

Based on this framework, the court's judgments regarding Lee Seok-ki and the UPP revolved primarily around two questions: (1) whether the introduction of "progressive democracy" into the UPP represented a term meant to signify activities designed to threaten the "basic democratic order," and (2) the question of whether Lee Seok-ki's speech to and actions in the Revolutionary Organization, especially in May 2013, represented incitement to launch a violent revolution to overthrow the South Korean political system.

The court interpreted the evolution of the term "progressive democracy" and its addition to the UPP party platform as a euphemism for efforts to manipulate democratic structures to gain organizational control and as a red flag suggesting undue North Korean influence on party formation. The argument centered on "progressive democracy" as a veiled reference for an agenda that seeks a "permanent solidarity mechanism" in pursuit of national autonomy, democracy, and unification.[42] At the UPP Closing Ceremony for Victory Campaign HQ following the election and prior to the split of the UPP North Korean–aligned policies of national autonomy, Lee Seok-ki stated that "progressive democracy groups have established a popular progressive party line, set up a populist party movement for the peaceful unification front, and created the Progressive Party as a unified consolidated party. . . . The incident of the Progressive Party is a class struggle by progressive democrats to seize political power."[43]

At a small group meeting for ideological study held on May 8, 2013, Hong Sun-seok further elaborated on progressive democracy, stating that "the progressive democratic process is autonomy, democracy, and unification. The origin of the word 'progressive democracy' could be traced to the work of the Leader in which he mentioned that our society should be constructed as a progressive democratic society. It is the origin of progressive democracy, and when we talk about democracy, we say that it should be progressive democracy. . . . We decided to call it progressive democracy for now."[44] The court concluded that the goals of the UPP's platform were to "first realize progressive democracy through violence, and then based on this, ultimately realize socialism through unification."[45]

Regarding the charges of incitement, the court reviewed rising tensions with North Korea following its third nuclear test on February 12, 2013, and its March 5 declaration of terminating the Korean Armistice Agreement. Against the backdrop of these tensions, North Korea reportedly sent instructions to South Korean operatives to show solidarity during a state of emergency, mobilize the public, and collect information on U.S. military bases in South Korea. As part of this mobilization, Lee Seok-ki spoke at a secret meeting in Mapo-gu on May 12, 2013, to approximately 130 attendees affiliated with a pro–North Korean network.[46] Lee's speech characterized North Korea's nuclear development and abrogation of the armistice as a major turning point in a confrontation with the United States that would lead to war. Lee advocated for a South Korean political revolution under his leadership, urging physical and technological preparation for war, followed by a social revolution that would remove capitalists and replace them with mass-based leadership of the proletariat. Lee stated "What's wrong with shooting when circumstances call for it? Let's shoot! It is reasonable to shoot. Nuclear weapons, what's wrong with it, it is the pride of the nation. . . . We must create opportunities and proudly shoot."[47] Lee did not object to participant discussions of how to take down critical infrastructure in South Korea and whether insiders might be won over to help destroy electrical plants and fuel storage facilities.

The single dissenting opinion in the case by Justice Kim Yi-su distinguished the activities of Lee Seok-ki from those of the UPP and made an argument that the UPP should not be held responsible for the actions of a single leader. But he did not dispute whether Lee was guilty of treason or inciting revolution within South Korea.

THE CONSTITUTIONAL COURT DECISION AND EVIDENCE OF NORTH KOREAN INFLUENCE OPERATIONS

The court opinion indirectly addresses three instances of past North Korean strategies to influence South Korean dissidents and cultivate pro–North Korean activism and more in South Korea. First, the court opinion details the history of pro–North Korean organizational work and Lee Seok-ki's involvement since the 1980s. Second, the court details communications with North Korea around the establishment of the UPP and North Korean instructions for how to maximize influence within the UPP. Third, the court details standard North Korean influence strategies and tactics also used by Lee Seok-ki and his followers as part of efforts to subvert political order in South Korea.

The court's review of Lee Seok-ki's history of involvement with pro–North Korea groups provides a solid record of past North Korean influence efforts in South Korea. Along with the former dissident Kim Young-hwan, Ha Young-ok, and others, Lee took part in the establishment of Kim Il-sung's *Juche* ideology as the guiding ideology of the "Anti-Imperialist Youth Alliance," established in March 1989. The Anti-Imperialist Youth Alliance (반제청년동맹) went on to become the foundation for the establishment of the Democratic Revolution Party in 1992. The party pursued its ideology of promoting revolution among oppressed groups in South

Korea with the aim of seizing control over dissident organizations and leading violent antigovernment struggles. The former Democratic Revolution Party Central Committee member Kim Young-Hwan illegally entered North Korea twice, met with Kim Il-sung, and received operating funds. According to Kim's testimony, his colleague Ha Young-ok also joined the Workers' Party of Korea. The party established regional chapters that acted as cell groups to prevent infiltration and exposure of the entire network to South Korean authorities.

In January 2002, on the instruction of North Korean agents, Jang Min-ho established *Ilsimhoe* (일심회), an organization that sought to root out American imperialism and promoted unification by federation. The organization regularly reported to and received instructions from North Korean agents on personnel matters, activities, and actions to be conducted. *Ilsimhoe* was identified as a pro–North Korea organization and the Supreme Court sentenced Jang to seven years in prison.[48] The Democratic Labor Party members Choi Ki-young and Lee Jung-hoon were caught leaking personal details of hundreds of party officials to North Korea and were subsequently charged with espionage for receiving, leaking, and delivering state secrets.[49]

The Action and Solidarity network (남북공동선언실천연대) was established on October 21, 2000, received instructions from North Korean agents, propagated the content of North Korea's New Year's Joint Resolutions, and supported North Korea's nuclear tests. The Seoul Central District Prosecutor's Office stated that six members of the group met with members of North Korea's United Front Department and received instructions such as to punish Kim Young-sam and Hwang Jang-yop, crush defector groups, hack the U.S. Embassy website to display anti-U.S. propaganda, and organize a committee to advocate for the withdrawal of U.S. troops in South Korea.[50] The South Korean Supreme Court declared it an enemy-benefiting organization on July 23, 2010.

The Korea Youth Movement Council (한국청년단체, Hanguk ch'ongnyon danch'e) was established in February 2001 under North Korean direction to advocate against American imperialism and foreign interference from the United States. The group was declared an enemy-benefiting organization by the Supreme Court on February 2, 2009, for violating the National Security Act, stating that the group praised and promoted North Korean activities.[51]

The court also reviewed reports of North Korean involvement in efforts to introduce "progressive democracy" into the platform of the Democratic Labor Party and the UPP. The court's opinion revealed that North Korea instructed agents in the Incheon region to "make progressive democracy, which has already been adopted by the Democratic Labor Party, the guiding ideology of the progressive grand unified party" and to promote concepts such as autonomy, equality, antiwar peace, democratic reform, and solidarity.[52]

Finally, the court decision detailed a range of North Korean strategies for achieving revolutionary objectives: the creation of a united front through alliances "encompassing all anti-imperialist and patriotic classes, political parties and organizations and a broad alliance of patriotic people of all classes"; the promotion of mass struggles to raise public awareness, catalyze organization, and teach people how to struggle using both legal and illegal means; advocacy for unification via federation with an autonomous democratic government in South Korea; and the pursuit of a go-slow approach to revealing its final objective of achieving socialist reforms.[53]

THE CONSTITUTIONAL COURT FINDING AND DEBATES OVER SAFEGUARDING SOUTH KOREAN DEMOCRACY

The Constitutional Court's judgment in this extraordinary case drew a boundary between freedom of expression and national security by calling for the UPP's dissolution. The court's decision provided clear evidence that the UPP had adopted a pro–North Korean party platform and that the National Liberation faction within the party had engaged in internal election rigging to secure a higher position on proportional representation lists than was justified. These actions themselves caused a party split as social progressives and liberals exited the party, further consolidating party control under pro–North Korea radicals.

The court's decision to dissolve the UPP catalyzed a notable debate over whether the decision was good for South Korea's democratic system. The progressive citizen journalist OhMyNews contributor Jang Ho-chul observed that the conservative *JoongAng Ilbo* supported the outcome as a reasonable defense of South Korea's democratic system and lamented that it was necessary to take such a step in the first place, while the progressive *Hankyoreh* argued that the decision represented a blot on the court and that UPP's existence itself had been a testimony to the progress of democracy. *Hankyoreh* argued that the court had acted prematurely in taking action against the party and that judicial curtailment of party activities was a setback for Korean democracy.[54]

The fact that the National Assembly unanimously decided to strip Lee Seok-ki of immunity following the vote-rigging scandal and publicity surrounding his May 12 speech suggests that the National Assembly itself realized that Lee had gone too far. The court decision finding him guilty of incitement and violating the National Security Act through the possession of a wide range of pro–North Korea materials and for singing revolutionary songs underscored limits imposed by South Korea's national security situation and North Korea's ongoing antipathy and competition against the South Korean system. These actions establish clear limits on the freedom of speech on national security grounds that are to some degree unique to South Korea as a country that remains in a state of war with North Korea but also represent universal limits and safeguards that any political system might establish when facing treasonous actions or incitements to insurrection. Lee's incitement of his audience went beyond issues of freedom of expression or possession of North Korean materials. The Constitutional Court's decision to dissolve the UPP drew a stark line limiting organizational activities and recruitment based on antistate platforms and revolutionary ideologies.

The UPP split into two successor parties. The Democratic Justice Party essentially purged the pro–North Korean elements within the new party while retaining its emphasis on social progressivism. The Minjung

Party absorbed many former UPP members but has been careful not to embrace progressive democracy so as to stay within the boundaries of acceptable political expression drawn by the Constitutional Court.

The Minjung Party was created on October 15, 2017, by the former UPP National Assembly members Kim Sun-dong, Oh Byung-yoon, and Lee Sang-kyu, who all lost their National Assembly seats after the dissolution of the UPP.[55] The Minjung Party platform distances itself from progressive democracy and does not follow several elements of former UPP platforms, including the abolition of the NSA.[56] The party's popularity remains low, and it is unclear whether broad public support for the party is sustainable within South Korea. The constitutional provision allowing for the dissolution of parties may indeed not be necessary to the extent that South Korean public sentiments toward North Korean revolutionary ideology are self-correcting.

Even more complicated questions arise about the sustainability of ideological limits on South Korean political parties to mobilize pro–North Korean support within South Korean society when one considers the dramatic shift in the composition of South Korea's Constitutional Court since 2014. Under the Moon administration, many conservative justices were replaced by more progressive justices who would likely be more sympathetic to party organizations, even if there were grounds for political leaders who espouse revolutionary views to be held criminally liable. The opposition-appointed justice Kim Yi-su's minority opinion that refused to accept individual or even collective leadership actions as sufficient to impute responsibility to the party organization would likely be in the majority view if a similar case were to come before a Constitutional Court in which a majority of judges were appointed by a progressive administration. The likelihood of shifting judicial interpretations under progressive leaders toward a more permissive approach to pro–North Korean expressions has catalyzed strong protest and counterdemonstrations on such issues among South Korean conservatives today.

South Korean public opinion continues to tilt conservative on these issues, opening up the possibility of further cleavage and polarization within South Korea over the proper limits of expression under the National Security

Act and the question of the extent to which it is necessary or desirable to outlaw North Korean influence, infiltration, and subversion efforts. These efforts are undeniable due to their exposure with the UPP's dissolution. The question now is whether South Korean democracy deems them tolerable or whether they provide an opening for North Korea to continue its pursuit of subversion of a government in South Korea that it continues to regard as illegitimate.[57]

NORTH KOREAN POLITICAL STRATEGIES AND THE U.S.–SOUTH KOREA ALLIANCE

Alongside North Korean infiltration efforts and influence operations, the U.S.–South Korea alliance has remained a consistent target of North Korean political and diplomatic strategies aimed at widening gaps between Washington and Seoul. North Korea has traditionally employed two types of political strategies toward the alliance as an effort to drive a wedge between the alliance partners. The first political strategy, known as *tongmi bongnam* or "communicate with the United States; ignore South Korea," involves focusing on political engagement with the United States while marginalizing South Korea. The second political strategy, known as *uri minjok-kkiri* or "our nation together," involves efforts to build ethnically based solidarity with South Korean political leadership at the expense of the United States through an emphasis on grand national unity. Both strategies have been utilized at various times during periods of North Korean engagement with the United States and South Korea, respectively, to generate tensions between alliance partners over policy coordination toward North Korea.

The strategy of *tongmi bongnam* has generally been utilized by North Korea as part of an effort to go over South Korea's head directly to the United States on issues of critical importance to South Korea. In the 1990s, North Korea used the *tongmi bongnam* strategy as part of nuclear talks with the United States that led to the Geneva Agreed Framework. By engaging directly with the United States and keeping South Korea at arm's length,

North Korea played on South Korean fears of political exclusion on security issues critical to South Korea. This strategy generated tensions and resentment between the U.S. president Bill Clinton and the South Korean president Kim Young-sam during the course of the U.S.–North Korea nuclear negotiations in Geneva that complicated the negotiation of the Agreed Framework and the initial implementation of the light water reactor project outlined in the U.S.–North Korea agreement. Specifically, the North Koreans strongly objected to the selection of a South Korean model light water reactor as the type to be constructed under the agreement and initially resisted the participation of a South Korean company as the project's main contractor implemented under the auspices of the newly established multinational Korean Peninsula Energy Development Organization (KEDO). North Korean resistance to South Korean participation in the project caused approximately a year of delay in implementing the agreement on issues that required additional U.S.–North Korea official negotiations to resolve.

North Korea's efforts to pursue *tongmi bongnam* are most likely to occur under circumstances in which South Korea is led by a conservative president and the North perceives opportunities to marginalize or punish South Korean hard-line policies by pursuing opportunities for engagement with the United States while resisting cooperation with South Korea. For instance, North Korea viewed the return to power of the South Korean conservative Lee Myung-bak following a decade of progressive engagement-oriented leadership under Kim Dae-jung and Roh Moo-hyun as a propitious moment to return to a *tongmi bongnam* approach. Under the Lee administration, North Korea cut off high-level dialogue channels with the Lee administration and shot down the Gumgang Mountain tourism project following the killing of a South Korean tourist by a North Korean soldier.[58] In that circumstance, North Korean state media outlets criticized the Lee administration's proposals to establish liaison offices and engaged in personal attacks against Lee while continuing to leave the door open for talks with the United States. The Supreme People's Assembly International Parliamentary Union chairman Choi Tae-bok was reported as stating that North Korea can be friends with the United States if it abandons its hostile policy, and North Korea's official newspaper *Rodong Sinmun* stated that the door was open for improved U.S.–North Korea relations.[59]

The second North Korean strategy designed to separate the United States and South Korea is known as *uri minjok-kkiri*. This strategy has been a part of inter-Korean engagement approaches since the two Koreas resumed contact in the early 1970s, in the form of joint efforts by the two Koreas to resist the influence of outside powers in inter-Korean affairs. The strategy uses the pretext of a one-Korea ethnic brotherhood to categorize the United States as an unwelcome outside influence and directly targets the alliance by goading South Korea to pursue autonomy and rejecting cooperation with the United States in favor of pan-national unification.

Since progressive Korean political leadership has historically been more amenable to inter-Korean engagement and cooperation, *uri minjok-kkiri* themes are usually more prominent during phases of inter-Korean engagement and are a running theme in inter-Korean declarations at the leadership level, including the July 1972 declaration and subsequent summit declarations in 2000, 2007, and 2018. North Korea appeals to ethnic unity as a basis for exclusion and minimization of influence of external parties, in particular the United States.

North Korea has successfully used cultural exchanges during periods of inter-Korean engagement under progressive South Korean administrations as a basis and pretext for the promotion of themes of pan-national ethnically based Korean unity. North Korea successfully supported cultural exchanges and family reunions to promote feelings of ethnic brotherhood among the South Korean public. But under the surface, North Korea exerted strict political controls and deflected activities that North Korean authorities felt might feed the spread of South Korean influences within the North. The North's strategy of promoting highly controlled family reunions of limited duration and restricted to once-in-a-lifetime contacts over the span of forty-eight hours generated surface propaganda benefits for North Korea while exposing the strictness of North Korean political controls over its own people. Periodic promotion of sporting exchanges and pan-national football matches under the "unification flag" of a pale blue representation of a unified Korean Peninsula on a white background has provided similar ethnic-nationalist-based jolts of pride and good feeling. The strategy generated propagandistic campaigns for national unity while seeking to maintain strict control over North Korean participants in such joint events. The joint entry of Korean athletes under one flag at the 2000 Sydney and 2018 Pyeongchang Olympics sought to capitalize on the sporting competition to present an idealized picture of Korean unity to the world.

During North Korea's 2018 pursuit of summit diplomacy and its failure in 2019, North Korea pursued *uri minjok-kkiri* and *tongmi bongnam* in combination with each other. Kim Jong-un's charm diplomacy toward the United States, initiated following an intense phase of successful missile testing and rising tensions in 2017, utilized the Moon administration as an intermediary and as a partner in North Korea's international diplomatic outreach to create the environment for Kim's summit outreach to both China and the United States. North Korea's participation in the 2018 Pyeongchang Winter Olympics was punctuated with moments of high-level inter-Korean engagement designed to evoke *uri minjok-kkiri* sentiments, including the exchange of athletes, the merger of the Korean women's hockey team for the first time in international competition, and the hosting in South Korea of high level North Korean officials including Kim Jong-un's sister Kim Yo-jong in the opening and closing ceremonies. These gestures from the North created an atmosphere of reconciliation and high expectations for institutionalization of inter-Korean exchanges and cooperation in South Korea. But following the failed 2019 Hanoi Trump-Kim summit, the North turned South Korea's role from intermediary to marginalized actor. In the end, Moon was not a main actor but a bystander at the Trump-Kim DMZ meeting on June 30, 2019, and Kim Yo-jong became a vociferous public critic of South Korea and even President Moon himself, blowing up the inter-Korean relationship symbolically and physically by ordering the destruction of the South Korean–constructed inter-Korean liaison office established in Gaesong in the run-up to the 2018 Pyongyang Summit.

Following the transition from the Trump to Biden administration and the apparent end to prospects for a close leader-to-leader relationship between the United States and North Korea, the tone of North Korea's approach has shifted slightly back toward *uri minjok-kkiri* as North Korean official statements emphasizing U.S. hostile policy firmly rebuffed the U.S. openness to the resumption of diplomatic dialogue while leaving the door ajar to the resumption of inter-Korean relations conditioned on the Moon administration's disavowal of so-called "double-standards" in which Moon reaches out toward the North while continuing to invest in defense and deterrence.[60]

However, with the election of the conservative Yoon administration in South Korea and the low likelihood that North Korea would perceive direct engagement with South Korean conservatives as likely to yield a favorable outcome, North Korea took steps that suggest a shift back to a *tongmi bongnam* strategy in which the North would be more likely to engage in negotiations with a U.S. counterpart than with a South Korean counterpart in the event that negotiations materialize.

NORTH KOREAN WEDGE-DRIVING STRATEGIES AND THEIR EFFECTS

North Korea has steadfastly pursued the objective of unification of the Korean Peninsula on its own terms, initially through force and subsequently through efforts to infiltrate and destabilize South Korea, and with South Korea's democratization, through cyberattacks and influence operations designed to foment revolution, subvert democratic processes, and to exploit divisions between the United States and South Korea. A primary North Korean objective, as seen in its alternation between the *tongmi bongnam* and *uri minjok-kkiri* strategies, has been to exploit divisions between the allies.

As a leading Asian democracy, South Korea has had to contend with North Korean subversion strategies while upholding democratic principles of open debate in addition to defending against subversion and efforts to instigate revolution from within. The deliberations of South Korea's Constitutional Court and its verdict in the case of Lee Seok-ki and the UPP highlight the complexity of distinguishing between external threats generated by North Korea's influence operations and acts of incitement by

South Korean citizens subject to those external influences. The Constitutional Court grappled with the challenge of defining the limits on political speech and freedom of expression necessary under the South Korean constitution to preserve the stability of the South Korean state from the threat of revolution and incitement. Although the South Korean Constitutional Court deliberations occurred in the unique context of an armistice between state parties that maintain conflicting claims over the legitimacy of their rule, the challenge of balancing between constitutionally guaranteed freedoms of political expression and the imposition of limits on incitement necessary to ensure constitutional order is one that fellow democracies share. It is a task that has been made even more difficult in the context of increasing domestic political polarization, as a result of which even empirical facts may become contested as a result of intensely competing narratives.

In his waning days in office prior to the March 2022 presidential election, Moon announced presidential pardons for Park Geun-hye and Lee Seok-ki on the same day. Although there was no accompanying explanation for why Moon simultaneously pardoned Park and Lee, the timing implies a moral equivalency between the impeachment of a sitting president and the dissolution of a party and its leadership for inciting revolution against the state. While the pretext for Moon's pardons appeared to be part of a tactical effort to influence voters ahead of the presidential election, they also presage the likelihood of yet another chapter in North Korea's ongoing efforts to use influence operations to exploit political divisions in an increasingly politically polarized South Korea.

6

SOUTH KOREA'S ORIENTATION AND CHINA'S RISE

The emergence of U.S.–China competition for influence over South Korea constitutes a serious puzzle for South Korean strategists tasked with preserving South Korea's interests, independence, and voice. Moreover, rising U.S.–China rivalry has generated pressures on South Korea to more actively coordinate its policy toward China with the United States, even to the extent that the focus on the threat from China within the alliance may supersede the past focus of alliance coordination almost exclusively on North Korea. As reflected in chapter 2, while South Korea has cooperated with the United States under both progressive and conservative administrations in the context of rising U.S.– China rivalry, South Korean conservative administrations have shown much greater willingness than their progressive counterparts to publicly align with the United States as a hedge against China's rising regional and global influence.

While Chinese direct intervention in South Korean domestic politics has been rare, the question of how to deal with China has generated active debate among South Korean strategists. Three main schools of thought have presented different visions for how South Korea should position itself in the context of U.S.–China geostrategic competition: (1) South Korean conservatives seek to shore up and strengthen security alignment with the United States; (2) moderates seek to buffer South Korea against U.S.–China rivalry by making common cause with other Asian middle powers and developing stronger relations with extraregional actors such as the EU and the Association of Southeast Asian Nations (ASEAN); and (3) progressives view inter-Korean reconciliation as the key to South Korea's ability to build the strategic depth on the peninsula necessary to retain and maximize Korean autonomy and independence amid major power rivalry.

Each school of thought on South Korean strategic options draws from historical response strategies to China that include accommodation, balancing, and choice avoidance or hedging. South Korea pursued policies of accommodation in China–South Korea relations following diplomatic normalization in the 1990s in an effort to induce strategic cooperation and alignment toward North Korea but to little effect. South Korea has generally eschewed balancing policies that involve full-scale alignment with the United States and Japan to limit China's regional influence, though some have advocated for such alignment as an essential element of South Korea's security strategy. In response to growing U.S.–China competition, South Korea under the Moon administration defaulted to hedging strategies and attempted to create multiple decision points on many different issues rather than aligning with either China or the United States in an effort to navigate a middle course between the two powers. In contrast, the conservative Yoon administration has embraced a much more overt alignment with the United States but maintains that the development of a "comprehensive strategic alliance" does not imply a zero-sum framework with a China–South Korea relationship built on "mutual respect." Alongside these primary strategies, both conservative and progressive South Korean administrations have advocated for some form of institutionalized cooperative multilateralism since the late 1980s. Finally, though South Korean strategists have considered the pursuit of neutrality and independence, they have generally set aside such strategies as unfeasible in light of current geostrategic realities.[1]

CONSERVATIVE VIEW: STRENGTHEN ALIGNMENT WITH THE UNITED STATES AND PURSUE REALIST ENGAGEMENT WITH CHINA

Conservative South Korean strategists, such as those who lead South Korean foreign policy under the Yoon administration, support the restoration and expansion of alliance-based cooperation with the United States to uphold shared values and a rules-based international order. They recognize that South Korea's close alignment with the United States and access to U.S. markets have historically enabled its economic success and that South Korea's export-led economy has succeeded in part because Pax Americana created an environment in which South Korean exports have been able to thrive. Though South Korean conservatives actively support taking advantage of the economic opportunities that have resulted from China's participation in globalization and entry into the WTO, they fear that the evolution of China's economic policies and use of economic leverage as an instrument of coercion will likely make Korean bets on China increasingly risky.

China's domestic illiberalism is a source of concern for South Korean conservatives, and they also worry that China is enabling North Korea to pursue nuclear and other military development. Some conservatives support the return of tactical nuclear weapons to the Korean Peninsula and/or strengthened U.S. commitments to extended nuclear deterrence in defense of South Korea, and insist that any revision of military operational control arrangements exercised by USFK not come at the expense of the combined U.S.–South Korea deterrence posture. While South Korean conservatives have also shown caution in calling out China as a violator of international norms, they strongly advocate for South Korean participation in U.S.-led multilateral cooperation efforts designed to challenge Chinese actions that subvert international norms and laws.

South Korean conservative media outlets scrutinized the Moon administration's handling of the U.S.–South Korea alliance for evidence of gaps between Washington and Seoul not only on North Korea but also on China. They advocated for South Korean participation in U.S.-led initiatives such as the Quad and criticized Moon's hesitancy to join such initiatives. For instance, on the eve of President Moon's first meeting with President Biden at the White House, *Joongang Ilbo* argued that "only South Korea balks at joining the Quad as the Moon administration habitually worries about China's economic retaliations. But without security, there's no economy anyway."[2] South Korean conservative outlets expressed dissatisfaction with Moon's effusive rhetoric toward China designed to frame common approaches to governance and international affairs. Conservative South Korean websites and chat rooms increasingly promulgated a narrative that characterized Moon as pro–North Korean and pro-Chinese, with subscribers to Korean conservative YouTube channels expressing their anxiety that the "socialist" Moon administration would sell out South Korean national interests by taking direction from Pyongyang and Beijing.

In sum, South Korean conservatives are wary of China under Xi Jinping, concerned by rising Chinese influence and the possibility of Chinese interference in South Korean domestic politics, and increasingly support an approach that aligns with a U.S.-led balancing strategy designed to stem the negative effects of China's rising regional influence. These conservative precepts have guided the trajectory of South Korea's policies toward China under Yoon.

MODERATE VIEW: LEVERAGE RELATIONS WITH OTHER MIDDLE POWERS TO BUFFER AGAINST CHINESE AND U.S. PRESSURES TO TAKE SIDES

An alternative view preferred by South Korean moderates such as the Ajou University professor Kim Heung-gyu is that South Korea should strengthen relations with other middle powers (countries that have the ability to partially influence aspects of foreign relations but are not major powers capable of setting the international agenda on their own) in Asia and beyond to buffer against the fallout of U.S.–China strategic competition.[3] Moderates have successfully advocated for South Korea to leverage its middle power capacities through outreach to and coordination with countries such as Australia, Indonesia, and Vietnam and the strengthening of relations with multilateral organizations such as ASEAN, EU, and NATO, all of which were incorporated to varying degrees in the Moon administration's policies.

Moderate South Korean strategists advocate for the forging of partnerships with other middle powers as an approach that should be implemented independent of existing U.S.-led alliance networks or groupings designed to counter China's rising regional influence. They argue that South Korean diplomatic efforts should aim to promote solidarity with like-minded actors that have an interest in maintaining good relations with both the United States and China but seek to develop a unified voice in urging self-restraint by both parties. A major challenge to this strategy is that in the strategic context of U.S.–China rivalry, the respective interests, priorities, and thresholds for joint action on individual issues of middle powers or other groupings may not always align.

The strategy of enhancing relations with other middle powers as a buffer against rising U.S.–China rivalry does not envision an end to the U.S.–South Korea alliance but an environment in which South Korea can maintain the U.S.–South Korea security alliance to offset South Korean economic dependency on China while independently promoting cohesion among groups of third-party countries on an issue-by-issue basis. However, there is little evidence that it would be possible for a middle-power coalition to serve as an effective buffer against U.S.–China rivalry.

PROGRESSIVE VIEW: PURSUE STRATEGIC DEPTH AND ENHANCE AUTONOMY VIA RECONCILIATION WITH NORTH KOREA

The progressive approach to strengthening South Korea's ability to navigate U.S.–China competition involves emphasizing inter-Korean reconciliation as the key to unlocking enhanced strategic weight and standing for a South Korea or unified Korean nation capable of charting its own course. The progressive strategy seeks Korean unification not only as an end goal for achieving peace and prosperity on the peninsula but also as a possible solution to Korea's geopolitical quandary as a "shrimp among whales" endlessly caught up in clashes between greater powers over the strategic orientation of the Korean Peninsula.

Progressive strategists have most immediately sought the gradual reduction of South Korea's reliance on the U.S.–South Korea security alliance through enhanced cooperation with North Korea and eventual elimination of the security threat from North Korea. For the time being, South Korean progressives recognize the necessity of a close alliance with the United States, but they anticipate a diminishing U.S. role in influencing South Korean foreign policy. The United States might serve as a counterweight to excessive Chinese influence, but Korean progressives seek to either ensure security and autonomy through enhanced multilateral cooperation or by playing great powers off each other.

With inter-Korean reconciliation and peaceful coexistence reducing South Korea's need for protection from the North and freeing up its ability to focus on external threats, progressives would most likely seek a diplomatic orientation of neutrality vis-à-vis neighboring great powers. Korea's growing capacity and willingness to resist pressures from great powers would lessen its need for security dependency on the United States. Furthermore, a more autonomous and independent Korean orientation in foreign affairs, accompanied by increasing degrees of inter-Korean political cooperation and mutual alignment, would empower South Korea to work toward reducing the North's economic and political dependency on China and enhancing South Korea's relations with China based on cooperation and mutual respect.

Through peaceful Korean coexistence or reunification, progressives seek to enable the Korean Peninsula to free itself from the geostrategic stalemates of the Cold War and post–Cold War eras, become capable of managing its own security needs, and rebuff external efforts to unduly influence its autonomy or geopolitical orientation. However, though South Korean progressive strategists believe that reconciliation will allow the Korean Peninsula to gain autonomy and independence, they have yet to provide the road map for precisely how this will work in practice. Furthermore, the progressive vision for a future China–South Korea relationship will likely generate friction with China to the extent that it challenges China's strategic interest in using North Korea as a buffer as well as China's Sinocentric approach to relations with neighboring countries.

CHINA'S EXPANDING REGIONAL INFLUENCE AND THE EVOLUTION OF SOUTH KOREAN POLICY VIEWS TOWARD CHINA

In the view of some, China's rising impact on the Korean Peninsula represents a restoration of China's historic dominance, reminding strategists of the Korean sensitivity and deference to Chinese centrality that characterized the China–Korea relationship for centuries during Chinese imperial rule. Events of the late nineteenth century, including the 1894–95 Sino-Japanese War, upended the traditional Sinocentric order and led to a shift in orientation of the Korean Peninsula from a regional order revolving around China to one shaped by imperial Japan. The post–World War II spread of U.S.–Soviet rivalry and the Korean War armistice contributed to the institutionalization of a bipolar global order in which South Korea migrated into the U.S. orbit and North Korea into that of Communist China and the Soviet Union. The U.S.-led Asian regional architecture, underpinned by U.S. alliances with Japan and South Korea, remained stable for decades, even surviving the collapse of the Soviet Union and the end of the Cold War.

Today, it is increasingly under stress from China's ambition to restore a Sinocentric regional order. South Korea has once again found itself caught in the vortex of a renewed and deepening geopolitical rivalry, this time between the United States and China. While China seeks to weaken and eventually induce U.S. withdrawal from the Korean Peninsula, the United States seeks to revitalize alliance coordination as a foundation for efforts to resist widening and deepening Chinese influence throughout the Indo-Pacific. South Korea sits atop a sharpening U.S.–China geostrategic fault line, magnifying the significance and implications of South Korea's policy choices.

Prior to the emergence of U.S.–China strategic competition under the Trump administration, South Korean views of China and the United States were not politically polarized. As discussed in chapter 4, the influence of domestic political polarization has been felt primarily on foreign policy questions that evoke Korean nationalist sentiments, like Japan and North Korea.[4] In contrast, conservatives and progressives alike were apt to see trade and other engagement with China as an economic and political opportunity to expand South Korea's geopolitical horizons at little or no cost to its relationship with the United States. Even when political problems arose, such as China's Northeast project that subsumed ethnic Korean history in Manchuria or China's treatment of North Korean refugees, there was no significant difference in response between South Korean progressives and conservatives.

Until the emergence of the THAAD imbroglio in 2017, progressives and conservatives were much the same in their handling of China-related issues. The conservative Roh Tae-woo administration cautiously coordinated its opening to the Soviet Union in 1990, and normalized ties with Beijing in 1992. With the establishment of diplomatic relations between Seoul and Beijing, the two countries deepened their economic interdependence; embraced the exchange of citizens through trade, tourism, migration, and educational programs; and declared successive levels of strategic partnership under Kim Young-sam, Kim Dae-jung, and Roh Moo-hyun. The conservative Lee Myung-bak administration embraced economics-driven improvements in relations with China despite China's description of the U.S.–South Korea alliance as a "Cold War relic," and Lee also explored prospects for the construction of oil and natural gas pipelines from Russia through North Korea with his Russian counterparts. The development of a strategic partnership between China and South Korea has reflected a growth in bilateral economic ties and progressed independently of the ideological orientations of successive South Korean governments. The conservative Park Geun-hye administration pursued its own Eurasia Initiative designed to connect the Korean Peninsula with continental Eurasia and developed a Northeast Asia Peace policy that borrowed directly from Roh administration efforts to promote the institutionalization of cooperative security in Northeast Asia. The Moon administration's New Northern Policies built directly on Park's Eurasia Initiative, which in turn drew inspiration from the Kim Dae-jung administration's desire to restore a land route for trade with Europe via the Trans-Siberian railway.

RISING U.S.–CHINA RIVALRY AND SOUTH KOREAN DOMESTIC POLARIZATION OVER CHINA POLICY

The revival of U.S.–China strategic rivalry on the peninsula, driven initially by China's objections to U.S. placement of a mid-range defensive Terminal High-Altitude Air Defense (THAAD) system in South Korea aimed at countering advances in the range and lethality of North Korean short-range missiles and multiple launch rocket systems (MLRS), catalyzed domestic polarization over how South Korea should navigate rising U.S.–China tensions and stimulated debate on China policy among South Korea's conservative, moderate, and progressive camps. China's economic retaliation against South Korea for allowing the THAAD deployment despite Chinese objections demonstrated its willingness to impose costs on South Korea for making decisions that the Chinese perceived as undermining China's national security, while South Koreans saw China's objections as unprecedented interference in decisions related to South Korea's defenses against the North. China's perceived interference fueled South Korean public anxieties about China.

The promulgation of the U.S. National Security Strategy in late 2017 formalized U.S.–China competition as a framework both for viewing China in the context of strategic competition and for viewing alliances as instruments through which the United States would respond to China's rising ambitions. South Korea has sought to view economic dependency on China and security dependency on the United States as complementary rather than mutually exclusive. However, South Korea is now under pressure from both the United States and China to make strategic choices in favor of one side over the other. Moon administration efforts to repair relations with Beijing and differing preferences between Korean conservatives and progressives on how to deal with China in the early stages of the COVID-19 pandemic revealed growing polarization in South Korean views of China.

DEBATE ON THAAD AND CHINA'S ECONOMIC RETALIATION

The Moon administration came to office following the Park administration's decision to accept the installation of THAAD in South Korea. THAAD was deployed in late 2016 and early 2017 amid the corruption scandal that led to Park's impeachment and paved the way for Moon's presidential inauguration. During the THAAD deployment process, the progressive opposition objected to its implementation, as evident in Jeong Se-hyun's concern outlined in chapter 4 that the deployment would entangle South Korea in a regional arms race. But ultimately progressives did not oppose the deployment itself. However, the incoming Moon administration refused to address unsatisfactory conditions for supplying and supporting troops stationed at the site in Seongju where the THAAD batteries were deployed, leaving the issue to fester as a point of friction in the U.S.–South Korea alliance.

As the Moon administration opted not to reverse the THAAD deployment, it had to contend with the fallout of China's economic retaliation across many sectors, including Chinese tourism to South Korea, cultural exports to China, sales of South Korean cosmetics and mobile phones in the Chinese market, and retaliation against retail stores in China owned by Lotte—which sold to the South Korean government the golf course where the THAAD units were deployed. Economists estimate that China's economic retaliation against South Korea in the form of restrictions on Chinese tourism and Korean pop music concerts in China resulted in over $24 billion in lost revenue to South Koreans.[5]

A deeper impact of the THAAD dispute emerged with the rise of China-related issues as sources of political contention between the progressive ruling party and the conservative opposition. Park's impeachment had opened her foreign policy decisions up to scrutiny from the incoming Moon administration. The Japan–South Korea comfort women agreement underwent a formal review and eventual reversal by the Moon administration, but despite its vulnerability to criticism resulting from rushed deployment during the transition period, the THAAD deployment escaped unscathed. Moon's party initially objected to the THAAD deployment on grounds that the decision was rushed and that the government had failed to conduct a proper environmental impact study, but once in office the progressives conducted no such review.

Against the backdrop of Park's impeachment, members of Moon's party had hurried to Beijing to posture against the THAAD deployment. But those efforts received bitter media criticism from South Korean conservatives, reflecting overall South Korean support for the deployment and resentment against China's heavy-handed intervention. Most notably, a delegation led by Song Young-Gil, a progressive heavyweight and leading Moon supporter, visited Beijing to meet with the Chinese foreign minister Wang Yi in January 2017 following Park's impeachment.[6] The South Korean media widely criticized Song's visit as ill-timed in a clear political signal that reversal of the THAAD deployment by the incoming Moon administration would engender heavy domestic criticism. But such objections from conservatives that Moon might prove to be too soft toward China persisted as Moon sought to stabilize the relationship with China following the THAAD imbroglio.

THE "THREE NO'S" AND MOON'S 2017 VISIT TO BEIJING

Moon found himself constrained by both South Korean public opinion and U.S. expectations that South Korea would not reverse the THAAD decision, but as South Korea's new president he still had a responsibility to reverse the damage to China–South Korea relations. In an effort to clear the decks before Moon's planned visit to Beijing in December 2017, his administration negotiated an agreement through coordinated statements by both nations' foreign ministries to "normalize" ties and work toward the "further development of the strategic cooperative partnership." But the controversial statement involved a pledge that became known as the "three no's," in which South Korea agreed not to join a trilateral alliance with the United States and Japan, permit future THAAD deployments in South Korea, or join a regional integrated missile defense system with the United States and Japan. Through the statement, the Moon administration attempted to meet Chinese conditions for putting the THAAD imbroglio in the past while maintaining South Korea's flexibility to meet its future security needs.

But debate ensued in South Korea over whether adherence to Chinese demands was a prerequisite for improved China–South Korea relations or simply a statement of the current reality that could change in accordance with South Korea's future assessments of its own defense needs. South Korea's minister of foreign affairs Kang Kyung-wha told a parliamentary session that "the 'three no's' were not matters on which we gave China our consent, but were simply a repetition and confirmation of [the South Korean government's] existing position."[7] Depending on one's interpretation, the Moon administration was pragmatically building the foundation for a restoration of the relationship or was engaging in what the opposition party politician Joo Ho-young referred to as "humiliating diplomacy."[8]

The agreement generated a firestorm of controversy in South Korea exacerbated by a Chinese government readout that distorted and expanded its interpretation of the agreement beyond its original scope and wording.[9] South Korean public opposition to the three noes generated defensive interpretations of the agreement from the Moon administration, deepened the controversy surrounding relations with China, and further limited what the Moon administration could accomplish without receiving public criticism.

Moon's December 2017 "fence-mending summit" in Beijing attempted to get economic relations back on track with heavy participation from the Korean business community, but it also contributed to further domestic polarization. *Chosun Ilbo* highlighted reports of Chinese security officials manhandling South Korean journalists, Moon and his entourage being stiffed in terms of hosting and hospitality, China's high-handed and blunt efforts to box South Korea in on the THAAD issue, and what was portrayed as Moon's overly fawning and obeisant language toward Xi.[10] In advance of the Moon visit, even the progressive *Hankyoreh* complained about Chinese state media distorting Moon's words in a CCTV interview as "not only partial, inappropriate, but even arrogant."[11] But the progressive-leaning *Kyunghyang Shinmun* delivered a harsh broadside against conservative criticisms of Moon's China visit, arguing that "as the opposition party who insisted on the almighty alliance and the exclusion of China, they should not expect Chinese hospitality. Their criticism on not being welcome is a self-contradiction."[12] These exchanges between conservative and progressive media revealed deepening polarization in South Korean preferences over how to deal with China and the divergent perceptions and interpretations within South Korea of the Moon administration's efforts to manage relations with China.

SOUTH KOREAN DIVERGENCE ON CHINA AND COVID-19

Another China-focused issue emerged as a point of political contention with the Moon administration's decision not to cut off travel between China and South Korea in February 2020 during the early days of the COVID-19 pandemic, despite a recommendation to do so from the Korean Medical Association. At the height of COVID-19 community spread within South Korea in March, this criticism appeared to be gaining traction among conservatives. But early successes by the Korean Center for Disease Control in setting a strategy for containing the virus laid the foundation for the ruling party's resounding victory in the April 2020 National Assembly election and seemed to squelch conservative critiques of the Moon administration's handling of the virus.

China's decision to impose an entry ban on South Korean travelers later in the spring irritated supporters of a China travel ban and revived conservative criticisms of the Moon administration's approach to China. However, the Moon administration's efforts to keep channels of travel between China and South Korea open paid off as China's economy recovered early from the pandemic while many other countries remained in recession through the fall of 2020. Nonetheless, China's emergence as a point of contention in South Korean domestic politics was clear in conservative critiques of the Moon administration's gentle handling of China (generally interpreted as part of an effort to score political points by luring Xi to

Seoul to buttress his foreign policy image) prior to the spring National Assembly elections.

THE QUAD AND MOON ADMINISTRATION BALANCING BETWEEN THE UNITED STATES AND CHINA

The Trump administration's announcement of its 2017 National Security Strategy set a framework for confrontation between the United States and China that would inevitably limit South Korea's ability to avoid making strategic choices. The senior *JoongAng Ilbo* columnist Kim Young-hie wrote upon the release of the U.S. National Security Strategy that "the new competitive structure between the United States and China and Russia is extremely ominous for South Korea, which has to tackle its urgent issue of the North Korean nuclear threat. No North Korean issue, including its nuclear and missile programs, can be resolved without China's cooperation or against China's will."[13]

The Moon administration felt the imperative of maintaining cooperation with China to keep hopes for inter-Korean reconciliation alive but also recognized the necessity of cooperation with the United States as the foundation for ensuring South Korea's security in light of the North Korean nuclear threat. Moon's efforts to preserve an opening for China–South Korea relations increasingly came under pressure from conservative assertions that a failure to align more closely with the United States would critically compromise South Korea's national security. Initial criticisms focused on the Moon administration's reluctance to align with the Trump administration's hardline approach to China, but pressure on the Moon administration ramped up further as the Biden administration reframed its approach around a positive mission, the upholding of international norms and rule of law, rather than a negative focus on demonizing the Chinese Communist Party.

The Trump administration's policy toward China hardened during 2020, with senior administration officials including Vice President Mike Pence and Secretary of State Mike Pompeo overtly calling out Chinese authoritarian abuses and human rights failures. Furthermore, the Trump administration promoted the establishment of the Economic Prosperity Network

(EPN) in a nascent effort to lobby against Huawei's participation in global supply chains.[14] Even as it distanced itself from Trump administration invitations to join in anti-China alignments or engage in public criticism of China, South Korea felt greater pressure to join U.S. efforts to marginalize China from global supply chains on the basis of security concerns.

The Trump administration expanded its efforts to enmesh South Korea in multilateral institutions aimed at countering China's rising regional influence. It considered inviting South Korea to join the Quadrilateral Security Dialogue (Quad), which consists of China-focused consultations among the United States, Japan, India, and Australia. But the Moon administration viewed the Quad with an abundance of caution out of fear of alienating China.[15] The former Moon policy advisor Moon Chung-in expressed his concern that "if the United States forces us to join some kind of a military alliance against China, then I see that will pose a very existential dilemma for us."[16]

However, the Trump administration's invitation to South Korea in the summer of 2020 to join an expanded version of the G7 yielded an immediate positive response from the Moon administration, motivated by perceived gains in South Korea's international stature from participation in the meeting. Although the U.S.-hosted G7 never materialized due to the pandemic, the Biden administration pushed the initiative at a UK-hosted meeting in April 2021 that included Australian, South Korean, and Indian leaders.

The Biden administration attempted to further sharpen choices of like-minded countries between the United States and China by casting the U.S.–China relationship in terms of a competition between authoritarianism and democracy and making the Quad a centerpiece of its Indo-Pacific policy. However, the Biden administration broadly shifted its engagement efforts in the Indo-Pacific away from a framework aimed at calling out and excluding China to mobilizing like-minded countries to cooperate under alternative frameworks such as the Quad and the Indo-Pacific Economic Framework, which focus on collaboration to uphold a rules-based international system, to preserve peace and prosperity in the Indo-Pacific, and to generate global public goods through collaboration on vaccine diplomacy, supply chain resiliency, climate change, and environmentally sustainable infrastructure projects.

South Korean responses to the growing U.S.–China rivalry grew even more polarized in the context of the Biden administration's emphasis on the restoration of alliances and framing of the rivalry in terms of a values-based ideological competition. Though progressive news outlets such as *Hankyoreh* and *Kyunghyang Shinmun* voiced concerns that increasing U.S.–China rivalry could result in a new cold war, lead to the consolidation of a northern triangular alignment among China, Russia, and North Korea, and reinforce peninsular divisions, conservative outlets advocated for the Moon administration to further align itself with the United States.

Progressives sought to preserve cooperative relations with China so as to gain China's acquiescence to inter-Korean integration aims. Moon Chung-in in particular responded to conservative criticism of President Moon Jae-in's diplomacy by asserting that conservatives sought to abandon balance for a level of alignment with the United States that Moon characterized as "liable to wreck key national interests."[17] South Korean moderates seek a hedge through cooperation with other Asian neighbors to reduce the risks and costs imposed on the region by the U.S.–China rivalry. In contrast, the conservative Yoon Suk-yeol administration has been inclined to align South Korea's overall foreign policy closely with the United States by emphasizing the U.S.–South Korea alliance, enabling South Korea to stand up to China more effectively than it otherwise would in the absence of the alliance.

CHINA'S INFLUENCE OVER NORTH KOREA AND RISING U.S.–CHINA TENSIONS

As the U.S.–China competition for influence in Seoul increased, the Moon administration faced a conflict between its desire to maintain good relations with China to encourage North Korea to restore inter-Korean engagement and to engage in dialogue with the United States and align with the United States and other allies to show a united front against China's tendencies to resort to economic coercion as a form of political retaliation.

Because South Korea sought to maintain a relationship with Beijing sufficient to make its influence felt on China's policies toward North Korea, the Moon administration sought to soft-pedal any sense of strategic alignment between the United States and China that might generate South Korean fears of containment or deepen the U.S.–China strategic competition. The main form of South Korean effort to moderate U.S. competition with China was South Korea's unwillingness to publicly join in criticisms of China on sensitive issues such as regional security concerns or human rights issues. As a result, U.S.–South Korean statements on regional security stood in stark contrast to parallel joint statements issued under the U.S.–Japan alliance by not publicly mentioning or calling out China.

The Moon administration showed willingness to cooperate on a wide range of issues with the United States during the May 2021 Biden-Moon White House summit but refrained from naming China as the object or motive for such cooperation. Based on this approach, Moon agreed to a surprisingly expansive list of joint measures at the summit meeting, including a statement urging the peaceful management of cross-straits relations. The U.S.–South Korea joint statement drew a rebuke from the Chinese ambassador to South Korea Xing Haiming following the summit even despite the non-mentions of China.[18] As a form of reassurance to Beijing, the Moon administration continued to emphasize the critical importance of China's role on the Korean Peninsula. However, during the campaign for South Korea's March 2022 election, both conservative leaders and presidential candidates were willing to criticize China publicly—regardless of the possible impact on China's future influence on Korean peninsular security.

IMPACT OF DOMESTIC POLITICAL POLARIZATION ON SOUTH KOREAN VIEWS OF STRATEGIC CHOICE

The three schools of strategic thought presented at the beginning of this chapter represent contending South Korean approaches to navigating the rising U.S.–China rivalry. South Korean analysts are advocating competing security strategies in an increasingly polarized domestic political context, and the South Korean public is therefore unlikely to cohere behind any single approach. Instead, over the long term, South Korean foreign policy will likely vacillate between the three schools of strategic thought or pursue elements of each on an ad hoc basis depending on the preferences of South Korea's political leadership and the circumstances and specific issues involved. External events will also influence the direction of South Korean foreign policy more so than relative support for the preferred road map of any single school of thought. The debate over how to navigate rising U.S.–China competition poses a deep dilemma for South Korean foreign policy that may prove fundamental to national survival: how can South Korea overcome political polarization to achieve the democratically representative domestic consensus necessary to become an autonomous geostrategic actor, rather than a mere object of rising major power competition? It may be precisely such an existential threat that drives the South Korean public to sufficient unity and consensus around an effective South Korean strategy for dealing with China.

Whether or not it will be possible for South Korean leaders to reconcile these contending strategies for managing U.S.–China rivalry will have implications for the future health of the U.S.–South Korea alliance, with two primary factors likely to influence South Korean public preferences over how to deal with China. On the one hand, Chinese political heavy-handedness in pursuing its own priorities to the perceived exclusion of South Korean interests and discriminatory practices toward South Korean private sector participation in the Chinese market have generated negative South Korean public views toward China. On the other hand, perceived pressure from the United States for South Korea to align on policies toward China without careful consideration of the costs and risks South Korea may incur will generate South Korean public criticism of an overly close South Korean alignment with the United States.

As reflected in table 2.1, South Korean conservative strategists shaping foreign policy in the Yoon administration prefer a path forward that has the greatest resonance with and dependence on the U.S.–South Korea alliance and U.S. strategic desires. U.S. interests are best served if South Korea chooses to opt into close alignment with the United States. While conservatives mostly support continued cooperation and alignment with the United States, the progressive view is less conducive to a mutually satisfactory outcome. Progressive strategic preferences may portend greater tension in U.S.–South Korea policy coordination efforts toward China due to a growing divergence of interests surrounding the process of achieving peaceful coexistence, opposing preferences for inter-Korean political accommodation, and differing views regarding the fundamental structure and purpose of the U.S.–South Korea alliance.

7

U.S.–CHINA TECHNOLOGY COMPETITION VS. CHINA–SOUTH KOREA ECONOMIC INTERDEPENDENCE

Since the late 1990s, South Korean analysts have expressed their concern that conflict might arise within the U.S.–South Korea security alliance as a result of South Korea's development of closer economic ties with China. These concerns grew when China became South Korea's largest trading partner in 2004. Initially, the likelihood that the mismatch between South Korea's economic exposure to China and its security reliance on the United States might force South Korea to choose between the two appeared slim in view of the extensive economic interdependence between the United States and China. But the possibility that Seoul might be forced to choose between Washington and Beijing became a real concern in South Korea during the Trump and Biden administrations as strategic rivalry between the United States and China grew and economic competition intensified over which country would take the lead as the global standard setter in technological innovation. U.S.–China competition has threatened to divide the globalized world on which South Korea's export-driven economy depends, raising the prospect of selective economic decoupling in the technology sphere between the United States and China and changing the way South Korean companies frame their strategies and make choices in a divided global economy. These challenges and South Korea's response have superseded domestic political divides due to the economic nature of the challenge and the recognition that private sector actors are responding to changing economic and geopolitical conditions.

South Korean companies incorporated China-based production into its global supply chain in the early 2000s on the premise that China's low-wage, low-cost production capabilities would enable the competitiveness of South Korean goods in U.S. and global markets. But the emergence of U.S.–China technology competition resulting from China's national development aspirations to localize and dominate technologies through initiatives such as "Made in China 2025" has raised questions for South Korean companies about the safety, reliability, and feasibility of relying on China as part of the manufacturing supply chain for Korean products.[1] To the extent that the United States regards the integration of China into the supply chain for certain products as a security concern, South Korean companies will be forced to either adapt to U.S. restrictions or accept that certain goods made in China or goods utilizing parts made in China may be restricted from the U.S. market. In the past, South Korean companies assumed that a single globalized supply chain was the best structure by which to promote export growth, assure profitability, and secure market share. These companies are now adjusting to the increasingly plausible reality that U.S.–China technological decoupling could result in a bifurcated technology market that would change the economic incentive structures around strategic planning in the sectors most important to South Korea's economic production and exports.

The United States has strengthened its rules for inward investment to protect critical technologies from acquisition by Chinese firms, enhanced controls on exports of critical technologies and components to Chinese companies on national security grounds, and pressed allies to do the same. The Biden administration launched a U.S. government–led analysis of supply chain resiliency and signaled more active investment in and regulation of cutting-edge technologies. As a result, South Korean companies have felt increasing pressure to make choices about whether to join Chinese supply chains and markets or to embed themselves more fully into U.S.-led supply chains and markets. The United States has challenged the South Korean government and private sector to make difficult and heretofore avoided choices, and the impact of the pandemic has provided a basis for reevaluation of South Korean corporate strategies toward China. In so doing, the United States has attempted to reframe South Korea's long-standing hedging strategy as its main framework for thinking about relations with China and the United States by at least partially restoring the alignment of security and economic benefits for South Korea associated with the U.S.–South Korea alliance. As the economic dimension of the U.S.–China rivalry intensifies in the context of technological competition resulting from the securitization of the technology sphere as a major component of U.S.–China major power rivalry, the South Korean government and private sector are being challenged to respond to new geostrategic and geoeconomic realities.

THE RISE OF CHINA–SOUTH KOREA
TRADE RELATIONS

Since diplomatic normalization in 1992, relations between the People's Republic of China and the Republic of Korea have been characterized by economic opportunity–driven growth in trade and investment largely independent from geopolitical considerations. Under the umbrella of a liberal international order in which economic interdependence would expand prosperity and peaceful relations, South Koreans pursued trade and investment with China with little concern for ideology, except to the extent that their own experiences under authoritarian rule provided a guide to mapping the political connections necessary to unlock economic opportunities in China. During the 1990s and 2000s, the China–South Korean trade relationship grew by 20 to 30 percent annually from $6.4 billion in 1992 to over $260 billion in 2018.[2]

The premise underlying China's economic reforms initiated by Deng Xiaoping in 1978 from a socialist to a quasi-capitalist economy was that economic development necessitated a peaceful external environment. The United States encouraged China's integration with the international economy by backing China's 2001 entry into the WTO and exhorting China to become a responsible stakeholder.[3] Under that framework, there was virtually no perception of political risk for South Koreans who sought to harness economic opportunities by incorporating China's cheap labor into a supply chain focused on production for the United States and other developed country markets. With the United States as the primary target audience for the production of South Korean goods, the rapid expansion of Sino–South Korean trade and investment during the early 2000s increased South Korea's dependency on economic relations with China as a source of growth but hardly at the expense of U.S.–South Korea security relations.

Having experienced rapid growth under the direction of an authoritarian state-directed model of economic development in the 1970s and 1980s, South Koreans were intuitively familiar with the contours of the Chinese system in which state-directed economic growth drove institutional and political transformation. The Chinese economy shifted from internally focused growth to a model reliant on integration with the capitalist world that used its ample labor supply to attract foreign investment. The growth of South Korean economic ties with China in the 1990s led to the establishment of domestic interest groups and constituencies in the South Korean private sector focused on promoting China–South Korea economic relations. These groups had a stake in reducing frictions and resolving political problems with China so that they would not become an obstacle to further export-led economic growth. But South Korean companies supportive of China's economic integration into U.S.-focused supply chains viewed their priorities as complementary rather than conflicting with the U.S.–South Korea security alliance.

As early as the mid-2000s and certainly by the 2010s, South Koreans had grown conscious of and concerned about the bifurcation of economic opportunities with China and security dependency on the alliance with the United States. Structural changes in China's economy in the late 2000s contributed to these concerns. China's economy, which had featured low labor costs and invited foreign investment to attract advanced production technologies to Chinese soil, became more competitive as the price of labor increased and China progressively resorted to demands that foreign companies transfer technologies used to make goods inside China as part of its trade and investment relationships. Chinese local competitors sprang up to compete with South Korean manufacturers in both Chinese domestic and international markets. Some of those local competitors secured stolen or borrowed technology combined with expertise gained on Korean and other foreign-owned shop floors in China to open their own factories producing knockoff mobile phones, cars, and other goods—often across the street from Korean and international factories—generating new sources of competition. But the high rates of growth and profits that South Korean companies experienced diminished some of those concerns even as they represented a long-term threat to the sustainability and competitiveness of South Korean companies.

As China's drive to secure advanced technologies became more organized and centralized, the environment for manufacturing goods within China became less hospitable. Then the Chinese government began using economic leverage to pressure foreign companies to comply with demands for technology transfer, essentially requiring foreign firms to trade long-term competitiveness for short-term economic gains. Finally, the Chinese government began to use economic leverage as a retaliatory weapon against countries such as Japan, South Korea, and Australia that challenged China's political interests, making foreign investors hostages to the risk of retaliation rather than catalysts for expanded economic opportunities, profits, and global market share.

This shift in the environment surrounding participation in the Chinese economy has introduced a dilemma for foreign investors in the China market. On the one hand, as China's economy was poised to transition from a manufacturing hub to a consumer-driven market, foreign investors naturally hoped to secure a share of China's domestic market. On the other hand, participation in China's economy through foreign trade and investment came with increasing political and economic risks, conditions for entry, and penalties for noncompliance. The South Korean government and firms were pressured to recalibrate their strategic choices while searching for ways to avoid facing a direct conflict between China-centered economic opportunism and continued security reliance on the United States. South Korean firms adjusted their strategies based largely on economic conditions and challenges to entering China's domestic market but were most vulnerable to pressure arising from tensions over political issues between the Chinese and South Korean governments.

Further complications arose in the context of concerns about supply chain resiliency following China's stated goal to capture a leading market share in emerging technologies such as artificial intelligence, big data, semiconductors, and supercomputing. The adoption of the Made in China 2025 industrial policy set off alarm bells among foreign investors faced with increasingly aggressive demands for transfers of technology that would enable China to eventually develop domestic capabilities and potentially exclude foreign companies from the Chinese market while increasingly taking global market share.

TRENDS IN SOUTH KOREA'S ECONOMIC AND TRADE RELATIONS WITH CHINA AND THE UNITED STATES

South Korean exports to China rose by double digits almost every year from 1992 to 2011. China's economic retaliation against the deployment of the U.S.-made THAAD missile defense system in South Korea resulted in negative trade growth in 2016. Although relatively rapid recovery took place in 2017 and 2018 on the strength of booming Chinese demand for South Korean memory chips, the continuing growth in bilateral trade revealed the selective nature of China's economic retaliation that targeted sectors not essential to China's continued development. In 2019 South Korean exports fell 16 percent from the previous year. As a result, China's share of South Korea's overall exports declined from 26.8 percent to 25.1 percent in 2019 but returned to 2018 levels in 2021.[4] However, South Korea's trade with China outstripped ties with the United States and Japan combined.

From the mid-2000s, Korean corporate efforts to diversify South Korean supply chain reliance on China drove a shift in South Korean trade and investment to Southeast Asia and, in particular, Vietnam. South Korea's trade diversification efforts away from China have enabled Vietnam to become South Korea's fourth largest trade partner, almost reaching the level of total trade between South Korea and Japan in 2020 (see figure 7.1).

The watershed decline in South Korean exports to China in 2019 reflected changes in the Sino–South Korean economic relationship that resulted in part from structural changes in the Chinese economy. South Korean analysis of reasons for the decline pointed to sluggish exports of intermediate goods, slowing exports of memory chips and other electronic components, and a decline in parts exported for assembly by South Korean manufacturers in China.[5] More broadly, the decline in South Korean exports to China reflected the impact of redirected South Korean investments to Vietnam and other countries as part of burgeoning diversification strategies, the growing perception that South Korean production in China for the U.S. market would be caught up in U.S. sanctions against Chinese imports, and the aftermath of China's economic retaliation against South Korea around the THAAD deployment.

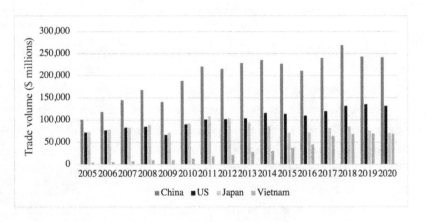

FIGURE 7.1 South Korea's trade volume with top four trade partners ($ in millions)

Another factor influencing the volume of bilateral trade has been the failure of South Korean efforts to capture a greater share of the Chinese consumer market. For instance, Hyundai's sales in China enabled the company to capture significant market share in China's automobile market in the early 2000s and 2010s, but China's THAAD retaliation and declining competitiveness with Chinese domestic brands took its toll on the market share of Korean automobiles in China's increasingly competitive market.[6] South Korean beauty products were taking off in China, but advertising strategies benefited from the popularity of Korean pop music and dramas that were no longer possible when China shut down concerts by Korean artists in China. Lotte abandoned its retail outlet strategy in China as a result of having experienced the Chinese government's imposition of strict health and safety checks on its outlets at the height of China's THAAD retaliation.

Although the decline in South Korean exports to China predates the impact of the COVID-19 pandemic and further escalation of U.S.–China trade tensions in 2020, the emergence of additional regulatory barriers on South Korea's export of memory chips incorporating U.S. intellectual property and other political pressures have likely facilitated downward trends. At the same time, China's initial recovery from the pandemic enabled an early South Korean economic recovery during a period of suppressed consumer demand from Europe and the United States.

Figure 7.2 shows that South Korea's investment in China following China's WTO entry outstripped its investment in the United States in the mid-2000s. But rising Chinese wages and the imposition of various conditions on South Korean inward investment, including demands for technology transfer, began to create headwinds for continued growth in South Korean investment in China from around 2008, at which time the United States again surpassed China as the preferred overseas market for South Korean investment.

By 2016 South Korean investment flows to the United States had greatly surpassed investment flows to China. Following the 2012 ratification of the KORUS FTA, South Korean investors appear to have con-

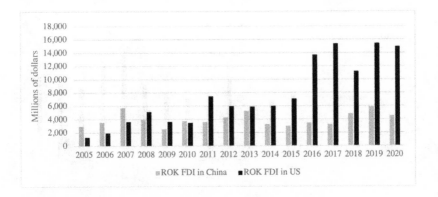

FIGURE 7.2 South Korea's foreign direct investment in China and the United States

Sources: "Foreign Investment Details," Statistics of Foreign Direct Investment, Export-Import Bank of Korea, https://stats.koreaexim.go.kr/sub/detailedCondition .do; "Foreign Investment Statistics," Ministry of Trade, Industry, and Energy, http://www.motie.go.kr/motie/py/sa/investstatse/investstats.jsp.

cluded that opportunities to gain profits and share of the U.S. market were substantially greater than opportunities associated with continued South Korean investment in China. Figure 7.3 provides an illustration of the relative share of South Korean investment flows to China and the United States. South Korea's investment in China peaked at almost 40 percent of its overall foreign investment in 2005, after which South Korean investors diversified from China. From 2011, there was a sustained shift toward the United States as the primary destination for South Korean investment abroad.

As shown in figure 7.4, U.S. investment in South Korea picked up after 2012, partly reflecting expectations by U.S. investors of improvements in the South Korean investment environment under the KORUS FTA. China also became a source of investment in South Korea, primarily in conjunction with increased flows of Chinese tourists to Jeju Island as government regulations on Chinese tourist travel overseas began to ease in the 2000s, but the momentum for these flows was cut off at least

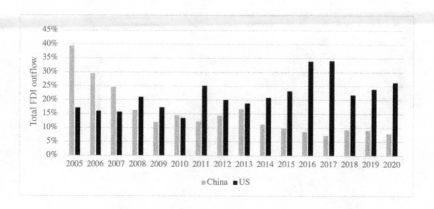

FIGURE 7.3 South Korea's foreign direct investment in China and the United States as a percentage of total FDI outflow

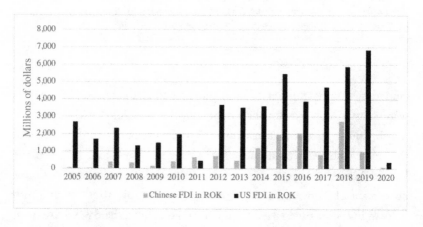

FIGURE 7.4 Chinese and U.S. FDI in South Korea

temporarily due to the global pandemic in 2020. There were also Chinese efforts to purchase some Korean companies, possibly to transfer their technological assets to China. Notably, the inflow of Chinese investment into South Korea dropped as part of China's economic retaliation in 2017 but subsequently rebounded strongly in 2018 before declining dramatically in 2019 and 2020.

CHINA'S ECONOMIC RETALIATION STRATEGY AND SOUTH KOREAN ECONOMIC DEPENDENCE ON CHINA

The use of economic retaliation to achieve political objectives or to coerce adherence to Chinese views has emerged as a common tool in Chinese statecraft after 2009. China has restricted exports of rare earth metals to Japan, punished South Korea for accepting the deployment of THAAD, and retaliated against Australia's call for an investigation into the origins of COVID-19. The South Korean experience has provided a case study of the selective and targeted nature of Chinese retaliation through regulatory pressure on South Korean entities operating in China's domestic market, restricted access of South Korean entertainment and cultural products to the Chinese market, and discouragement of Chinese tourists from traveling to South Korea. Notably, China's actions did not encompass areas of Sino–South Korean trade where China had a particular need or benefit, such as South Korean export of intermediate manufacturing goods and components to China.[7] The Korea International Trade Association (KITA) reported that South Korea's share of China's domestic consumer goods market dropped from 4.9 percent in 2015 to 2.9 percent in the summer of 2017.

China's economic retaliation against South Korea made a deep psychological impression on South Korea. South Korean public opinion toward China has remained negative in response to China's 2017 THAAD deployment retaliation, even following the Moon administration's efforts to return the economic relationship to normal. The impact of China's economic retaliation also sent a lasting signal to South Korea regarding the risks of crossing China on political issues critical to Chinese goals or preferences. As discussed in chapter 6, China's efforts to extract pledges from the Moon administration to exercise future restraint by refraining from accepting the introduction of future THAAD batteries, not joining a regionalized U.S.-led missile defense system, and refusing to forge a trilateral security alliance with the United States and Japan illustrate the Chinese intent to induce South Korean self-restraint on security matters considered sensitive by China. The Moon administration's controversial "three no's" pledge to China and fears of additional economic retaliation may have contributed to Moon's self-restraint in making public criticisms of China on issues such as the human rights of ethnic minority Uyghurs in Xinjiang or China's enactment of a National Security Law in Hong Kong that directly violated its 1997 pledge to follow a "one country, two systems" approach of allowing Hong Kong to exercise a high degree of autonomy until 2047.

Among the recommendations regarding how South Korea should respond tactically to China's economic retaliation, KITA encouraged the Moon administration to employ more China experts, advised the private sector to expand new and existing economic channels and networks with China, and recommended that South Korean corporations pursue further diversification and risk response measures to mitigate against the risks of another round of Chinese economic retaliation.[8] An alternative recommendation involved holding Chinese partners close and attempting to embed South Korean products even more deeply into the Chinese domestic market, despite the risks of further exposure to industrial espionage and technology leakage that such a strategy would entail.[9] But to the extent that decoupling between the U.S. and Chinese markets proceeds, especially in hi-tech sectors, South Korean companies risk having to make choices as the U.S. and Chinese governments, respectively, attempt to raise the costs to South Korean firms of doing business with the other side.

U.S. SUPPLY CHAIN RESILIENCE AND IMPLICATIONS FOR SOUTH KOREA

The Biden administration made supply chain resilience a top priority, ordering within its first one hundred days a multiagency review of and report on critical supply chain infrastructure in four essential areas deemed critical to national security and economic resiliency: semiconductor manufacturing, large capacity electric batteries, critical minerals and materials, and pharmaceutical manufacture. The resulting report, "Building Resilient

Supply Chains, Revitalizing American Manufacturing, and Fostering Broad-Based Growth: 100-day Reviews Under Executive Order 14017" (or "Building Resilient Supply Chains"), provides the framework, context, drivers, and objectives underlying the Biden administration's approach to technology, resiliency, and the parameters of economic competition with China in the area of emerging technologies.[10]

The primary theme of the report is that "more secure and resilient supply chains are essential for our national security, our economic security, and our technological leadership."[11] The report provides extensive context and detail around the Biden administration's prioritization of supply chain resiliency as an essential national and economic security priority and the implications for both the U.S.–China technological rivalry and the desired roles and contributions of South Korean industries toward those objectives. The Biden administration further signaled its intent to make supply chain resiliency a priority within the alliance by including in the joint Fact Sheet released at the first Biden-Moon summit that both sides would "explore the creation of a U.S.–ROK Supply Chain Task Force between the U.S. White House and the ROK Office of the President, to implement and review bilateral cooperation in the high-tech manufacturing and supply chains."[12]

The implications for South Korea and the alliance of the Biden administration's emphasis on supply chain resiliency in the context of a high technology competition with China were double-edged. On the one hand, the U.S.–South Korea alliance has been prioritized as an instrument by which the United States can strengthen the economic integration of South Korean companies into U.S. supply chains as part of its competition against China. On the other hand, U.S. reliance on South Korean and other foreign-based production capabilities has generated tension between the United States and its allies as the Biden administration sought to onshore critical technology and manufacturing processes to minimize supply chain vulnerabilities.

The Biden administration sought to use tax and labor policies to promote investment in U.S.-based manufacturing and to build American jobs. For instance, the Department of Commerce recognized the competitive advantage that South Korean and Taiwanese semiconductor manufacturers have gained as a result of large-scale public investment in the sector and expressed concern that the United States will be unable to keep up with the level of quality, cost, or workforce necessary to compete in semiconductor fabrication.[13] South Korean companies have carefully assessed the Biden administration's emphasis on supply chain resiliency, both to identify potential areas of opportunity and to mitigate possible downside risks associated with the U.S. approach. South Korean companies may welcome opportunities to integrate themselves into the U.S. market but may not necessarily view those opportunities as exclusive to the pursuit of opportunities in other markets. Instead, South Korean firms are likely to pursue further business cooperation and integration where economic opportunities present themselves.

Among the four priority areas dealt with in "Building Resilient Supply Chains," South Korea's role in the semiconductor industry stands out as critical, South Korean contributions to the electric vehicle sector are notable, its contributions to supply of critical minerals are negligible, and its potential future partnership in the pharmaceuticals sector is promising if plans for development of cooperation are realized. South Korea is an ally and a partner of the United States, but South Korean companies are also autonomous actors and private sector competitors. As such, South Korean companies are influenced and supported by the government but focused on profit making and are not always beholden to the government.

The recommendations of the report have cross-cutting impacts on South Korean semiconductor and electric battery/EV manufacturers in the following areas: (1) the impact of possible U.S. government investments of up to $50 billion for domestic leading-edge semiconductor production along with additional U.S. government investments in the electric battery and electric vehicle sectors; (2) "Made in America" guidelines for the procurement of U.S. goods, the implementation of the proposed Supply Chain Resilience Program at the Department of Commerce, and the application of both trade enforcement actions and invocation of the Defense Production Act (DPA), which could influence both the competitive environment within the U.S. market and the degree of South Korean integration into U.S. supply chains; and (3) U.S. efforts to cooperate with allies through a Presidential Forum on supply chain resiliency and through U.S. Development Finance Corporation (DFC) investments to support supply chain resilience with allies. The three main sectors in which South Korea has a role are semiconductors, electric vehicles, and public health cooperation including vaccine production.

SEMICONDUCTORS

The Biden administration focused on five dimensions of semiconductor production as part of its review of supply chain resiliency: (1) design, (2) fabrication, (3) assembly, test, and packaging (ATP) and advanced packaging, (4) materials, and (5) manufacturing equipment. The semiconductor supply chain is complex and geographically dispersed, with a process that takes up to one hundred days and products that may cross international borders up to seventy times. Each of these steps in the process involves supply chain vulnerabilities resulting from supply bottlenecks or overdependence on limited sources as well as varying degrees of South Korean private sector involvement. The semiconductor industry is relevant as a growth sector because it has implications for U.S. national security and because of the increasing importance of semiconductors as components of products important to the quality of life of American consumers who would be negatively affected by supply chain disruptions. As the Biden administration attempted to incentivize domestic semiconductor production, promote resiliency, work with allies, and protect U.S. technological advantages, these efforts have generated potential opportunities and costs for South Korean semiconductor sector participants.[14]

As shown in table 7.1, the structure of the integrated circuit semiconductor market is divided into three types of semiconductors: logic (42 percent), memory (26 percent), and analog (14 percent). Logic chips are primarily used for personal computer central processing units (CPUs), dedicated graphics processing units (GPUs), field programmable gate arrays (FPGAs), and application-specific integrated circuits (ASICs). U.S. companies primarily lead in the production of logic ships, with Samsung holding a 13 percent market share in the mobile CPU logic sector. But in the memory sector, South Korean companies hold a substan-

TABLE 7.1 Integrated Circuit Market Share Leaders, 2020

LOGIC				MEMORY		ANALOG
PC CPU	MOBILE CPU	GPU	FPGA	DRAM	NAND	ANALOG
Intel (78%)	Qualcomm (29%)	NVIDIA (82%)	Xilinx (52%)	Samsung (42%)	Samsung (33%)	Texas Instruments (19%)
AMD 0 (22%)	MediaTek (26%)	AMD (18%)	Intel (36%)	SK Hynix (30%)	Kioxia (20%)	Analog Devices (10%)
	HiSilicon (16%)		Microchip Technology (7%)	Micron (23%)	Western Digital (14%)	Infineon (7%)
	Samsung (13%)		Lattice (5%)		SK Hynix (12%)	Skyworks (7%)
	Apple (13%)				Micron (11%)	ST (6%)
					Intel (9%)	NXP (5%)

Note: Based on data from Mercury Research, Counterpoint Research, Jon Peddie Research, Gartner, TrendForce, Mordor Intelligence, and IC Insights

Source: "Building Resilient Supply Chains, Revitalizing American Manufacturing, and Fostering Broad-Based Growth: 100-day Reviews Under Executive Order 14017," Report by the White House

tial market share in both the DRAM and flash memory (NAND) categories (72 percent and 45 percent, respectively), while Japan-based Kioxia (formerly Toshiba) holds a 20 percent share in the NAND segment of the market.[15] China-based Yangtze Memory Technologies (YMTC) has received over $24 billion in government subsidies. Analog chip producers are less concentrated, with U.S.-based Texas Instruments leading production with a 19 percent market share followed by Advance Micro Devices with a 10 percent share.

A major concern reflected in the Biden administration's "Building Resilient Supply Chains" report was the geographic concentration of semiconductor fabrication in Asia, specifically in Taiwan and South Korea. An additional concern motivating the report involved the significant Chinese-government funding available to buy up critical expertise across the supply chain necessary to make Chinese firms competitive in the semiconductor sector as well as the extent to which Chinese firms have powered their global advance on U.S.-sourced intellectual property and low-cost Asian chip manufacturing. The concerns expressed in the report have three major implications for South Korean semiconductor companies: (1) the Biden administration expressed sensitivity toward overreliance on Taiwan-concentrated foundry and logic chip-production capabilities, creating a potential opportunity for IDM companies such as Samsung to provide options for diversification, keeping in mind that expanding the U.S.-based share of the foundry market is the preferred goal, (2) the Biden administration has shown greater sensitivity to South Korean semiconductor company investments in China involving cutting-edge technology while desiring greater investment in U.S.-based semiconductor manufacturing capacities, creating opportunities for new investment by Samsung in the United States, and (3) the Biden administration showed greater sensitivity to South Korean–sourced supply to China as well as to reliance on China-based firms for participation in ATP. These factors may influence Korean perceptions of the costs and opportunities in the semiconductor manufacturing sector, particularly as related to opportunities to enhance its share of the U.S. market and the risks associated with the upward of $100 billion in Chinese-government investments in semiconductor production in over sixty new manufacturing facilities.[16] Table 7.2 shows trends in Samsung's and SK Hynix's investments in the semiconductor sector in the United States and China, respectively.

Table 7.3 shows that Samsung's sales of semiconductors in the U.S. and Chinese markets have been weighted toward the United States as the largest global market for semiconductor sales but have also remained consistent in terms of exposure to the Chinese market. But U.S. pressure to restrict sales of semiconductors to China will come at a cost not only to Samsung but also to the U.S. producers Qualcomm and Micron, which both gain a significant share of their revenues from China and therefore are likely to resist a complete cut off of semiconductor exports to the Chinese market.[17]

As shown in figure 7.5, other important aspects of supply chain resilience include the advanced packaging of semiconductors, a relatively low-tech component of the supply chain, as well as materials and Semiconductor Manufacturing Equipment (SME). By revenue, Taiwan is the leader in market share of ATP with a 29 percent market share, followed closely by the United States with 28 percent. China is third at 14 percent and South Korea is fourth at 13 percent, but China has identified ATP as an investment area to compensate for its limited production of leading-edge semiconductors.[18] Both the United States and South Korea are dependent on dominant Japanese producers of silicon wafers, photomasks, and photoresists, with China lacking most of these critical items. But China is a leading producer of gallium, tungsten, and magnesium—all critical components in the semiconductor manufacturing process.[19]

The Biden administration's emphasis on supply chain resiliency and South Korea's significant market share in semiconductor production have raised South Korea's profile as an important economic partner in a sector critical to U.S. national security. But rising concerns regarding massive Chinese investments, acquisitions, and purchase of talent in this critical sector have catalyzed U.S. concerns and desires to maintain a technological advantage and recover domestic manufacturing capacity. South Korean companies have an opportunity to expand their share of the semiconductor market and integrate more deeply in the U.S. supply chain while also capitalizing on opportunities presented by the Biden administration's emphasis on supply chain resilience by investing in U.S.-based semiconductor production capabilities.

TABLE 7.2 South Korea's Semiconductor Investment in the United States and China

	UNITED STATES		CHINA	
YEAR	SAMSUNG	SK HYNIX	SAMSUNG	SK HYNIX
1997	Opens its first U.S. fabrication plant in Austin[a]			
2006				Opens its production line of DRAMs in Wuxi[b]
2007	Opens second wafer factory to build NAND flash chips[c]			
2011	$3.6 billion to expand its Austin factory to make logic chips[d]			
2012		Acquisition of LAMD a California-based storage solution company[e]	*$10.8 billion in the first Chinese plant in Xi'an[f]	
2016				Begins expansion of Wuxi plant[g]
2017			Cumulative investment of $15 billion in the second plant[h]	
2019			Announces a $8 billion investment plan[i]	Cumulative investment of $14 billion in Wuxi[j]
2020				Begins to transfer $170 million worth of equipment from Korea to Wuxi

(continued)

TABLE 7.2 *(Continued)*

YEAR	UNITED STATES		CHINA	
	SAMSUNG	SK HYNIX	SAMSUNG	SK HYNIX
2021	Announces a $17 billion investment plan for a new plant in Taylor City, Texas[k]	Announces a $1 billion investment plan to establish a new R&D center in Silicon Valley[l]		Announces a $9 billion Intel Unit Purchase plan[m]

*At the time, it became the largest investment project in the history of Samsung's overseas investment, and the largest foreign investment project in China's electronics industry. "Samsung Constructs Phase-2 Memory Chip Base in Xi'an, Northwest China," *Global Times*, March 11, 2021, https://www.globaltimes.cn/page/202103/1218073.shtml.

[a] "History," Samsung, https://www.samsung.com/us/sas/Company/History.

[b] "SK Hynix's Expanded Fab Plant in Wuxi Complete," *China Daily*, updated April 19, 2019, http://www.wuxinews.com.cn/2019-04/19/c_448971.htm.

[c] "History."

[d] Kristina Shevory, "To Meet Demand for Chips, Samsung Bets Big on Austin," *New York Times*, May 3, 2011, https://www.nytimes.com/2011/05/04/realestate/commercial/04chips.html.

[e] "Company," SK Hynix Memory Solutions America, Inc., accessed July 14, 2021, http://www.skhms.com/company/.

[f] "Korean Chipmakers Facing a Big Problem Called China," *Korea JoongAng Daily*, April 25, 2021, https://koreajoongangdaily.joins.com/2021/04/25/business/industry/Samsung-Electronics-SK-hynix/20210425155800418.html.

[g] Ahn Sung-mi, "SK Hynix's Investment Into Chinese Plant to Exceed $10b," *Korea Herald*, October 9, 2016, http://www.koreaherald.com/view.php?ud=20161009000167.

[h] "Korean Chipmakers Facing a Big Problem Called China."

[i] Hyunjoo Jin and Josh Horwitz, "Samsung to Invest an Extra $8 Billion in China Chip Plant," Reuters, December 12, 2019, https://www.reuters.com/article/us-samsung-china/samsung-to-invest-an-extra-8-billion-in-china-chip-plant-media-idUSKBN1YG1GM.

[j] Song Mengxing, "Society Industrial Investment Amounts to Billions," *China Daily*, November 14, 2019, https://global.chinadaily.com.cn/a/201911/14/WS5dcca9a2a310cf3e3557742c.html.

[k] "$17 Billion U.S. Investment by Samsung Electronics Confirmed," *Korea JoongAng Daily*, May 22, 2021, https://koreajoongangdaily.joins.com/2021/05/22/business/industry/Samsung-Electronics-SK-Joe-Biden/20210522004601892.html; "Samsung Electronics Investing on a New Foundry Line at Tailor, United States," Samsung Newsroom, November 24, 2021, https://news.samsung.com/kr/삼성전자-미국-테일러市에-신규-파운드리-라인-투자.

[l] Doh Hyun-woo, "Semiconductor Industry: SEC and SK Hynix Announce US Investment Plans," *Business Korea*, May 24, 2021, http://www.businesskorea.co.kr/news/articleView.html?idxno=67833.

[m] Sohee Kim, "SK Hynix Wins U.S. Approval for $9 Billion Intel Unit Purchase," Bloomberg, March 11, 2021, https://www.bloomberg.com/news/articles/2021-03-12/sk-hynix-wins-u-s-approval-for-9-billion-intel-unit-purchase.

TABLE 7.3 Sales Percentage of South Korean Semiconductors

YEAR	SAMSUNG		SK HYNIX	
	AMERICAS*	CHINA	UNITED STATES	CHINA
2014	33%	16%	37%	22%
2015	34%	15%	40%	24%
2016	34%	18%	31%	35%
2017	34%	16%	37%	33%
2018	34%	18%	35%	39%
2019	32%	17%	30%	47%
2020	33%	16%	40%	38%

*Samsung does not release disaggregated, U.S.-only data. The figures are for the percent of sales in the Americas.

Source: Samsung Electronics Co., Ltd. Income Statement 2013–2020. https://www.samsung.com/global/ir/financial-information/financial-valuation-snapshot/; SK Hynix Inc. Annual Periodic Report 2014–2020, https://www.skhynix.com/ir/UI-FR-IR12_T4.

Beyond Borders: Semiconductors are a Uniquely Global Industry
Typical semiconductor production process spans multiple countries: **4+** Countries, **4+** States, **3+** trips around the world, **25,000** miles travelled, **100** days TPT, **12** days in transit

Japan to USA

3. Fab wafer sorted, cut into die

7. Customer buys end product

2. Bare wafer into fab wafer

China to USA

1. Silicon ingots cut into wafers

6. Chip integrated into consumer good by end product manufacturer

Singapore to China

5. Final product shipped for inventory

USA to Malaysia

4. Die are assembled, packaged, tested

$1,340 Billion in Global Trade **$36.8 Billion** in Global Trade **$23.7 Billion** in Global Trade

Top Participants in Global Trade: Semiconductor Goods			Top Participants in Global Trade: Fabrication Material Goods			Top Participants in Global Trade: Assembly, Test, Packaging Goods		
China	USA	Mexico	China	Taiwan	Norway	China	France	Mexico
Hong Kong	Malaysia	Thailand	USA	UAE	Mexico	Germany	Korea	Netherlands
Singapore	Japan	France	Japan	Singapore	Netherlands	USA	Hong Kong	Poland
Taiwan	Germany	Viet Nam	Germany	UK	France	Japan	Italy	Canada
Korea	Philippines	Netherlands	Korea	Italy	Brazil	Taiwan	UK	Belgium

FIGURE 7.5 Global supply chain representation

Source: "Building Resilient Supply Chains, Revitalizing American Manufacturing, and Fostering Broad-Based Growth: 100-day Reviews Under Executive Order 14017," White House, June 2021, https://www.whitehouse.gov/wp-content/uploads/2021/06/100-day-supply-chain-review-report.pdf.

LARGE CAPACITY BATTERIES AND ELECTRIC VEHICLES

A second critical industry that has drawn attention as part of the Biden administration's focus on supply chain resilience is the electric battery and electric vehicle production sector. The Biden administration's emphasis on this sector stemmed largely from the fact that the Chinese and European sectors have benefited from state investment and, as a result, their EV sectors have grown more rapidly than in the United States, which constitutes only 12 percent of EV demand compared to 40 percent in China and 40 percent in Europe. To address these challenges, "Building Resilient Supply Chains" reviewed five stages of the high-capacity battery supply chain: (1) raw material production, (2) material refinement and processing, (3) battery material manufacturing and cell fabrication, (4) battery pack and end use product manufacturing, and (5) battery end-of-life and recycling. The report concluded that U.S. weaknesses lie in the processing and manufacturing components of the supply chain. China has over 75 percent of the global cell fabrication capacity.[20] South Korean EV investments receive government subsidies, but its strategies have focused on third-country markets.

The Moon and Yoon administrations have made it clear that South Korean investment in the battery sector is a strategic priority. Moon underscored his administration's commitment to developing the industry on July 8, 2021, during a report on K-battery development strategy, declaring "Our objective is clear; we will become the number one battery producing nation by 2030."[21] According to the document released by the Ministry of Trade, Industry, and Energy, LG Energy Solution, Samsung SDI, SK Innovation, Hyundai, and about fifty other businesses pledged to invest 40.6 trillion won (roughly $34 billion) in battery technology by 2030. The government also promised to support large-scale R&Ds and provide support to businesses so that they can acquire the needed technology.[22] The government along with the private sector pledged to pool together an 80 billion won R&D innovation fund with the government providing 30 billion won; LG Energy Solution, Samsung SDI, and SK Innovation collectively providing 20 billion won; and the fund managing company investing another 30 billion won.[23]

Major South Korean players in battery production include LG Chem, Samsung SDI, and SK Innovation. All these companies have extensively invested in China in the form of joint ventures and mergers and acquisitions (M&A) to either improve the procurement of vital components or cooperate with Chinese electric vehicle producers who would use Korean batteries as a component of sales within China's domestic market. In the aftermath of the THAAD deployment, the Chinese government excluded cars using Korean batteries from the list of models eligible for subsidy. But the rapid growth of China's EV market makes it very attractive, especially in light of China's efforts to achieve carbon neutrality.[24]

Beijing's generous subsidy program has proven challenging for Korean battery makers, but the subsidy was scheduled to phase out by the end of 2020, prompting LG, Samsung, and SK to invest in China ahead of the subsidy's expiration. China announced that it would extend its subsidy for another two years, though it started to relax its restrictions on models using Korean batteries in late 2019. The subsidy extended to models like Tesla 3 and Beijing Benz E-Class using batteries from LGES and SK Innovation respectively.[25] The Chinese market remains both an opportunity and a risk for Korean battery manufacturers. Major recent investments by these companies in China and the United States, respectively, are detailed in table 7.4.

A comparison of South Korea's downstream investments provides additional insight on corporate investments in the Chinese and U.S. EV sectors, respectively. Table 7.5 shows that Hyundai and Kia have made limited and gradual progress toward capturing market share in the United States with Korean EV sales capturing 3.3 percent of U.S. total EV sales by 2020. Hyundai and Kia have attempted to capture EV sales in China but with limited success. Table 7.6 shows that Hyundai and KIA's share of the Chinese EV market has reached only 0.4 percent.

U.S.–SOUTH KOREA VACCINE PARTNERSHIP

The timing and circumstances around Moon's first White House meeting with Biden in May 2021 and the agreement of the two governments to

TABLE 7.4 South Korea's EV/Battery Investment in the United States and China

YEAR	UNITED STATES			CHINA		
	LG CHEM	SK INNOVATION	SAMSUNG SDI	LG CHEM	SK INNOVATION	SAMSUNG SDI
2012	Completes construction of EV battery plant in Holland, Michigan[a]					
2013					Establishes joint ventures with BAIC Group and Beijing Electronics Holding[b]	
2015				Completes construction of a battery plant in Nanjing[c]		
2018	Confirms it will invest over ₩10 billion to expand production lines in Holland[d]			Establishes a joint venture with Zhejiang Huayou Cobalt to manage supply of cobalt; invests ₩239.4 billion[e]	As part of the joint ventures, SK invests ₩82 billion to build a battery plant in Changzhou[f]	Announces it will invest ₩1.3 trillion to increase battery production capacity in Xi'an and Tianjin[g]

(continued)

Year						
2019	Establishes a joint venture with GM with plans to invest ₩2.7 trillion to build battery plant[h]	Invests ₩2.2 trillion to build its first U.S. battery manufacturing plant in Georgia[i]		Establishes a joint venture with Geely Auto Group and invests ₩103.4 billion to build a new factory[j]	Invests an additional ₩579.9 billion to build a second battery production plant in Changzhou[k]	Invests ₩84 billion to expand the Xi'an plant.[m]
2020		Invests another ₩1.1 trillion to expand its plant[l]				
2021	Announces it will build at least two more plants with plans to invest ₩5.1 trillion by 2025[n]	Establishes a joint venture with Ford; the joint venture will invest ₩6 trillion to build a new plant[o]	In talks with Stellantis to invest at least ₩3 trillion to build a cell plant that would be Samsung's first U.S. cell plant[p]	Confirms it will invest ₩40 billion in Jiujiang DeFu Technology that produces electroplated copper foil, a key component in batteries[q]		

[a] "History of LG Chem," LG Chem, https://www.lgchem.com/global/lg-chem-history/timeline.

[b] "Battery," SK Innovation, http://eng.skinnovation.com/business/battery.asp.

[c] "History of LG Chem."

[d] "LG Chemical to Extend Its Electric Vehicle Battery Plant in the U.S.," *Electronic Times*, January 5, 2018, https://m.etnews.com/20180101400031?obj=Tzo4OiJzdG RDbGFzcyl6Mjpzczo3OiJyZWZlcmVyljtOO3M6NzoiZmoyd2FyZCl7czoxMzoid2lHRvIGrvYmlsZSl7fQ%3D%3D.

[e] Cho Ji-won, "LG Chemical Investing 239.4 Billion KRW to Form a Joint Corporation with Chinese Huayou Cobalt . . . Stabilizing Raw Material Supplies," Chosun Biz, April 1, 2018, https://biz.chosun.com/site/data/html_dir/2018/04/11/2018041100555.html.

TABLE 7.4 *(Continued)*

f Choi Man-soo, "SK Innovations, Completing Its First Global Production Base," *Hankyung*, December 6, 2019, https://www.hankyung.com/economy/article/2019120556871.

g "Samsung SDI to Invest $1.15 Bn to Expand Battery Facility in China," Pulse, Maeil Business News Korea, December 12, 2018, https://pulsenews.co.kr/view.php?year=2018&no=776192.

h "LG Chemicals and GM Constructing a Battery Plant in the U.S. with an Investment of 2.7 Trillion KRW," *JoongAng Ilbo*, December 7, 2019, https://news.joins.com/article/23651189.

i Battery," SK Innovation.

j Byun Kuk-young, "Why LG Chemicals Is Partnering Up with Geely Auto," Energy Daily, June 14, 2019, http://www.energydaily.co.kr/news/articleView.html?idxno=99618; Kim Jae-hu, "LG Chemicals Collaborating with Top Automobile Manufacturers in the U.S. and China . . . 'Fast and Furious' Electric Vehicle Batteries," *Hankyung*, January 9, 2020, https://www.hankyung.com/economy/article/2020010093861.

k "SK Innovation Building a Second EV Battery Factory with Chinese EVE Corporation," *Hankyung*, September 27, 2019, https://www.hankyung.com/economy/article/2019092782487Y.

l "SK Innovation to Invest Another $940 Million in Jackson County Expansion, Create 600 Jobs," Office of the Governor, June 25, 2020, https://gov.georgia.gov/press-releases/2020-06-25/sk-innovation-invest-another-940-million-jackson-county-expansion-create.

m Oh So-young, "Electric Vehicles with Samsung SDI Batteries Receiving Chinese Financial Subsidies," The Guru, January 7, 2021, https://www.theguru.co.kr/news/article.html?no=17646.

n "LG Creating Two New Battery Factories in the United States . . . Investing 5.1 Trillion KRW Until 2025," *Dong-A Ilbo*, March 12, 2021, https://www.donga.com/news/Inter/article/all/20210312/105844105/1.

o Heo Ji-yoon, "SK Innovation, Cooperating with Ford in the United States to Expand Battery Business," Chosun Biz, May 20, 2021, https://biz.chosun.com/industry/company/2021/05/20/XSKRO2CWK5B2LBJ3T4T3RHPA5A/.

p Heekyong Yang, "South Korea's Samsung SDI Considers Building Battery Cell Plant in United States," Reuters, July 8, 2021, https://www.reuters.com/business/skoreas-samsung-sdi-considers-building-battery-cell-plant-us-2021-07-08/.

q Song Ki-young, "LG Chemical Investing 40 Billion KRW to Chinese Copper Foil Manufacturers," Chosun Biz, May 16, 2021, https://biz.chosun.com/industry/company/2021/05/16/KBLTHQVQWFBMVGXK47BC5EBSU/.

TABLE 7.5 Plug-in Electric Vehicle Sales of Hyundai and Kia in the U.S. Market

YEAR	U.S. TOTAL EV SALES	HYUNDAI AND KIA	PERCENTAGE OF TOTAL U.S. VEHICLE SALES
2013	97,102	0	0.0%
2014	118,882	359	0.3%
2015	114,023	1,030	0.9%
2016	159,616	4,728	3.0%
2017	195,581	6,355	3.2%
2018	361,315	7,883	2.2%
2019	326,644	10,758	3.3%

Source: "U.S. Plug-in Electric Vehicle Sales by Model," Transportation Research Center at Argonne National Laboratory, U.S. Department of Energy, January 2020, https://afdc.energy.gov/data/.

TABLE 7.6 Plug-in Electric Vehicle Sales of Hyundai and Kia in the Chinese Market

YEAR	CHINA TOTAL EV SALES[a]	HYUNDAI[b] AND KIA[c]	PERCENTAGE OF TOTAL CHINA VEHICLE SALES
2013	18,000	33	0.2%
2014	75,000	0	0.0%
2015	331,000	4	0.0%
2016	507,000	100	0.0%
2017	777,000	2,172	0.3%
2018	1,256,000	1,817	0.1%
2019	1,206,000	3,771	0.3%
2020	1,367,000	5,305	0.4%

[a]"中汽协会行业信息部. 2020年汽车工业经济运行情况," China Association of Automobile Manufacturers, January 13, 2020, http://www.caam.org.cn/chn/4/cate_39/con_5232916.html.

[b]"Y2013 Global Plant Sales–Y2020 Global Plant Sales," Hyundai Motor Company, https://www.hyundai.com/kr/ko/company-intro/ir-information/sales/sales-record/overseas-factory.

[c] "Retail Sales by Country '13–Retail Sales by Country '20," Kia Corporation, https://worldwide.kia.com/kr/company/ir/archive/sales-results.

pursue a vaccine partnership illustrate a third area in which the U.S.–China technological rivalry on South Korea has influenced the U.S.–South Korea alliance. In response to President Moon's urgent political need and request to the United States to make vaccines available to South Korea on an early timeline due to South Korea's inability to obtain sufficient vaccine through commercial channels, the Biden administration advanced a framework in which South Korea might enhance a partnership with the United States in the production and supply of vaccines internationally on a long-term basis. This framework involved the combining of U.S.-developed vaccine formulas with available South Korean production capabilities to enable South Korea to ramp up vaccine production to enhance the global availability of vaccines. South Korea's opportunity to form a vaccine partnership with the United States came about in part due to the U.S. political need to provide vaccine internationally in response to China's vaccine diplomacy and the temporary disruption of availability of vaccine production in India due to India's acute domestic needs. The framework also linked South Korea in practical terms to a priority objective identified by the Quad summit in March 2021 of global vaccine provision, alongside climate change and enhancement of supply chain resiliency. Although South Korea remained institutionally outside the Quad, the establishment of a global vaccine partnership associated South Korea with a Biden administration political priority that was also identified as a Quad deliverable.

The May 21, 2021, U.S.–South Korea Leaders' Joint Statement announced the establishment of the KORUS Global Vaccine Partnership "to strengthen joint response capabilities for infectious disease through international vaccine cooperation, including focus areas on global expansion of production and related materials, as well as scientific and technological cooperation." The joint statement called for the establishment of a KORUS Global Vaccine Partnership Experts Group, and South Korea pledged to increase its financial support for COVAX, the primary international mechanism under the World Health Organization (WHO) responsible for the global distribution of vaccines.[26]

Alongside the U.S.–South Korea Global Vaccine Partnership, Moderna and Samsung Biologics concluded a memorandum of understanding and follow-up expert meetings were held.[27] The Moon administration has pointed to the vaccine partnership as "recognition of Korean bioindustry's superior production capacity, human assets, and quality control ability."[28] As a tangible step toward realizing U.S.–South Korea cooperation in vaccine production, the U.S.-based vaccine raw material manufacturer Cytiva submitted a $52.5 million investment plan to the Ministry of Trade, Energy, and Industry for a production facility to make raw materials for vaccines in South Korea.[29] But the partnership was largely aspirational, dependent on the realization of production capacity and export of U.S.-developed vaccines to other countries. Within South Korea, the agreement was criticized primarily for insufficiently meeting South Korea's immediate need to increase the supply of vaccines to the South Korean public.[30] While public health remains a promising area for international cooperation and vaccine manufacture holds the promise of combining U.S. development of effective vaccines with South Korea's production capabilities, prospects for realizing an effective and beneficial partnership in the global public health sector remain to be developed.

U.S.–CHINA TECHNOLOGY TENSIONS AND IMPLICATIONS FOR SOUTH KOREA

South Korean analysts have closely watched the escalating U.S.–China trade tensions, especially as related to the emerging U.S.–China technology competition. The United States ramped up efforts to thwart Chinese investment and technology transfer demands from U.S. firms and their partners through the Committee on Foreign Investment in the United States (CFIUS), tightened U.S. export regulations, and imposed penalties for nonsanctioned technology transfers. These restrictions have blocked future South Korean investments in Chinese semiconductor plants that employ the most advanced semiconductor technologies but have not blocked South Korean factories based in China from continuing to produce legacy semiconductors used to power the smart technologies most commonly available in the global consumer market.[31] South Korean analysts have paid particularly close attention to the impact of and have sought exemptions from U.S. restrictions on semiconductor exports to China, which would directly target South Korea's largest export item to China.[32]

Exports of semiconductors to China and Hong Kong represent 60 percent of South Korea's memory chip exports, so prohibitions on the export of memory chips to China likely require significant strategic readjustments for the South Korean semiconductor sector.[33] In particular, Samsung and SK Hynix have faced the prospect of considerable losses due to prohibitions on the supply of memory chips to Huawei. American semiconductor exporters have also experienced lost business estimated by the Boston Consulting Group at 30 percent as a result of the export curbs.[34] At the same time, the restrictions could significantly limit competition from Huawei for South Korean technology firms in third country markets. The Konkuk University professor Bae Young-ja evaluated that such measures have thwarted China's Made in China 2025 goal of achieving 70 percent self-sufficiency in semiconductor supplies.[35]

For this reason, the opportunity to step up integration into U.S.-based supply chains represents an important incentive for South Korean semiconductor firms. As the United States emphasizes domestic supply chain production, South Korean investment in semiconductor production in the United States constitutes both an opportunity to develop an alternative market through integration into the U.S. supply chain to reduce the impact of losses from the Chinese market and a risk unless U.S. efforts to promote expanded domestic production provide South Korea with new opportunities for participation. One South Korean analysis of the 2021 version of the U.S. Creating Helpful Incentives to Produce Semiconductors (CHIPS) for America Act—conducted prior to the release of the Biden administration's initial 100-day review of supply chain resiliency—speculated that South Korea might face greater competition in the memory chip sector with

Micron, but that U.S. interests in the diversification of foundry capacity primarily concentrated in Taiwan might represent a potential opportunity for South Korean companies to cultivate their own foundry industry.[36]

With the passage of the Inflation Reduction Act (IRA) in the summer of 2022, South Korea's debate over the opportunities and risks of supply chain integration with the United States exploded. Companies such as Samsung, SK Hynix, and Hyundai had pledged billions of dollars of investment in the United States in hopes of integrating with the U.S. supply chain while domestic production–only tax credits for electric vehicles contained in the IRA generated comparisons with exclusionary treatment faced by South Korean firms in the China market and spurred a debate within South Korea over the danger that investments directed toward the United States represented a loss of domestic investment needed to generate jobs in South Korea.[37]

In response, the Biden administration struggled to find an effective mechanism by which to deal with South Korean concerns and the seeming contradiction between a China strategy that promoted practical steps toward the building of a technology alliance among like-minded partners and the passage of legislation that excluded the eligibility of foreign-made electric vehicles for tax credits in favor of U.S.-made vehicles. Only three months prior to the passage of the IRA, Hyundai's chairman Chung Eui-son, during a meeting with President Biden in Seoul, had made significant pledges to build electric vehicles in the United States, yet Hyundai EVs made outside the United States prior to the completion of the factory would be excluded from the tax credit. The exclusion of Hyundai from the tax credit appeared to have an immediate negative impact on Hyundai's U.S. sales of EVs in monthly sales data following the passage of the IRA.[38]

Political outcry from the South Korean public amplified the issue, generating pressure on senior administration officials including President Biden to mollify South Korean critics, who openly wondered why South Korean conglomerates chose to invest in the United States rather than at home. In response, President Biden sent a letter to President Yoon on October 4, pledging to address the issue through bilateral consultations, with Korean media speculating that Korean concerns might be assuaged either through favorable consideration by the U.S. Treasury as part of the drafting of guidelines for implementation of the IRA or through congressional passage of an amendment to the law.[39] The political pressure from South Korea on the Biden administration generated by the unintended impact of the IRA on Hyundai Motors underscored the complexity of the political challenge and unforeseen conflicts with allies the Biden administration undertook as part of its efforts to sharpen the technology competition as a critical dimension of U.S. rivalry with China.

Increased U.S. government investment in the semiconductor sector is intended to provide greater capital infusion for leading U.S. firms in the industry and to generate incentives for existing market players to provide new U.S.-based investment for the production of critical components in the supply chain. The impact and distribution of U.S. government investments in the sector is another factor likely to draw close scrutiny from the South Korean private sector. The entry of the U.S. government into the sector, both in terms of investment and oversight, signifies a willingness to compete with China's state-centered efforts to develop advanced technologies on its own terms.

The U.S. decision to withhold exports of technological components to Chinese competitors seeking to establish an international commercial and strategic advantage and market share may slow China's advancement, limit the international scope of its growth, and hinder its development of market share and competitive advantages accruing from the adoption of Chinese products and technologies. However, it will not prevent China from mounting its own domestically driven effort to innovate cutting-edge technologies that might eventually challenge those of the United States, advancing or profiting from its own domestic market, or financing the spread of Chinese technologies to customers in China's economic orbit. In the end, both a U.S.-centered and a China-centered semiconductor industry will grow and compete with each other, with South Korean technology companies navigating opportunities and costs between the two markets, but it is unlikely that either market will achieve the size or efficiency of a single, globalized technology market.

SOUTH KOREA'S RESPONSE TO U.S.–CHINA TECHNOLOGY RIVALRY AND IMPLICATIONS FOR KOREAN FOREIGN POLICY

To the extent that South Koreans have viewed economic opportunity as the engine catalyzing the development of China–South Korea relations while security is the primary rationale for the U.S.–South Korea alliance, the Biden administration's supply chain resiliency efforts appeared in part designed to challenge that perception and to realign South Korea's economic engagement with the United States as a means by which to reinforce and revitalize a comprehensive U.S.–South Korea relationship. But China's growing regional economic influence, its geographic influence, and opportunities for South Korean companies to gain a share of China's rapidly expanding domestic economy remain powerful sources of attraction in the Sino–South Korean relationship.

The specter of Chinese economic retaliation against South Korea for making political and security decisions perceived as infringing on Chinese interests has introduced a new dimension of China's growing regional influence by demonstrating to Seoul the costs of challenging Beijing. But its manifestations have repelled rather than attracted South Koreans, who encountered new obstacles and limits in dimensions of the economic relationship that enhanced South Korea's standing such as pop culture, tourism, and direct consumer marketing sectors, while leaving the door open to sectors in which China's economy benefited from continuing South Korean inputs. South Korean concerns about such a possibility predated China's 2017 economic retaliation, but those concerns were reinforced as the Sino–South Korean economic relationship appears to have peaked in 2018 rather than recovering its pre-THAAD growth.

China's economic retaliation against South Korea has also opened the door for the politicization of China policy as an issue in South Korean domestic politics. The bipartisan consensus on policy toward China that had been buoyed for decades by Korean economic opportunities in the China market has begun to fray. While China's retaliation for the THAAD deployment on South Korean soil has elicited a strong negative reaction among the Korean public, the Moon administration's accommodationist approach toward China opened the door for conservative criticisms in support of a much more confrontational approach toward Beijing. In response, the Chinese government has been drawn into the sphere of South Korean domestic politics, both through its courting of Democratic Party members who opposed THAAD prior to Moon's election and through its response to South Korean conservative criticisms of China's political crackdown and human rights abuses in Hong Kong and Xinjiang.

But the biggest influence on the structure and strategy of South Korean producers of cutting-edge technologies such as semiconductors has been U.S. government measures under the Biden administration to prioritize new investments in supply chain resiliency. South Korean research institutions such as the Korea International Trade Association have carefully scrutinized the implications of the CHIPS Act and other Biden administration initiatives in an effort to maximize the effectiveness of South Korean business strategies going forward.[40] Despite ongoing concerns that U.S. protectionism might disadvantage Korean companies, the eagerness of the South Korean tech sector to pursue foreign direct investments of its newest technologies in the United States rather than China marked a turning point that engendered concern in China. The response of the *Global Times* to Yoon's election consisted of a mixture of anxiety and veiled warnings to South Korea not to challenge Chinese core interests. Both sides insisted on "mutual respect" in the relationship, but they had opposing interpretations of what the phrase meant for the conduct of the relationship. South Korean trade with China, and especially South Korean exports of semiconductors that China desperately needs, will not suddenly dry up, but rapid growth of bilateral trade that had characterized the relationship for decades appears to have reached its peak.

Yoon administration advisors have expressed confidence that China does not have the same tools available to implement a second economic retaliation against South Korea because of the lost leverage resulting from China's earlier economic retaliation against South Korean cultural exports and tourism sectors. Moreover, the pandemic and China's own exclusionary policies have dampened South Korean market share of Chinese domestic products and tempered optimism about China's willingness to allow foreign firms to maintain market share in the Chinese market against domestic competitors. The Yoon administration's decision to align more closely with the United States has coincided with greater opportunities for South Korean firms to invest in the U.S. market at the same time that Chinese policies and practices have reduced South Korean prospects for significant opportunities in China's domestic consumer market. At the same time, the Yoon administration has been at pains to emphasize that the relationship between Seoul and Beijing should remain positive and cooperative even as South Korea strengthens alliance ties with the United States against the backdrop of rising U.S.–China strategic competition.

PART III

THE CREDIBILITY OF THE AMERICAN ALLIANCE COMMITMENT AND THE IMPLICATIONS OF ALLIANCE BREAKDOWN

8

THE CREDIBILITY OF THE AMERICAN
ALLIANCE COMMITMENT

Under the Donald J. Trump administration, the U.S.–South Korea alliance for the first time faced direct presidential criticism of the U.S.–South Korea security and economic relationship. This criticism marked a striking departure from decades of consistent rhetorical U.S. commitment to South Korea's defense. While President Trump acknowledged the closeness and longevity of the U.S.–South Korea relationship, he minimized South Korea's value as an ally, downplayed U.S. benefits accrued from forward-deployed defense strategies, expressed a desire to minimize U.S. exposure to potential conflict on the Korean Peninsula, and approached cost-sharing negotiations from a mercenary, transactional perspective in an attempt to maximize South Korean financial contributions to U.S. force presence on the peninsula. The only other president to publicly consider removal of U.S. forces from South Korea was Jimmy Carter, who did so in the mid-1970s to honor his campaign pledge to withdraw U.S. military support for the authoritarian Park Chung-hee regime in light of its many human rights abuses.

As discussed in chapter 2, Trump rhetorically devalued a U.S.–South Korea alliance deeply rooted in shared democratic values based on his view that U.S. allies globally had for decades taken advantage of and profited economically from military deals with the United States that left it with substantial military burdens overseas. In so doing, Trump simultaneously fed long-standing fears and doubts of both Korean progressives and conservatives regarding the credibility of the United States by seemingly reaffirming what Koreans perceived as worrisome continuities in the trajectory of U.S. foreign policy and by saying the quiet part out loud. For progressives, Trump's rhetorical diminution of the alliance and his disparagement of South Korea's value as an alliance partner provided proof that the United States would never leave South Korea but would instead take advantage of South Korea while continuing to pursue its own national security interests. South Korea would remain entrapped by the constraints of the alliance with the United States, underappreciated, and therefore devalued by the United States. For conservatives, Trump's rhetoric stimulated fears of abandonment and betrayal by the United States, the reverberations of which have continued even under the Biden and Yoon administrations. These fears were amplified both by the prospect that, despite South Korea's remarkable democratic transformation, the alliance remained as vulnerable to threats of U.S. withdrawal as it had been under the authoritarian Park Chung-hee regime and by concerns that Trump would betray South Korea's security and unilaterally embrace South Korea's principal enemy through summitry with Kim Jong-un.

Compounding the challenge to U.S. credibility, both Korean progressives and conservatives would point to continuities in U.S. foreign policy extending to the Trump administration to support their own narrative. Progressives recalled how the United States under President George W. Bush redirected a brigade previously stationed in South Korea for decades to fight in Iraq in the mid-2000s while simultaneously pressuring South Korea's president Roh Moo-hyun to make military contributions to the stabilization of Iraq in the aftermath of the second Persian Gulf War. Despite South Korea's contributions to U.S. priorities in Iraq, however, the United States never honored the implicit quid pro quo that progressives sought by placing diplomatic reconciliation with North Korea at the top of its list of priorities. Trump made U.S.–North Korea relations a priority, but U.S. attention to the North came with a high price tag in the form of unprecedented U.S. demands for South Korea to increase its financial support for U.S. forces in South Korea.

In contrast, South Korean conservatives carefully observed pressures on the United States in support of global U.S. retrenchment, focusing on the continuities between the Obama administration's efforts to reduce U.S. commitments abroad and Trump's accusations of free riding directed at both European and Asian allies. In the meantime, conservatives observed with unease North Korea's consistent but unfettered expansion of its asymmetric military development and the U.S. failure to contain such developments. South Korean conservatives called on the Obama and Trump administrations to redeploy U.S. tactical nuclear weapons in South Korea or give South Korea permission to go nuclear, which revealed their discomfort with North Korea's nuclear advances and the U.S. failure to make the North Korea challenge a policy priority, encapsulated in references to the Obama administration's policy as one of "strategic patience." For conservatives, Trump's summitry with North Korea contrasted with his failure to deliver tangible achievements in denuclearization negotiations and his willingness to trade away deterrence measures by unilaterally suspending joint U.S.–South Korea military exercises following Trump's June 2018 Singapore summit with Kim.

Conservative South Korean security analysts began to question whether the United States would shed its commitments to international security, insist on prioritizing domestic issues, and abandon its leadership role in preserving the liberal international order. Polling of the South Korean public has consistently shown relative favorability for American international leadership (with ratings consistently over five on a zero to ten scale), especially compared to South Korea's neighbors. These results suggest few concerns thus far about U.S. credibility, but the potential for doubt stirred by a divided American narrative regarding U.S. political will to meet its overseas commitments may lie just under the surface.[1] South Koreans must also weigh U.S. capabilities and intentions against the context of changes in the strategic environment resulting from China's rising capabilities, as discussed in chapters 6 and 7. The alliance could come under siege from both a narrowing

U.S. commitment to preserve its international role and a South Korean perception that U.S. security guarantees are no longer credible.

TRUMP'S PUBLIC STATEMENTS REGARDING THE U.S.–SOUTH KOREA ALLIANCE

Trump came into office profoundly skeptical of U.S. alliances, viewing security commitments abroad as bad deals that provided other countries with distinct economic advantages over the United States. Trump saw defense commitments as economic subsidies that enabled alliance partners to take advantage of and compete unfairly against the United States rather than as structural frameworks that furthered U.S. interests and predisposed allies to engage in mutually beneficial economic trade with the United States.

A 2019 Center for Strategic and International Studies (CSIS) study of 122 statements by Donald Trump regarding U.S. alliance commitments going back to 1990 concluded that Trump perceived allies as free-riding on U.S. security guarantees, wanted allies to pay more for U.S. troop presence in their countries, and believed that allies have taken advantage of U.S. security guarantees by running large trade deficits with the United States.[2] These beliefs appear to have influenced Trump's presidential remarks about South Korea. A review of Trump's public comments about South Korea during his presidency—compiled from the White House website for this book—shows that of 148 comments about or referring to South Korea, 23 were negative, 58 were mixed, and 67 were positive. Many of Trump's positive comments about South Korea were self-promotional or focused on his administration's accomplishments rather than on South Korea. Strikingly, this was the case even for statements Trump made at public appearances during two visits to South Korea and two meetings with President Moon Jae-in at the White House.

Prior to the announcement of a renegotiated KORUS FTA on September 24, 2018, to replace the agreement ratified in 2012 under the Obama

administration, Trump's comments about South Korea were often dispar-
aging and portrayed South Korea as having taken advantage of the U.S.–
South Korea alliance to generate economic benefits at the expense of the
United States. Trump viewed bilateral economic relations exclusively
through the lens of merchandise trade balances and saw other countries as
exploiting the United States wherever that balance was in the red. This
approach posed a particular problem for Trump's views of South Korea
because the KORUS FTA, negotiated under the George W. Bush administration and ratified under the Obama administration, was premised on
the idea that South Korea's opening of its market in areas such as legal and
financial services would generate surpluses for U.S. firms that would balance against South Korea's strong manufacturing profile and targeting of
the U.S. market as favorable for South Korean exports. But by excluding
the growing U.S. surplus in services in favor of an exclusive focus on merchandise trade, Trump minimized the contributions of the KORUS FTA
to the overall U.S.–South Korea trade balance and continued to pressure
South Korea to balance its surplus in merchandise trade, as discussed in
chapter 2.

Following the announcement of the renegotiated KORUS FTA, Trump
repeatedly made positive references to the new trade agreement while den-
igrating the agreement made by his predecessors. On one such occasion,
Trump asserted "We've totally renegotiated the deal with South Korea. It
was not a good deal for the United States; now it's a great deal for the United
States."[3] Trump often falsely claimed that the Obama administration trade
deal, which Trump regularly ascribed to Hillary Clinton, created jobs for
South Korea but not for the United States, and that his own deal fixed that
flaw. These claims contradicted the findings of the independent U.S. International Trade Commission (USITC), which concluded that the impact
of the KORUS FTA on "aggregate U.S. output and employment changes
would likely be negligible."[4]

Trump's criticisms regarding the U.S.–South Korea relationship extended
to his negative evaluation of South Korean contributions to support the continued USFK presence on the peninsula. For instance, Trump stated that
"We helped—and you had the Korean War; we helped South Korea. We

helped everybody. And nobody changed. They had no money, they had no anything. They were rebuilding from a war. And the agreements basically stayed the way they were. And they became very wealthy, and they could pay a tremendous amount, and they could pay us back. But nothing happened."[5] With these comments, Trump primarily sought to portray South Korea as dragging its feet in meeting U.S. expectations for fairness in shouldering the financial burden of the U.S. commitment to South Korea's defense. Trump's comments on South Korea as a valuable security partner were much rarer and primarily came in the context of his visits to South Korea in November 2017 and June 2019.

Another recurring theme of Trump's public commentary on the Korean Peninsula involved the periodic retelling in various campaign speeches of Trump's own version of events surrounding his meetings and exchange of letters with the North Korean leader Kim Jong-un. Usually, this narrative focused exclusively on the Trump-Kim dynamic, but Trump also occasionally referenced his support for the suspension of what he and the North Koreans have called "war games," the joint U.S.–South Korea military exercises conducted regularly on the Korean Peninsula. Trump's references to "war games," which he began discussing in a press conference immediately following his first meeting with Kim in Singapore in June 2018, indicated his opposition to U.S.–South Korea joint military exercises. The exercises, which had strong bipartisan support, continued throughout his administration, though their scope, timing, and frequency were adjusted to make room for diplomacy with the North. In advance of a meeting with the Japanese prime minister Abe Shinzo in France, Trump responded to North Korea's resumption of short-range missile testing by stating "I'm not happy about it [North Korean testing]. But again, he's not in violation of an agreement. We speak. I received a very nice letter from him last week. We speak. He was upset that South Korea was doing the 'war games' as you call them. I don't think they were necessary either, if you want to know the truth. And I said to my people, 'You can have them or not. I would recommend against them, but I'm going to let you do exactly what you want to do. . . . But I think it's a total waste of money.'"[6] Perhaps because Trump's characterization of U.S.–South Korea defensive exercises as "war games" drew significant opposition within the defense bureaucracy and on Capitol Hill as well as from his own national security advisor John Bolton, Trump refrained from using his executive power to actually end the exercises.

Trump's fixation with the economic dimension of the U.S.–South Korea alliance spilled over into his focus on burden sharing for U.S. security commitments in South Korea. During his presidency, Trump attempted to impose public pressure on South Korea to induce it to substantially increase its cash commitments in support of the U.S. deployment of personnel and equipment to South Korea and the annual joint exercises. But Trump's minimization of the need for joint exercises undercut his own demands for South Korea to increase its share of financial support for the U.S. presence in South Korea. Trump's interest in adjusting the financial basis for the military relationship dovetailed with his efforts to manage the North Korean nuclear issue and burgeoning personal relationship with Kim Jong-un. Most notably, during the Singapore summit Trump personally pledged to suspend U.S.–South Korea joint military exercises alongside the formal signing of the Singapore Declaration, in which the United States and North Korea agreed to work toward building a new U.S.–North Korea relationship, permanent peace arrangements, and complete denuclearization of the Korean Peninsula.

STAKEHOLDERS CONSTRAINING TRUMP'S ATTACKS ON THE U.S.–SOUTH KOREA ALLIANCE

The effect on the American public consciousness of Trump's repeated discussion at campaign rallies of alliance free-riding, disproportionate costs to the United States of its security commitment to South Korea, and unfair trade cannot be discounted as a potential source of trouble down the road. However, Trump's personal views toward South Korea fell well outside conventional mainstream attitudes toward the U.S.–South Korea security alliance. The headwinds Trump faced in opposition to his criticism of the

U.S.–South Korea alliance came from the U.S. Congress, the institutional bureaucracy and notably his own advisors, and from countervailing support for South Korea among the American public.

U.S. CONGRESS

As Trump moved to diminish alliance commitments abroad, congressional leadership attempted to limit the perceived damage Trump could do to U.S. alliances. Bipartisan congressional opposition to Trump's crusade against alliances took a variety of forms, including public statements of, support for, and reassurance of allies. Following Trump's first visit to NATO in 2017, where he cranked up the heat on European countries by calling on them to pay up while diminishing U.S. alliance commitments, the conservative U.S. senator John McCain (R-AZ) provided public pledges of reassurance to allies at the Munich Security Conference. Congress also stepped up to pass measures aimed at reassuring U.S. allies, bounding presidential actions, and mitigating the damage done by Trump's criticisms of U.S. alliances. Members of Congress such as the Democratic senator Ed Markey (D-MA) bluntly called out Trump for his demands on allies to pay more for the U.S. military presence, stating in advance of the first Trump-Moon summit in June 2017 "Unity of purpose between the United States and our South Korean allies was undermined today by President Trump's discourteous remarks about so-called 'burden sharing' for the United States' military commitment. The U.S.–South Korean alliance is a mutual defense commitment, not a protection racket."[7]

Several congressional resolutions provided reassurances regarding the continuity of the U.S. military presence in Asia and the steadfastness of U.S. alliances with Asian nations. The U.S. Congress passed the Asia Reassurance Initiative Act (ARIA) in December 2018 authorizing appropriations for specified security programs, promotion of democracy, strengthening of civil society, human rights, rule of law, transparency, and accountability in the Indo-Pacific region; enhancement of cybersecurity cooperation with Indo-Pacific nations; and support for exchanges including the Young Southeast Asian Leaders Initiative (YSEALI) and the

ASEAN (Association of Southeast Asian Nations) Volunteers program. A Congressional Research Service advisory regarding the provisions stated that "the act shows congressional support for many elements of the Administration's approach to China as a strategic competitor. Many observers have also read it, however, as a sign of congressional unease with President Trump's treatment of U.S. allies and traditional partners."[8]

Congress also imposed limits on Trump's ability to reduce or remove U.S. forces from the Korean Peninsula in the 2019 and 2020 National Defense Authorization Act (NDAA). Trump reportedly objected to those provisions but ultimately signed the authorization with the provisions intact.[9] The 2020 NDAA raised the number of troops to be maintained on the peninsula from the 22,000 stipulated in the 2019 bill to 28,500 troops, essentially mandating no reduction in U.S. forces at a time when Trump might have desired to use withdrawal threats as leverage in the stalled U.S.–ROK Special Measures Agreement cost-sharing negotiations.[10]

As Trump tried to apply pressure to increase burden-sharing contributions from Japan and South Korea, Congress held hearings with senior administration defense officials in which individual representatives articulated their disapproval of a mercenary approach to allies and reasserted the value of U.S. alliances. At a March 2019 congressional hearing on "National Security Challenges and U.S. Military Activities in the Indo-Pacific," the House Committee on Armed Services chairman Adam Smith expressed his concern that an overly aggressive approach to burden sharing might "drive a wedge between us and our allies, which we don't need to do." In an effort to send a signal of opposition to rumored Trump demands to readjust defense-cost sharing with allies on a more transactional basis, Smith asked Assistant Secretary of Defense Randy Shriver about reports that the administration might incorporate a "cost-plus-fifty" approach to demanding that allies shoulder greater costs for the operations and deployment of U.S. forces in the Indo-Pacific. Shriver responded that he was satisfied with burden-sharing commitments by allies to date and that the Department of Defense had not been directed to employ such an approach.[11] This exchange signaled both concern within Congress and caution within the Department of Defense regarding reports that Trump was preparing to dramatically escalate financial demands for increased contributions from American allies and defense partners.

INSTITUTIONAL BUREAUCRACY

The institutional bureaucracy consists of career government workers and other actors within the U.S. government that contribute to the formation and implementation of U.S. policies at the direction of the president—such as the Department of State, Department of Defense, and various parts of the intelligence community (IC). While the institutional bureaucracy implements the policies of particular presidents, it also provides institutional memory and cautionary advice based on past experience at a practical level regarding which methods have worked and which have not worked as instruments of policy implementation. At a fundamental level, the institutional bureaucracy serves as a repository of expertise regarding highly complex and technical problems that are removed from politics and partisanship.

But the institutional bureaucracy—often referred to by Trump as a "swamp," which he pledged to drain during his campaign—was drawn into politics in an unprecedented fashion under Trump and constituted a constant source of opposition within the administration that thwarted Trump's efforts to follow through on many of his political promises. Because of Trump's hunger for publicity and his subordinates' willingness to broadcast their efforts to curb the president's most contentious foreign policy instincts, disputes between Trump and his closest advisors played out in a series of near-public confrontations with successive national security advisors and secretaries of defense. Congressional hearings during Trump's first impeachment illustrated the dysfunctionality of relationships between Trump emissaries within the White House and other elements of the bureaucracy. From day one to day 1,461, the main drama of the Trump presidency pitted the president against his own government, including in striking showdowns over policy toward the Korean Peninsula.

As previously discussed, one of Trump's biggest pet peeves involved his perception of trade with South Korea as unfair. Having already jettisoned ratification of the Obama administration's Trans-Pacific Partnership (TPP) and announced the renegotiation of the North American Free Trade Agreement (NAFTA), Trump turned his attention to another of Obama's accomplishments, the KORUS FTA. Trump came close to abrogating that agreement in September 2017 despite the message of betrayal such an action would send to South Korea during the "fire and fury" period of escalating tension with North Korea. But in an unprecedented move, revealing the depth of Trump administration infighting over policy even between the president and a member of his own Cabinet—the director of the National Economic Council Gary Cohn removed the paperwork that would revoke the KORUS FTA from the president's desk in the Oval Office, foiling Trump's plans to terminate the agreement. This occurred following appeals from Chief of Staff John Kelly, Secretary of Defense Jim Mattis, and Secretary of State Rex Tillerson to Trump to reconsider.[12] Ultimately, for unknown reasons, Trump did not go forward with termination of the agreement and the Trump and Moon administrations moved to renegotiate the KORUS FTA, presenting the president with a new agreement that he declared a major improvement over the previous deal.

Trump's objectionable rhetoric toward allies kept his Cabinet busy providing reassurances to America's closest friends. Defense Secretary Mattis made statements reaffirming the credibility of U.S. defense commitments and Vice President Mike Pence visited U.S. allies to provide reassurance regarding American steadfastness. The institutional bureaucracy at the highest levels sent messages of continuity and reassurance that contradicted Trump's impulsiveness, unpredictability, and most serious threats to the conventional wisdom underlying U.S. long-term security policy.

Trump's threatening messages toward North Korea also caused conflicts between Trump and his senior advisors in 2017, some of which remained private and others that became very public. Trump's senior advisors held conflicting views regarding North Korea as North Korea intensified its long-range missile testing during 2017. National Security Advisor H. R. McMaster reiterated that Trump would not accept a nuclear North Korea. Defense Secretary Mattis and JCS Chairman Joseph F. Dumford advised that a nuclear North Korea could be contained. But it was not clear that

Trump would be influenced by any of his senior advisors. Trump escalated his rhetoric to threaten North Korea's destruction and called Kim Jong-un "Rocketman" in his 2017 address to the UN General Assembly. The American investigative journalist Bob Woodward reported that Trump viewed the confrontation as a contest of wills, with all the showmanship of a professional wrestling confrontation: "This is all about leader versus leader. Man versus man. Me versus Kim." As the crisis ramped up, Trump's own secretary of state and fellow Washington outsider Rex Tillerson attempted to frame a diplomatic strategy toward North Korea by offering reassurance regarding "four no's": no regime change, no regime collapse, no accelerated Korean reunification, and no U.S. troops in North Korea. Days later, Trump tweeted on October 1 "I told Rex Tillerson, our wonderful Secretary of State, that he is wasting his time trying to negotiate with Little Rocket Man. Save your energy, Rex, we'll do what has to be done!"[13] The message to the bureaucracy was clear. On North Korea, Trump wanted to run his own show.

Despite the harsh rhetoric toward Tillerson, Trump in fact pursued diplomacy but with himself at the center of the effort. Trump used the occasion of the visit of the UN under-secretary-general for political affairs Jeffrey Feltman to Pyongyang in December 2017 to send an offer of talks to Kim. At the same time, Kim began a turn toward summitry by declaring his country's missile development complete following the November 28, 2017, test of the Hwasong-15. Kim's turn to summitry following the 2018 Pyeongchang Olympics provided Trump with an unprecedented opportunity to meet with Kim, but at the same time he selected the well-known North Korea hawk John Bolton to replace McMaster as his national security advisor. But Bolton had little influence on Trump's infatuation with Kim. In his memoir, Bolton detailed his frustration over his inability to influence Trump's handling of North Korea despite being his closest advisor on foreign policy. Bolton opposed Trump's decisions to meet with Kim in Singapore and Hanoi. When the president went ahead, Bolton claimed credit for talking Trump out of making any concessions toward North Korea that Bolton felt would truly jeopardize U.S. national interests.[14] However, Trump's refusal to take counsel even from his own national security advisors underscored the limits to the ability of the president's closest advisors to block the president's will to pursue his own policies, regardless of whether such decisions are ill-advised.

AMERICAN PUBLIC OPINION

A third constraint on Trump's criticisms of the U.S.–South Korea alliance as one-sided, free-riding, or imbalanced came in the form of American public views of South Korea and the alliance. Gallup found that American perceptions of South Korea have improved continuously since the early 2000s.[15] The Chicago Council on Global Affairs found in October 2020 during Trump's final year in office that favorable views of South Korea were at an all-time high, with 59 percent of Americans surveyed viewing alliances in East Asia as either benefiting both countries or mostly benefiting the United States and 74 percent of Americans seeing the United States and South Korea as partners. Americans viewed South Korea almost as favorably as Japan but held negative views of China and North Korea.[16]

A May 2021 poll by the Korea Economic Institute of America found that 62 percent of Americans surveyed viewed the military alliance with South Korea as beneficial to the United States and 56 percent of Americans either supported current levels of U.S. forces in South Korea or would have liked to see an increase in troops, compared to 19 percent of Americans who would like to see U.S. troop reductions or withdrawals.[17] Chicago Council on Global Affairs polling shows that over 60 percent of Americans have consistently supported maintaining the current U.S. military presence in the Asia-Pacific, regardless of Trump's negative rhetoric about free-riding by allies.[18] These polls show that despite Trump's criticism of South Korea as an unfair trading partner and free rider, American views of South Korea as a partner improved steadily throughout his presidency. Positive American views of South Korea suggest that Trump's negative rhetoric toward South Korea did not get through to the American public.

However, the apparent constraints imposed by strong American public support for South Korea, bureaucratic resistance from subordinates to the president even at the highest levels, and congressional opposition to presidential policies may in all likelihood not be sufficient to prevent a future American president from dismantling the alliance at any time. If Trump had successfully won reelection in 2020, he stated that one of his goals would have been to dismantle the alliance.[19]

SOUTH KOREA'S EVOLVING VIEW OF THE U.S. ROLE ON THE KOREAN PENINSULA

South Korean public opinion polling by the Asan Institute for Policy Studies has shown remarkable continuity in South Korean attitudes toward the United States. Trump's criticisms of South Korea as a free rider and demands for an exorbitant increase in South Korean financial contributions in support of USFK troop presence did not appear to have significantly influenced South Korean perceptions of the United States or the alliance. Over 78 percent of South Koreans polled supported maintaining or strengthening the alliance in 2020, with over 70 percent of respondents supporting either maintaining or increasing current troop levels. Over 87 percent of South Korean respondents believed that the United States would intervene in the event of a military contingency on the Korean Peninsula.

On the other hand, South Koreans generally opposed increasing financial contributions to USFK despite Trump's demands, with over 40 percent of respondents polled expressing a belief that the current level of financial support for U.S. forces was sufficient and 23 percent of respondents feeling that South Korean contributions should be lower than the current level. Only about 3 percent of South Koreans polled supported raising South Korean contributions to the full level of U.S. demands.[20] A 2019 CFR-Asan poll of South Korean attitudes toward USFK showed a gap between the strong degree of conservative support (6.98 on a scale of 0 to 10) and a lesser degree of progressive support for the USFK presence (4.85).[21] Perceiving the burden-sharing issue as a potential source of friction in the alliance, the Biden administration, within two months of his inauguration, concluded a new agreement that involved a more reasonable increase in South Korean contributions. South Korean public opinion data suggests that Trump's criticisms and demands toward South Korea, while irritating to the South Korean government, were either not taken seriously or were unacknowledged by the public in the face of strong underlying favorability toward the U.S.–South Korea alliance as an important foundation for South Korea's national security and prosperity.

Notably, South Korean public opinion polls conducted at the beginning and at the end of the Trump administration revealed a gap between South Korean perceptions of the United States and of the U.S. president. At the close of the Obama administration, South Korean public perceptions of Obama tracked closely with views of the United States, but in the early months of the Trump administration a huge gap emerged between negative perceptions of Trump and much more favorable views of the United States. The gap narrowed following Trump's efforts to engage in diplomacy with Kim Jong-un, in large part because Trump's summitry with Kim demonstrated that he was grappling with South Korea's most serious and intractable security problem. But with the Hanoi summit failure and U.S.– North Korea summitry waning after the June 2019 Trump-Kim meeting at the demilitarized zone dividing the two Koreas, South Korean perceptions of Trump declined and the gap between Trump's favorability and U.S. favorability returned. Biden's election and emphasis on restoration of alliances again closed the gap between South Korean perceptions of the United States and its president. However, this does not mean that there was not growing concern in South Korea about U.S. credibility, only that those doubts did not gain traction with the broader public.[22]

CONCERNS ABOUT U.S. CREDIBILITY DURING THE TRUMP ADMINISTRATION

The implementation of Trump's America First approach to foreign policy was greeted with a combination of anxiety and denial in South Korea. Progressive thought leaders highlighted Trump's perceived insensitivity and narrow focus on American self-interest in response to Trump's periodic and ongoing slights of South Korea, including Trump's characterization of South Korean opportunism at America's expense in trade or his perception of South Korea as a security free rider. But these commentators tended to gravitate toward a skeptical view that Trump's combination of inattention to and diminishing of South Korean contributions justified preexisting views of a United States primarily concerned with its own interests and not those of South Korea. While observing global trends, progressive media outlets generally did not express alarm that U.S. retrenchment would extend to South Korea, reflecting that the main progressive concerns regarding the relationship with the United States revolve around entrapment in the alliance rather than abandonment.

The progressive *Hankyoreh* argued that American "isolationism" might make room for inter-Korean arms control while opening space for a debate over the continuing presence of U.S. forces on the Korean Peninsula, urging the Moon administration to prepare meticulously for bilateral negotiations on OPCON transition, joint exercises, and negotiation of new defense cost-sharing arrangements.[23] The progressive labor-oriented *Kyunghyang Shinmun* staff reporter Park Sung-jin used Trump's inability to correctly recall the number of U.S. troops in South Korea and his unilateral suspension of joint exercises following the Singapore summit with Kim Jong-un to question the meaning of the often-repeated statement among alliance managers and government officials that "there is no room for light" in the U.S.–South Korea military alliance.[24] Notably, progressives (44 percent) had a more positive assessment of Trump than conservatives (31 percent) regarding Trump's impact on the Korean Peninsula, probably because of his willingness to prioritize North Korea and engage at a summit level directly with Kim Jong-un.[25]

Korean conservatives, on the other hand, viewed the Trump administration through two lenses, both of which magnified their anxieties about the future of the U.S.–South Korea alliance. First, they harbored profound mistrust of Moon's ability to handle the relationship with the United States and worried that he would facilitate the U.S. turn toward isolation and its application to U.S. policy toward the Korean Peninsula. Second, they were dismayed and alarmed not only by Trump's demeaning statements toward South Korea but also by his dalliance with Kim Jong-un. Both Trump's isolationism and his fascination with dictators—first among them Kim—generated profound disorientation, alienation, and fears of U.S. abandonment among conservatives. The former national security advisor under the Lee Myung-bak administration Chun Young-woo summed up South Korean conservative anxieties by pointing to loss of trust between allies, a conflict over alliance goals stemming from the minister of unification Lee In-young's desire to convert the alliance into a "peace alliance," and concerns that the Moon administration's underperformance of U.S. expectations for South Korean contributions to its broader strategic goals in East Asia would eventually undermine U.S. public support for the alliance.[26]

Despite public discussion of the sources of U.S.–South Korea alliance weaknesses and expressions of concern about the broader global implications of an America-First turn toward isolationism, there was virtually no significant South Korean public discussion of alternatives to the alliance with the United States while the Trump administration was in office. The absence of a more active exploration of alternatives to the alliance with the United States probably reflects a combination of the degree to which the dissolution of the U.S.–South Korea alliance has been regarded as unthinkable, wishful thinking, and "whistling past the graveyard" in hopes that Trump would prove to be an aberration rather than a new normal driving U.S. foreign policy, and the degree to which South Koreans continue to regard possible alternatives to South Korean reliance on the alliance with the United States as unpalatable.

NEAR-TERM IMPACT ON U.S.–SOUTH KOREA ALLIANCE MANAGEMENT UNDER TRUMP AND MOON

Trump's hostility toward alliances posed a unique challenge for the U.S.–South Korea relationship, which has traditionally been underpinned by shared worldviews, threat assessments, and institutional mechanisms for pursuing alliance cooperation. Trump tested the long-held assumption that differences between allies are best managed within the institutionalized frameworks for coordination that have sustained U.S. alliances for decades. For the Moon administration, Trump's style posed unique challenges and opportunities. On the one hand, Trump's criticisms of South Korea and threat to pull out of the KORUS FTA, if it had been realized, might have done more harm to the U.S.–South Korea relationship than a renegotiation of the existing agreement within normal institutional frameworks. On the other hand, Moon capitalized on and benefited from Trump's willingness to bypass his own bureaucracy and consider direct summit diplomacy with Kim Jong-un. By sending special envoys first to North Korea to meet directly with Kim and then to the White House to meet with President Trump in March 2018, Moon sidestepped many potential obstacles and objections from the institutional bureaucracies that might have impeded Trump's surprise decision to accept an invitation to meet personally with Kim. But an unintended consequence of Moon's success that clearly took not only him but also Trump's own government by surprise was Trump's agreement during the Singapore summit to postpone U.S.–South Korea joint military exercises at Kim's request.

After Moon went too far in his efforts to move forward based on Kim's pledges to pursue complete denuclearization at the September 2018 Pyongyang summit, the United States strengthened institutional coordination between the two governments by proposing a U.S.–South Korea working group on North Korea policy, as discussed in chapter 4. But bureaucratic efforts to strengthen policy coordination did not address emerging risks of what the CSIS senior vice president and Korea chair Victor Cha has referred to as a "perfect storm" threatening the U.S.–South Korea alliance: the possibility that Trump might attempt to secure greater South Korean financial support for a continued U.S. troop presence on the peninsula by unilaterally negotiating with Kim Jong-un the withdrawal of those forces in return for North Korean pledges to roll back its ICBM threat or for incomplete North Korean denuclearization. This America-First move by Trump might have been welcomed by progressives within the Moon administration but at a direct cost to South Korean security, U.S. credibility, and the sustainability of the U.S.–South Korea alliance.

EFFORTS TO RESTORE THE U.S.–SOUTH KOREA ALLIANCE UNDER BIDEN AND MOON

Following his inauguration, the Biden administration embarked on a mission of restoring alliances, including with South Korea. As discussed in chapter 2, the initial rollout of Biden administration policies toward the

Korean Peninsula reflected clear intentions to both restore and expand cooperation with South Korea as a major alliance partner, alongside Japan. Biden made early phone calls following his inauguration to both Suga Yoshihide, prime minister of Japan, and Moon Jae-in, president of South Korea. Secretary of State Antony Blinken and Secretary of Defense Lloyd Austin made their first overseas trip together for two-plus-two meetings with Japan and South Korea, and President Biden welcomed Suga and Moon as his first and second visitors to the White House in April and May 2021. This diplomatic outreach was accompanied by expansive joint statements and fact sheets outlining a comprehensive agenda for alliance-based cooperation on a wide range of regional and functional issues, signifying a desire by the Biden administration to elevate alliance partnership as a central mechanism by which to implement U.S. foreign policy.

The Biden administration deftly cleared the decks for these moves by reaching an early conclusion to the Special Measures Agreement (SMA) specifying South Korea's expanded cost-sharing obligations in support of the alliance but on terms that reflected an expansion of the traditional formula through which South Korea would support on-peninsula logistical support and pay salaries of Korean workers on U.S. bases. As the Biden administration implemented its North Korea policy review, it also provided evidence of strong coordination with the Moon administration as well as evidence that South Korean input into the process was being taken seriously through the Biden administration's decision to pursue "diplomacy and strict deterrence" with North Korea by building on the Singapore declaration and announcing the appointment of a special envoy for North Korea, Ambassador Sung Kim, at the joint press conference following the Biden-Moon summit on May 21, 2021.

But questions remained in South Korea around the restoration of the alliance under the Biden administration. The Biden administration issued an open invitation to North Korea for a return to diplomacy consistent with South Korean preferences under the Moon administration. But the Biden administration did not appear to welcome South Korean diplomatic efforts to jump-start inter-Korean relations through a relaxation of sanctions, approval of tangible cooperation projects between the two sides, or suspension of joint military exercises in line with North Korean public demands. Moreover, the Biden administration was swamped with contending priorities and appeared unwilling to take initiative or risks related to higher-level engagement with North Korea that had been exhibited by the Trump administration and were likely the necessary prerequisite for a resumption of dialogue with North Korea. Likewise, the Biden administration welcomed the election of President Yoon Suk-yeol and his placing of the "comprehensive strategic alliance" with the United States as a centerpiece of his foreign policy. Under Biden and Yoon, the focus of policy toward North Korea shifted from an emphasis on diplomacy to extended deterrence and the prospects for closer coordination of U.S. and South Korean policies toward China expanded as Yoon abandoned strategic ambiguity for overt alignment with the United States while seeking a mutually beneficial relationship with China based on "mutual respect."

Longer-term questions loom about U.S. staying power in the context of China's rising regional and global influence as well as American political will to maintain international leadership. Despite the Biden administration's reassuring actions, South Koreans were well aware of the limits of their ability to influence U.S. politics and policies. While South Korean officials have kept mum regarding U.S. staying power, close South Korean observers probed for information regarding the significance of American domestic political trends, the long-term future of American political leadership and policy, and its implications for the U.S. ability to meet its security commitments to South Korea. These doubts were even reflected by Biden himself. In reference to his initial conversations with foreign leaders after becoming president, Biden said "The comment that I hear most of all from them is they say, 'We see America is back, but for how long?'"[27] For a Yoon administration that robustly placed the revitalization of the U.S.– South Korea alliance as its central foreign policy priority and treated the United States as an essential partner, Biden's question looms as one that could have daunting political reverberations in both countries for some time to come.

9

IMAGINING U.S. FOREIGN POLICY TOWARD ASIA ABSENT THE U.S.–SOUTH KOREA ALLIANCE

A t a point of high tension in the U.S.–South Korea alliance in the mid-2000s, the former U.S. ambassador to South Korea Alexander Vershbow said to a workshop tasked with imagining the security implications of an end to the U.S.–South Korea alliance that if there were no alliance with South Korea, the United States would need to reestablish one. This assertion underscored his view that the weakening or loss of the U.S.–South Korea alliance would come at a significant cost to both parties and that the alliance plays an essential role in supporting U.S. strategic aims in Northeast Asia. A March 2021 Government Accountability Office (GAO) study of burden sharing in the U.S.–Japan and U.S.–South Korea alliances further concluded that a forward U.S. military presence in Japan and South Korea benefits U.S. national security in the following six areas: (1) regional stability and security; (2) defense capability and interoperability; (3) contingency response; (4) denuclearization and nonproliferation; (5) strong alliances; and (6) a free and open Indo-Pacific.[1] For the United States, the rationale underlying the commitment to South Korea's defense lies with the benefits outlined in the GAO study.

U.S. national security objectives have expanded far beyond the original focus on peninsular and regional stability and strengthening of South Korea's defense capabilities that led to the signing of the Mutual Defense Treaty in 1953 and its ratification the following year. Over the past seven decades, U.S. interests and objectives have broadened in line with the opportunities created by South Korea's growing ability to contribute to shared alliance objectives. The GAO report provides an extensive accounting for the benefits to the United States underlying the continuation of the alliance. However, were U.S. and South Korean interests and priorities to drift apart such that growing tensions resulted in alliance degradation, both countries would have no choice but to adapt to new circumstances.

Many contemporary analysts would argue that given the convergence in U.S. and South Korean strategic interests and the emergence of geopolitical rivalries and threats that are likely to underscore rationales for alliance continuation, the likelihood of the degradation of the U.S.–South Korea alliance is unthinkable. But we live in an era in which what was previously unthinkable is now regarded as plausible and has even come to be regarded as inevitable, making it necessary to stress test the prior assumptions underlying the rationales for existing structures and institutions. In the context of a shift in the existing geopolitical order, both the United States and South Korea may encounter new challenges to the continuation of the alliance, many of which are likely to result from shifting domestic politics in response to transitions in the international order and resulting changes to the respective roles of the United States and South Korea. Under such circumstances, institutions that once seemed enduring may find themselves subject to new challenges from unexpected quarters. The prospects of a weakening of the U.S.–South Korea alliance that once seemed implausible might come to be seen as possible or even inevitable.

Moreover, there is arguably value in projecting the impact of the degradation of the U.S.–South Korea alliance on the foreign policy profiles of each country, if for no other reason than that imagining a world with no U.S.–South Korea alliance may deepen appreciation for the value, utility, and tangible contributions of the alliance to the respective national interests of both countries. The following chapters contribute to an understanding of the value and utility of the alliance by presenting the likely adjustments to U.S. and South Korean foreign policy that would be necessary in the event of alliance degradation.

FACTORS LEADING TO THE DEGRADATION OF THE ALLIANCE AND ITS GEOSTRATEGIC IMPACT

The U.S. commitment to preserving South Korea's security has endured so steadfastly that it rarely comes under scrutiny. As mentioned in chapter 8, public opinion polling from the Chicago Council on Global Affairs in October 2020 shows U.S. support for the U.S.–South Korea alliance at almost 60 percent, and 74 percent of Americans surveyed described South Korea and the United States as partners.[2] However, the U.S.–South Korea alliance might face future pressures that could erode U.S. will and capabilities to meet its commitments.

First, as discussed in the previous chapter, the credibility of the U.S. commitment to the alliance was brought into question to an unprecedented degree in South Korea during the Trump administration. Trump's repeated characterization of South Korea as a free rider pursuing its own security and economic interests at the expense of the United States feeds into these trends. Other arguments seeping into public discourse about the alliance could be based on the belief that South Korea is capable of defending itself against North Korea's far weaker conventional forces without U.S. assistance and that North Korea's nuclear capabilities would be of little concern to the United States if it does not needlessly entrap itself in a possible conflict by committing to South Korea's defense.

Second, the U.S. pledge to defend South Korea against regional security threats may become a more sizable financial burden than in past years, particularly taking into account the need to match increased military spending in the region by China and the fact that U.S. defense budgets are distributed globally while China predominantly focuses on its own backyard. Although it has been unthinkable that the United States, which boasts the largest defense budget in the world, might feel constrained financially when it comes to investing in capabilities to meet its defense commitments, it is increasingly clear that China's regional investments may outpace U.S. investment in South Korea's defense.[3] The relative distribution of U.S. material capabilities in support of defense modernization in Asia could shift. South Korea might begin to question U.S. capabilities and willingness to come to its defense. The impact of U.S. financial constraints on defense procurement might emerge in a variety of forms, including increased demands for South Korean contributions to support the U.S. force presence, the inability or unwillingness of the United States to make additional force or weapons deployments to South Korea due to reasons of cost or priority, or the inability to outspend or outinvest peer competitors and prospective adversaries such as China in the latest military technologies or capabilities.

Third, the risk of entrapment in overseas commitments might ultimately tip the U.S. approach to South Korea in favor of domestic retrenchment. The United States finally pulled out of Afghanistan in 2021 following two decades of commitment to its stabilization, with political control of Afghanistan reverting to Taliban control. Despite the long-standing U.S. commitment to South Korea's defense, withdrawal from South Korea—a country with a modern military, significant military spending, and a sizable capabilities advantage vis-à-vis North Korea—could be presented by some analysts as even more justifiable than the U.S. withdrawal from Afghanistan.[4]

Finally, North Korea's expanding nuclear reach may highlight vulnerabilities in the U.S. commitment to extended deterrence. Concerns are growing in South Korea that the United States might be willing to make trade-offs for North Korean assurances and actions that reduce North Korea's long-range missile capabilities, thus reducing the military threat to the U.S. mainland, while leaving its regional threat capabilities intact. This is precisely the scenario that had Korea specialists holding their breath as Trump pushed an America-First agenda while meeting one-on-one with Kim Jong-un. If Trump was willing to come out of a summit with Kim in Singapore complaining about U.S. "war games" on the peninsula, couldn't he just as easily have accepted a North Korean pledge to dismantle ICBM capabilities in return for U.S. troop withdrawals from the peninsula, or made some other deal that limited Kim's ability and/or willingness to strike the United States but left his regional threat capabilities intact? Trump may have attempted to justify this sort of bilateral U.S.–North Korea deal as a way to diffuse the North Korean nuclear threat to the U.S. mainland while shedding commitments to South Korea. Although Trump's reported intention of dismantling the U.S.–South Korea alliance in his second term was forestalled by his election defeat, Trump or Trumpism could plausibly make a political comeback in 2024 or 2028, resuscitating prospects for U.S.–North Korea rapprochement at the expense of South Korea and the alliance.

COSTS AND ADJUSTMENTS FOR THE UNITED STATES

The immediate degradation of the U.S.–South Korea alliance is unthinkable for many security planners given the widespread assumption that the security relationship is enduring and the high degree of institutionalization of alliance coordination between the two governments. But a shifting context for the alliance would have implications for the sustainability and effectiveness of the alliance. If such shifts were indeed to occur, it would involve a number of potential costs and adjustments for the United States.

A loss by the United States of an effective, long-standing security partnership with South Korea and the accompanying U.S. military withdrawal from the peninsula would diminish U.S. influence and power in Northeast Asia. The ability of the United States to project political and military influence in the Indo-Pacific region would decline with the loss of its partnership with South Korea. Current security planning includes alliance-based cooperation between the United States and South Korea on initiatives that project joint influence in Southeast Asia, such as efforts to link South Korean policies toward Southeast Asia to the U.S. Free and Open Indo-Pacific Policy, but those initiatives would no longer be possible. In practical terms, the ability of the United States to provide effective responses to the regional impact of natural disasters, public health crises, or climate change would be reduced. The United States would revert to a posture of offshore balancing that would either be reliant exclusively on its military presence in Japan or would depend on a U.S. military posture exclusively reliant on U.S. states and territories in the Pacific to secure a forward presence in Northeast Asia. The security balance on the Korean Peninsula would likely shift drastically, with the degree of impact dependent on whether the causes for the degradation of the U.S.–South Korea alliance were confined to the Korean Peninsula or were part of a broader retrenchment that might extend to reductions and/or withdrawal of U.S. forces from Japan. Each potential consequence will be explored in greater detail below.

PENINSULAR IMPACT OF U.S.–SOUTH KOREA ALLIANCE WEAKENING

While the weakening of the U.S.–South Korea alliance would relieve the United States of its security commitments to South Korea, the alliance's degradation might also both increase the likelihood of inter-Korean conflict and reduce the ability of the United States to shape the outcome of such a conflict. The United States might benefit in the near term when relieved of the political and financial burdens of providing for South Korea's security, but the reduction of a U.S. presence on the Korean Peninsula that has deterred an inter-Korean conflict for decades might raise the immediate probability of renewed peninsular conflict or war. The heightened risk of renewed conflict might come about as a consequence of North Korean probing for South Korean conventional military weaknesses and North Korean perception that its window of opportunity to utilize nuclear coercion to improve its strategic position vis-à-vis South Korea might quickly close if South Korea were to acquire nuclear weapons to compensate for the loss of its alliance with the United States. But if North Korea were to reprise its 1950 decision to overrun South Korea in the wake of a U.S. military withdrawal or draw South Korea into military conflict, the political effect in the United States would likely be a presidential political decision backed by an outraged American public and a U.S. Congress suddenly supportive of a return of U.S. armaments and possibly U.S. forces in the defense of a South Korean democratic victim to the North Korean dictatorship's revisionist aspirations. To the extent that a U.S. withdrawal might result directly in the unintended precipitation of an inter-Korean conflict, it is plausible to imagine the ironic possibility that both the U.S. military presence and a U.S. military withdrawal might serve as a "tripwire" for renewed U.S. military involvement on the Korean Peninsula.

Overall, U.S. retrenchment or military reductions from the Korean Peninsula would restore the responsibility for peninsular peace and stability to the Koreans themselves but under conditions where it may not be clear whether both sides have fully set aside the political goal of reunifying the Korean Peninsula as a single nation. The North Korean side has most definitely not abandoned the long-term goal of Korean peninsular unification on North Korean terms, and it may see U.S. retrenchment or withdrawal both as a success in the context of North Korea's long-term strategy of driving a wedge between alliance partners and as a threat stemming from South Korea's relative conventional military superiority. The United States would finally be distant from the Korean political process, but it is hard to imagine at this time that either a precipitous or gradual U.S. retrenchment or withdrawal would ultimately be followed by sustained conditions of peace and stability between the two Koreas.

IMPACT OF U.S.-SOUTH KOREA ALLIANCE DEGRADATION ON U.S. INFLUENCE IN NORTHEAST ASIA

The degradation of the U.S.–South Korea alliance and possible reduction or withdrawal of U.S. forces from the Korean Peninsula would enhance Chinese influence at the expense of U.S. interests on the Korean Peninsula, but it would also reduce the likelihood of the Korean Peninsula becoming a flashpoint for a potential U.S.–China military conflict.[5] The United States might maintain residual ties to and a cordial relationship with South Korea, but the United States would no longer have a strategic obligation to defend South Korea, nor would South Korea be beholden to U.S. concerns as it pursues a more balanced, independent foreign policy. After safeguarding South Korean security for decades, the United States would have to adjust to its new reality as an observer to the most consequential events on the peninsula, with fewer instruments by which to influence ongoing developments. By the same token, though U.S. influence in Northeast Asia would decrease, the risk of U.S. entrapment in renewed conflict would be considerably lessened.

The degradation or zombification of the U.S.–South Korea alliance would lessen or remove the U.S. presence on the Korean Peninsula as a source of Chinese concern. To date, China has expressed its understanding of the U.S. presence on the Korean Peninsula but only insofar as the scope of the U.S.–South Korea alliance remains exclusively North Korea–focused and does not have strategic implications for China. For instance, China's opposition to the U.S. deployment of THAAD to South Korea revolved around its insistence that the system's radar could be used for reconnaissance in Chinese territory, suggesting that THAAD's utility might extend beyond the sole purpose of deterring North Korea. China has also demonstrated its sensitivity to the possibility that U.S. missile defense systems deployed in Japan and South Korea could be linked together to target Chinese missile capabilities, enhancing the likelihood that China would utilize the end of the U.S.–South Korea alliance to magnify bilateral differences between Tokyo and Seoul.

The removal of U.S. forces from the Korean Peninsula—if not driven by a U.S. retrenchment or turn toward isolationism—would potentially free up resources currently committed to South Korea for possible redistribution in the broader U.S.–China competition. Depending on the ability of the United States to forge new basing partnerships with other nations in the region, a more geographically distributed troop structure would give the United States an opportunity to extend troop deployments southward to South and Southeast Asia where they might be better positioned to respond to an escalation of U.S.–China tensions than from South Korea. U.S. military withdrawal from the Korean Peninsula would cede geopolitical influence over both North and South Korea to China, potentially enabling China to view the entire Korean Peninsula as a strategic buffer against U.S. regional influence in Northeast Asia.

IMPACT OF U.S.–SOUTH KOREA ALLIANCE DEGRADATION ON JAPAN

The end of an effective U.S. commitment to defend South Korea, if driven primarily by tensions specific to the U.S.–South Korea relationship, would put greater political and logistical pressure on the U.S.–Japan alliance as the primary locus of support for a U.S. forward-deployed presence in Northeast Asia. In this case, the United States would come under increasing pressure to affirm the credibility of its defense commitment to Japan, not least because Japanese strategists view the Korean Peninsula as a primary vector for possible attacks on the Japanese mainland. But if the degradation of the U.S.–South Korea alliance were part of a broader U.S. retrenchment from Japan and reduction of its security commitments in the Indo-Pacific, the impact on Japan would be much more severe.

IMPACT OF U.S.–SOUTH KOREA ALLIANCE
DEGRADATION ON THE U.S.–JAPAN ALLIANCE

The degradation of the U.S.–South Korea alliance would have a direct impact on Japan's security and its expectations for the United States to maintain its defense commitment to Japan. Most significantly, the existence of the U.S.–South Korea alliance and the forward deployment of U.S. troops to the Korean Peninsula would no longer provide assurance and protection to Japan's mainland. This circumstance would not only raise questions about the credibility of the U.S. commitment to Japan's defense but would also generate strategic concerns that a shift in the orientation of the Korean

Peninsula toward greater Chinese influence would create new security vulnerabilities for Japan.

Following an end to the U.S.–South Korea security alliance, Japan would likely be forced to take a more active role in its own defense. No longer would Japan see itself as a rear base of support for U.S. efforts to maintain deterrence on the Korean Peninsula or across the Indo-Pacific.

Japanese security planners would likely greet substantial reductions or a withdrawal of U.S. forces from South Korea with great anxiety. They would no longer have the assurance of knowing that an effective U.S. deterrent was in place on the peninsula to prevent a potential conflict on the Korean Peninsula from spilling over to Japan. Instead, U.S. retrenchment of forces from South Korea would make Japan a potential frontline theater for rising tensions and possible clashes with North Korea. The main role and responsibility for deterrence of North Korea would fall to U.S. forward-deployed forces not in South Korea but in Japan.

Japan's transition from a rear base to the frontlines of a deterrent relationship would potentially generate new tensions in the country's relationship with China. As the primary host for U.S. bases in the Indo-Pacific, Japan would likely need to revamp its regional political and security strategies to address expanded Chinese regional influence. These developments would put greater pressure on Japan to attain robust defense capabilities for deterring both China and North Korea.

Japan's peace constitution and exclusive focus on self-defense would likely come into conflict with its growing need to establish mutual deterrence with China.[6] New geostrategic threats would spur domestic debates on Japan's peace constitution and the expansion of Japanese military capabilities in a new strategic environment.

Japan's first political priority would be to bind itself even more closely to the United States to strengthen deterrence against China and North Korea. To make such a strategy more credible, the Japanese government might push the United States to provide more frequent and stronger rhetorical and tangible measures to underscore the credibility of U.S. commitments to Japan's defense. At the same time, the United States might encourage Japan to host some of the forward-deployed troop presence currently on the Korean Peninsula, both to make up for lost capacities on the

Korean Peninsula and to demonstrate the continued U.S. commitment to assuring Japan's defense.

IMPACT OF U.S. RETRENCHMENT ON
JAPAN AND NORTHEAST ASIA

If U.S. retrenchment from the Korean Peninsula were to be accompanied by U.S. force withdrawals from Japan, it would signify a reframing of great power competition in the Indo-Pacific along continental versus maritime spheres. In such a case, it is likely that China would move to fill the security vacuum, leaving the United States with considerably reduced influence and instruments for pursuing national security objectives or safeguarding regional stability. The loss of a continental foothold through the withdrawal of U.S. forces from the Korean Peninsula would signify that the major domains of conflict would be air, maritime, and possibly space and that the U.S. Navy would come under increasing pressure as the PLA Navy attempts to expand its maritime operations to dominate adjacent maritime areas, to include the Taiwan Strait and the South China Sea. Increasing Chinese pressure on U.S. naval operations would have the goal of clearing U.S. influence from the Western Pacific, but it would also generate contestation in the Western Pacific that could impinge on U.S. strategic interests in perpetuating naval dominance to protect U.S. Pacific territories and the U.S. mainland. Periodic tensions would rise if China attempts to expand its sphere of influence to dominate its periphery as well as to push the U.S. Navy out of the Pacific littoral. Chinese maritime expansion in the Western Pacific would raise concerns among U.S. strategists regarding the vulnerability of U.S. territories such as Guam or American Samoa to attack, evoking concern that just as a strong Japan exploited U.S. vulnerabilities to attack Hawaii in 1941, Chinese domination in the Western Pacific might expand U.S. vulnerability to Chinese aggression.

U.S. military reductions on the Korean Peninsula and Japan would mark a shift from a dominant U.S. role in stabilizing the Indo-Pacific and enabling it to become the fastest growing economic region in the world to a contested Northeast Asian security order in which conflicts would be more frequent, either as manifestations of deepening U.S.–China rivalry or resulting from the revival of the historic strategic competition between China and Japan. The primary U.S. role would be defensive, with limited capacity to influence Asia's strategic environment. To the extent that China can marginalize the United States, the Indo-Pacific would shift to a Sinocentric regional order in which either China would set the tone and rules, or the United States and its allies would contest China's growing influence but from an increasingly disadvantageous and comparatively weaker position. In sum, Northeast Asia would become a cockpit of conflict rather than economic growth, and China would increasingly be the primary norm setter rather than the United States.

The loss of protection resulting from the degradation of both the U.S.–South Korea and U.S.–Japan alliances would be a wrenching development for Japanese national security planners. Two particular areas of concern regarding the Korean Peninsula would influence the Japanese security debate. First, Japan would be highly sensitive to the potential for South Korea to undertake domestic nuclear weapons development. Second, Japan would face North Korea's expanding missile capabilities on its own in the context of a U.S. retrenchment. These factors might challenge the long-held Japanese public allergy to the idea of nuclear acquisition. A nuclear-armed China's expanded regional influence, North Korea's growing nuclear capabilities, and potential nuclear acquisition by South Korea might trigger serious Japanese consideration of the development of its own nuclear deterrent.

U.S. retrenchment or withdrawal from South Korea and Japan might induce efforts by the two countries to overcome long-standing historical differences in order to enhance security cooperation as an antidote to U.S. withdrawal and perceptions of an expanded threat environment from China and North Korea. This outcome appears counterintuitive, as the United States has long supported Japan–South Korea cooperation in the face of enduring disputes over history in their bilateral relationship, and the degradation of the U.S.–South Korea alliance would reduce the influence of U.S. encouragement to South Korea to maintain comity with Japan. But the magnitude of Japanese and South Korean concern over rising regional security threats might inspire more active mutual outreach as well as motivate a more realist South Korean response to such overtures. However, Japan would probably only see prospects for outreach to Seoul as having a greater chance of succeeding if South Korea is under conservative leadership, given the past difficulties in managing the Japan–South Korea relationship under progressive administrations in Seoul as discussed in chapter 4.

A further concern for Japanese security planners would be the possibility of coordinated manipulation of tensions by China and North Korea so as to create pressure on Japan on two fronts: in the East China Sea and in the Sea of Japan/East Sea. Concerns about simultaneous ramping up of tensions around two distinct flashpoints would become a focal point for Japanese security planners on how to manage such a risk and would also be a possible driver for Japan to increase the pace of its efforts to modernize and strengthen its own capabilities.

In this environment, Japan would face both multidimensional maritime threats in both the East China Sea and the Sea of Japan/East Sea as well as from North Korean missile capabilities.[7] Alongside ongoing Chinese patrols aimed at asserting ownership over the Senkaku/Diaoyu Islands, Japan would also have to worry about possible attacks across the Sea of Japan/East Sea from North Korea. In sum, Japan would face a daunting security agenda in the event of U.S. retrenchment that would drastically reorient Japan's national security posture and military policies.

U.S.–SOUTH KOREA ALLIANCE DEGRADATION: IMPLICATIONS FOR TAIWAN

The degradation of the U.S.–South Korea alliance would have potentially volatile implications for cross-straits relations. At first glance, it may seem counterintuitive that developments on the Korean Peninsula would have direct influence on cross-straits relations, unless one recalls that China's historic opportunity to pursue Chinese unification by defeating Guomindang (KMT) forces across the straits to Taiwan was interrupted by Mao Zedong's decision to intervene on behalf of Kim Il-sung only one year following the KMT's defeat and withdrawal from mainland China. Mao's decision to intervene on the Korean Peninsula precluded the possibility of additional military operations to take Taiwan. Thus, a U.S. withdrawal from the Korean Peninsula might be perceived in some quarters as directly connected to the future of Taiwan.

To the extent that Beijing and Taipei might read the weakening of the U.S.–South Korea alliance as evidence of U.S. weakness and withdrawal from Asia, Beijing might be emboldened while Taipei might be unsettled. While Beijing would probably be unlikely to treat U.S. military withdrawal from South Korea as a moment of opportunity to pursue military actions toward Taipei, China's leadership would likely capitalize on Korean developments to strengthen its position across the region while pressing its advantages with Taiwan in an effort to promote conditions favorable to the establishment of a revised, largely Sinocentric regional order.

In contrast, Taiwan's political leadership would be deeply concerned by an apparent shift from a U.S.-led to a China-centered Northeast Asian regional order. Taiwan might seek to consolidate relations with Japan or seek reassurances from the United States of political and military support for the defense of Taiwan under the Taiwan Relations Act, which obligates the United States to provide military armaments necessary for Taiwan's defense. Depending on the circumstances, it is even possible to imagine Taiwan expressing openness to hosting U.S. forces formerly deployed to South Korea, though such a development would likely be strongly opposed by Beijing. If seriously considered and adopted, this would mark a dramatic shift and turning point in U.S. policy following decades of balancing between the demands of a U.S. One China policy and the imperatives of the Taiwan Relations Act.

ECONOMIC IMPLICATIONS OF U.S.–SOUTH KOREA ALLIANCE DEGRADATION

The degradation of the U.S.–South Korea alliance would result in a reconfiguration of U.S. financial priorities in support of its presence in the Indo-Pacific region. The reduction in U.S. financial commitments necessary to support a troop presence in South Korea could be redirected and used for other purposes, either within the Indo-Pacific security context or independent of defense needs in the Indo-Pacific. It would likely also damage the U.S.–South Korea trade relationship, as the security and political relationship would no longer provide a supporting rationale for some forms of economic cooperation between the United States and South Korea.

A reduction or withdrawal of U.S. forces from Korea would also reduce annual financial obligations associated with the cost of guaranteeing South Korea's defense. According to the GAO, the United States spent $3.1–3.5 billion annually during 2016–2019 on five categories of military spending to support U.S. troops in South Korea: military personnel; operation and maintenance; family housing, operation, and maintenance; family housing construction; and military construction.[8] But only the operation and maintenance category of U.S. spending in South Korea would be reduced by removing the obligations of upkeeping U.S. bases in South Korea. This category of spending represents the infrastructure and logistics support costs of keeping bases and troops in South Korea. The GAO reports that the U.S. military spends $1–1.5 billion annually on operations and maintenance. But U.S. forces would still require financial support for operations and maintenance even if they were to be based on the U.S. mainland.

On the South Korean side, the end of the U.S. force presence in South Korea would free up the approximately $1.3 billion in annual spending budgeted to cover South Korean labor, logistics, and maintenance costs for other purposes related to the defense of South Korea. As interoperability with the United States would no longer be as relevant in South Korean military procurement decisions, South Korea would be more free to purchase military equipment from non-U.S. suppliers. As South Korea seeks to diversify its weapons imports away from the United States, competition between U.S. companies and non-U.S. suppliers for South Korea's military procurement would intensify.

Reduction or withdrawal of U.S. troops from South Korea would reduce the attractiveness of the South Korean market in the eyes of some U.S. private sector investors. Though regulatory barriers and inflexible labor laws have restricted the size and scope of U.S. investment in South Korea, the U.S. Department of Commerce has long pointed to the U.S. presence as an added rationale for attracting U.S. investment.[9] More significantly, the U.S. security commitment to South Korea has drawn South Korean companies to enhance investments in the United States.[10] This investment has grown in recent years, as the United States has ramped up its technology competition with China in ways that limit South Korean investment opportunities in China while making investment in the United States more attractive. In the event of an end to the U.S.–South Korea alliance, there would be greater political distance between Washington and Seoul and less motivation for South Korean companies to privilege the United States as an investment destination, raising the political risks associated with such investments compared to investments made under a strong U.S.–South Korea alliance.

In the context of a degraded U.S.–South Korea alliance, South Korean companies might respond differently to the Biden administration's efforts to integrate South Korean firms into its efforts to strengthen supply chain resilience, instead bringing a more critical eye and a possibly more cautious stance to investment decisions made against the backdrop of the rising U.S.–China technology competition that currently would favor the United States. The degradation of the U.S.–South Korea alliance could be seen as a bellwether indicator that South Korea's economic future would be shaped by China's rise and that China would increasingly be able to shape global economic markets. South Korean companies would likely continue to invest in the United States, but the business and geopolitical context for such decisions would be less favorable in the absence of the U.S.–South Korea alliance than is currently the case. For U.S. investors in South Korea, the presence of USFK has been perceived as a source of confidence and a hedge against perceived political risks. Likewise, the U.S.–South Korea trade relationship might become more distant without the security context provided by the U.S.–South Korea alliance. The alliance was a factor that facilitated the KORUS FTA negotiations and justified ratification of the agreement in 2012.

A weakened or ineffective U.S.–South Korea alliance would lead South Korea to pursue a more independent foreign policy and the United States would no longer enjoy special attention from policymakers in Seoul or exert decisive influence on South Korean strategic or economic decisions. U.S. appeals to South Korea to cooperate with its initiatives to promote a Free and Open Indo-Pacific, for instance, would enjoy less support and interest in Seoul. South Korea would seek to enhance its own opportunities in Southeast Asia while more actively balancing respective Chinese and U.S. influences in an effort to preserve South Korean autonomy.

Finally, the weakening of the U.S.–South Korea alliance would deal a blow to person-to-person and familial ties that have developed between the two countries, leading to further loss of mutual influence. For decades, South Korean students have pursued higher education in the United States and then returned to Seoul to take up leading positions as part of a pro-U.S. elite that has staffed senior positions across academia, government, and the private sector. It is less likely that Koreans would continue to perceive higher educational experience in the United States as a logical pathway for upward mobility and elite status in a South Korea that adjusts its geopolitical orientation and foreign policy toward greater independence from the United States. Instead, South Koreans would be more likely either to develop internal pathways for cultivating elite status through further development of its own domestic educational system or to seek quality education from a greater variety of world-class institutions with less regard or expectation for professional benefits that might accrue from the experience of education in the United States.

In sum, the weakening or degradation of the U.S.–South Korea alliance might generate some savings as well as offsetting costs. But most significantly, the alliance would no longer be part of the strategic geopolitical and geo-economic context shaping individual decisions in the South Korean private sector.

PURSUIT OF U.S. STRATEGY TOWARD ASIA WITHOUT SOUTH KOREA

The United States would face a much more difficult security environment and would have at its disposal considerably fewer instruments by which to pursue its goals as a result of a degraded or ineffectual U.S.–South Korea alliance. The impact on U.S. strategy would be even more detrimental in the event of a withdrawal of U.S. forces from both South Korea and Japan. Such an eventuality would introduce heightened risks to South Korea emanating from increased prospects for renewed conflict on the Korean Peninsula, parallel and possibly converging direct and indirect threats toward Japan from North Korea and China, and the ability of China and North Korea to apply more intense, multidirectional pressure on Japan.

If the United States were to withdraw forces from South Korea but retain forces in Japan, regional dynamics around Japan's sensitivity to developments on the Korean Peninsula would not eliminate the possibility of a clash that might still implicate the United States in an inter-Korean conflict. Instead, the combination of the U.S. commitment to the defense of Japan and pressures to withdraw forces from the Korean Peninsula would generate a contradiction similar to the one the United States faced in 1950 when Secretary of State John Foster Dulles omitted the Korean Peninsula from U.S. defense commitments yet found it necessary to intervene to prevent North Korea from unifying the peninsula under communist control. The U.S. commitment to Japan's defense might result in U.S. participation in such a conflict but from an off-peninsula far less strategically favorable vantage point. Yet it seems unlikely that the Korean Peninsula's significance to the United States would diminish as long as the United States maintains its alliance commitment to the defense of Japan.

The United States would face an even more difficult strategic environment in the event that retrenchment or withdrawal from Asia involved U.S. force withdrawals from both South Korea and Japan. Japan would face dramatically greater security concerns resulting from both rising tensions within the region and the need to dramatically increase military capabilities to pursue its own defense in the context of U.S. retrenchment from Japan. The increased threat to Japan resulting from a possible shift in the strategic orientation of the Korean Peninsula would likely catalyze the transformation of both Japanese defense and foreign policy.

As part of the dramatic deterioration of Japan's security environment resulting from the degradation of the U.S.–South Korea and U.S.–Japan alliances, perhaps the most consequential question would be whether Japan should acquire its own nuclear capabilities. Especially if South Korea goes nuclear, the threat environment would probably have changed sufficiently to forestall Japan's traditional reticence regarding the acquisition of nuclear capabilities as well as its hesitancy to adopt a more "normal" defense posture. In such an event, Japan's continued status as the only nonnuclear power in the region might depend primarily on the sustainability of the U.S.–Japan alliance.[11]

The prospect of a U.S.–Japan alliance transformed into a frontline force prepared for multidimensional warfare and focused on deterring Chinese aggression and North Korean brinkmanship illustrates the significance and potential consequences of the degradation of the U.S.–South Korea alliance. It reveals the strategic gains China and North Korea might seek to achieve through expanded influence on the Korean Peninsula as well as the potential shockwaves of such developments at the peninsular, regional, and global levels. A close examination of the potential ramifications of U.S. force withdrawal from the Korean Peninsula highlights the extent to which shifting regional security dilemmas and pressures may arise from the erosion of U.S. influence in Northeast Asia. It also reveals the extent to which U.S. allies and U.S. forward-deployed forces in the region might come under growing pressure in the event of the degradation of the U.S.–South Korea alliance.

10

IMAGINING SOUTH KOREAN FOREIGN POLICY ABSENT THE U.S.–SOUTH KOREA ALLIANCE

S outh Korea has for decades been anchored to the U.S. security commitment to defend the country from external aggressors. The degradation of the U.S.–South Korea alliance might take place gradually as a consequence of the emergence of alternative interests and priorities or the development of mutual U.S.–South Korean distrust that might diminish opportunities for alliance collaboration and chip away at shared interests. Alternatively, it might come more rapidly as a consequence of a leadership change and reorientation of strategic priorities away from shared alliance interests. Regardless of the pace of alliance degradation, such developments would ultimately free South Korea to pursue a more independent course and facilitate a long-cherished goal of advancing autonomy over its own strategic choices.

This chapter envisions the likely foreign policy profile that a future South Korean government might take in the absence of the alliance with the United States, with the goal of more deeply illustrating the foreign policy implications for South Korea that would accompany alliance degradation and the likely implications for South Korea's foreign policy profile and priorities. Consideration of South Korea's possible foreign policy orientation and priorities in the absence of the U.S.–South Korea alliance may help us envision both the challenges and opportunities that an autonomous South Korea might face in safeguarding its national security interests and might provide a clearer view of the likely costs that would accompany alliance degradation.

The main impact of the degradation of the U.S.–South Korea alliance would be to enable South Korea to pursue a fully autonomous foreign policy independent of U.S. influence. An autonomous foreign policy has been a long-standing goal of South Korean foreign policy strategists, but pursuit of that goal has been tempered by the necessity of maintaining an alliance with the United States as the most effective means by which to ensure South Korea's security.[1]

The primary tasks for an autonomous South Korea in charting a sustainable foreign policy course would be (1) to determine whether such a strategy is actually feasible; (2) to build a broad public consensus behind such an approach to ensure its sustainability; and (3) to mitigate and navigate cross-cutting influences from powerful neighbors to keep the South Korean ship of state sailing in the desired direction under its own power. But South Korea's foreign policy independence would also result in its heightened vulnerability to enemy attack or coercion from China and/or North Korea, increasing the stakes for South Korean strategic decision making and reducing the room for miscalculation in foreign policy implementation.

CONTEXTUAL FACTORS AND THE HYPOTHETICAL IMPACT OF U.S.–SOUTH KOREA ALLIANCE DEGRADATION

Major factors that would shape South Korean response pathways in the event of a U.S.–South Korea alliance degradation include the scope, timing, and sequencing of U.S. military withdrawals in relation to the formal end of U.S. political and treaty commitments to South Korea's defense; the relative balance of political responsibility for an alliance breakup; the domestic and external circumstances South Korea faces at the time of the degradation; and the extent to which third parties might plausibly have contributed to the weakening of alliance ties.

The U.S.–South Korea Mutual Defense Treaty formally authorizes the United States to deploy land, air, and sea forces around South Korea based on mutual agreement and envisions that the treaty would remain in force indefinitely, with a provision for termination one year after the other party has provided notice.[2] While the treaty provides a bilateral framework justifying the continued presence of U.S. forces in South Korea during peacetime with the codification of the U.S. defense commitment to South Korea, it does not obligate the United States to deploy forces within South Korea because the treaty commitment and the deployment of U.S. forces in the defense of South Korea are not directly linked. Thus, formal notification of terminating the treaty by either party would start the clock on the end of the alliance within one year, but removal of U.S. forces from South Korea could occur by mutual agreement either before or after formal abrogation of the treaty.

Formal abrogation of the U.S.–South Korea alliance would have a relatively short fuse because of the one-year timeline for the treaty's abrogation, but an end to the political commitments that underpin the alliance might be years in the making and could result in the degradation of the alliance resulting from decisions by either or both governments to withhold continued investments necessary to keep the alliance strong. U.S. troop withdrawals or a loss of U.S. credibility and political will to meet its formal treaty commitments despite a continued military presence could foreshadow a breakdown in the U.S.–South Korea alliance. The presence of USFK has served as tangible proof of the U.S. commitment to South Korea's defense, but it may not necessarily serve as credible evidence of U.S. political will to actually come to South Korea's defense. On the other hand, the withdrawal of U.S. forces would not necessarily signal an end to the U.S. political commitment to South Korea's defense.

These factors make the invocation of the termination of the Mutual Defense Treaty a lagging indicator of preexisting trends in the U.S.–South Korea alliance that would have already set the stage for alliance degradation.

They also blur the significance of troop presence in relation to the health of the alliance. South Korea has historically treated USFK presence as evidence of the U.S. commitment to South Korea's defense, with South Korean presidents even pushing for a numerical floor to the U.S. troop presence and seeking legislation stipulating numerical minimum troop requirements as a salve for South Korean anxieties regarding U.S. abandonment.[3] But such symbols are irrelevant if they are not buttressed by political will, cohesion in threat perceptions, and common interests shared by leaders of both countries. In this regard, both governments have felt an ongoing political responsibility to maintain support for cooperation measures that ultimately underpin the alliance.

The question of which party might formally initiate termination of the Mutual Defense Treaty would influence the political dynamics of the post-alliance U.S.–South Korea relationship, South Korea's strategic outlook, and South Korea's domestic political debate over the future of its relationship with the United States. The question of responsibility for alliance termination is likely to be much more salient in the domestic South Korean foreign policy debate than it would be in the United States because of the greater size and importance of the United States in South Korean foreign policy compared to the importance of South Korea to U.S. foreign policy.

A U.S.-initiated termination of the treaty would send a stark signal that the United States has reevaluated its security commitment to South Korea and has decided to reduce its overall posture in Northeast Asia. A U.S. withdrawal of its commitments to South Korea's defense would likely force a soul-searching strategic debate in South Korea premised on a need to identify a viable alternative national security strategy. The seriousness of that debate would be underscored by the fact that U.S. support has been South Korea's sole viable option for guaranteeing its security since recovering its nationhood following World War II.

A South Korean–initiated withdrawal from the Mutual Defense Treaty would likely be accompanied by a deeply politicized domestic debate and recriminations within South Korea. Critics would emphasize the risks of cutting security ties with the United States and would criticize abandoning the alliance as enhancing South Korean vulnerability to both external attacks and interference in South Korea's domestic political debate by malign external influences. Conservatives and progressives would likely coalesce around rival strategies for ensuring South Korea's security. Fractious internal divisions over how best to secure South Korea's independence from foreign influence would pose a serious challenge to South Korea's capacity to present a united front to the rest of the world.

A third influence on the process and outcome of alliance degradation would involve the external security environment as well as domestic circumstances that would influence South Korean efforts to chart a post-alliance security strategy. A regional security environment characterized by high tensions might generate specific points of difference in policy or strategy and perpetuate domestic political contention over the direction of South Korea's defense and foreign policy strategies. A more relaxed regional environment would provide greater time for gradual adjustment in the respective postures of the two countries in the wake of alliance degradation.

Finally, external actors such as North Korea and China may seek to foment differences between allies or generate moments of crisis to test alliance cohesion and drive wedges between alliance partners. As described in chapters 5 and 6, both North Korea and China have their own strategic interests in inducing or capitalizing on U.S.–South Korea alliance degradation. These parties may seek to force choices, expose divided allegiances, or exercise leverage to expose gaps in the respective interests of alliance partners.

CIRCUMSTANCES LEADING TO U.S. MILITARY WITHDRAWAL AND ITS POLITICAL IMPACT IN SOUTH KOREA

The dynamics of alliance weakening would have a direct bearing on South Korea's policy response and the country's new foreign policy trajectory in the absence of the alliance. Circumstances surrounding the impetus for the weakening of the U.S.–South Korea alliance, the pace of the U.S. military withdrawal from the peninsula, the nature of South Korean political leadership during the withdrawal process, and the inter-Korean military balance would all influence the immediate impact of a U.S. withdrawal on the peninsula. A precipitous U.S. military withdrawal might engender active, opportunistic probing by North Korea—building on the existing influence operations described in chapter 5—designed to take advantage of the transition to a new security reality on the peninsula. Without the deterrent provided by U.S. forces, a risk-acceptant North Korean leadership might view South Korea's capability to repel an attack from the North as diminished and probe for weaknesses to test and exploit.

South Korea would need to guard against North Korean opportunism. To the extent that North Korea's leadership perceives U.S. withdrawal as a tactical opportunity or is concerned by the North's relative conventional weakness vis-à-vis South Korea, an early provocation designed to test South Korean readiness might be a tempting means by which to shape the field for the negotiation of a new status quo on the peninsula. North Korean leaders might feel that an early, containable conflict of their own choosing that precedes South Korea's efforts to consolidate its defense posture would allow the North to establish a position of strength in the inter-Korean relationship. Such a temptation might be exacerbated by North Korean concerns that the South would pursue the development of its own nuclear capability in the absence of a U.S. extended deterrence guarantee, thereby eliminating one of the few strategic advantages North Korea holds over South Korea.

The nature of the South Korean political leadership at the time of U.S. withdrawal from the Korean Peninsula would no doubt shape its possible response to any North Korean attempt to capitalize on potential South Korean defense weaknesses. If South Korea were led by a conservative administration at the time of U.S. force withdrawal, it would likely greet North Korean aggression and attempts to take advantage of perceived South Korean weakness with less restraint than a progressive South Korean government would. In response to North Korea's shelling of the South Korean island of Yeonpyeong near the North-South border in November 2010, the conservative Lee Myung-bak administration initially considered a much more robust response than was ultimately implemented. Lee opted for restraint in part due to USFK pressure to contain the risk of crisis escalation, but absent the U.S.–South Korea alliance, such U.S.-imposed curbs on South Korean responses to North Korean provocations would no longer apply. Following the Yeonpyeong Island shelling, the Lee administration put into place a more aggressive doctrine of response to North Korean provocations under a policy of "proactive deterrence." The conservative Park Geun-hye administration subsequently authorized the implementation of "Kill Chain," a missile detection and preventive strike doctrine, and enhanced South Korean capabilities to respond to North Korean provocations under the Korean Massive Punishment and Retaliation (KMPR) doctrine.

A progressive South Korean administration might be less inclined to mount a robust military response to North Korean provocations but could then find itself having to respond to North Korean efforts to press an advantage through conflict while navigating South Korean public concerns that appeasement of North Korea might result in South Korean acquiescence to or even absorption by the autocratic North. A South Korean progressive administration would find itself the target of political attacks from South Korean conservatives wary of efforts by the North to subvert progressive dreams of reconciliation to enhance North Korean influence over the South. To a certain extent, this is the dilemma that the Moon administration found itself facing in 2020 after Kim Yo-jong made public demands that South Korea crack down on North Korean defector-led leaflet launches from the area near the DMZ. As discussed in chapter 4, the Moon administration's efforts to pass a law banning leaflet launches and other efforts to disseminate information to North Korean citizens faced objections from critics who accused the Moon administration of appeasement. The Moon administration's seeming obeisance to North Korean demands fed conservative anxieties about progressive intentions. Conservative anxieties have also revolved around the inclusion in successive inter-Korean summit declarations of language implying that inter-Korean cooperation could lead to political union in the form of a federation or give North Korea leverage to take advantage of the South and extend political influence and control over the entire peninsula. Despite the likely desire among progressives to avoid military conflict with North Korea, there are ongoing concerns among conservatives that progressives would be inclined to appease rather than confront North Korean hostility or belligerence.

A precipitous U.S. withdrawal from the peninsula might raise the immediate likelihood of inter-Korean tensions or military conflict. A U.S. decision to withdraw military forces would generate little resistance if the United States perceives South Korea as sufficiently capable and resilient to bear the costs of its own defense. Furthermore, efforts to support South Korea would likely be viewed in the United States as unnecessary as the conflict would no longer bear directly on U.S. core interests.

A more gradual withdrawal of U.S. forces and recalibration of U.S. security commitments to South Korea may reduce the likelihood that the degradation of the U.S.–South Korea alliance would spark renewed inter-Korean conflict. The U.S. signal of a gradual withdrawal of forces from the Korean Peninsula would provide more time for the leaderships of both Koreas to make necessary adjustments to their mutual deterrence postures and to the inter-Korean political relationship. But in the end, U.S. retrenchment would have the same implications for South Korean strategists charting an independent pathway for South Korean foreign policy no longer reliant on the alliance with the United States.

Decreased U.S. influence on South Korea would provide a counter to progressive views of the United States as an obstacle to or constraint on the development of inter-Korean relations discussed in chapter 4. South Korean progressive critics of the enduring U.S. military presence on the Korean Peninsula would no longer be able to point to the United States as the main source of Korean division. In this respect, U.S. retrenchment might contribute to a more realistic assessment in both North and South Korea of the Korean Peninsula and of the other side's capabilities and intentions.

Though a gradual transition on the Korean Peninsula following the weakening of the U.S.–South Korea alliance would allow both North and South Korea to address conventional weaknesses and adjust political relations toward the goal of sustaining peaceful coexistence based on mutual deterrence, the end of U.S. nuclear security guarantees to South Korea would raise questions about South Korea's vulnerability to North Korea's nuclear program. Just as South Korea has developed short-range and mid-range missile capabilities to match or exceed those under development in North Korea, it would be highly motivated to establish mutual nuclear deterrence with North Korea if it were meeting the threat from the North independently of U.S. or other international assistance. Given the magnitude of the perceived threat to South Korean security that would be generated by North Korea's asymmetric nuclear advantage, a South Korea no longer under nuclear protection from the United States would assert a compelling national security rationale for breaking its Nuclear Non-Proliferation Treaty (NPT) commitments, and on that basis, might minimize or avoid the economic and political penalties that would otherwise raise the costs to South Korea of withdrawing from the NPT.

North Korea may believe that nuclear blackmail strategies would bring South Korea into political submission to the North, but such views underestimate the degree to which South Koreans perceive North Korea's leadership claims as anachronistic, illegitimate, and threatening to South Korea's democracy and prosperity. Korean conservatives continue to perceive the German model as the most plausible and acceptable pathway to a South Korean–led unification process. The vast majority of South Koreans anticipate that any unification outcome would likely be shaped more by characteristics of South Korean democracy than by North Korean authoritarianism. Peaceful coexistence between the two Koreas may be desirable, but it is difficult to imagine a peaceful and harmonious process of integration between two such widely divergent political systems.

REVIEWING THE ALLIANCE VS. AUTONOMY BALANCE SHEET: ALTERNATIVES TO THE U.S.–SOUTH KOREA ALLIANCE

The loss of U.S. security guarantees to protect South Korea from external threats would be the most significant near-term challenge for South Korea's leaders to address in the event of an end to the alliance. Even despite the formal end of the alliance, South Korea might attempt to seek an extension of U.S. commitments to defend South Korea even if the waning U.S. political commitment to South Korea's defense is accompanied by U.S. retrenchment or force withdrawal. In doing so, South Korea would aim to buy time before having to meet its own security needs without U.S. assistance and to secure a lesser U.S. commitment to hedge against immediate security challenges from more powerful neighbors. Arrangements short of continuing the alliance might involve the preservation of some forms of military cooperation on the peninsula, such as South Korean pledges to the United States of continued access and maintenance of preferential basing arrangements in return for U.S. commitments to support South Korean efforts to achieve security independently of the withdrawal of U.S. troops from the Korean Peninsula. But South Korea would face difficulty in securing such assurances if alliance degradation is driven by U.S. retrenchment or results in bitter mutual recriminations.

As South Korea surveys possibilities for replacing the security protections provided by the alliance with the United States, few attractive alternatives are likely to emerge. No country is likely to provide South Korea with commensurate protections or to inspire the same level of confidence that South Korea has had with the United States. China might arguably have a strategic interest in offering security assurances to South Korea in return for greater deference to Chinese geopolitical goals. But South Korean public distrust of China has remained consistently high in recent years, and China would likely infringe on South Korean desires for foreign policy autonomy at levels South Korea would find unacceptable.[4]

Possible alternative alliance partners such as China would be even less willing or able to provide the commitments South Korea would desire. Japan and South Korea would have to overcome their long-standing historical mistrust sufficiently to promote closer security alignment with each other in response to rising South Korean threat perceptions from China. Similarly, Russia is too distant, too weak, and too distrusted to serve as a suitable security guarantor for South Korea.

Given the paucity of satisfactory replacements for the U.S. security guarantee, South Korea would most likely opt to navigate an autonomous foreign policy and security pathway that would involve overlapping tactical deals with its immediate neighbors. South Korea's goal would be to maintain security independence by offsetting the relative influences of the United States and China. Such a strategy would involve increased investments in national defense, omnidirectional and equidistant economic and security involvements with its neighbors including China and Japan, attempts to achieve a peaceful coexistence with North Korea, and efforts to draw external security actors such as NATO into network arrangements designed to bolster South Korea's capacity and independence.

CHARTING A PURPOSEFUL AND INDEPENDENT STRATEGIC PATHWAY

An essential prerequisite for South Korea's success as it navigated a complex new security environment would be the development of a unified domestic consensus supportive of an independent foreign policy and security strategy. Domestic political polarization would weaken South Korea and inhibit its ability to navigate effectively among stronger powers or thwart efforts by external actors such as China or North Korea to penetrate South Korean debates and sow internal divisions. Public perceptions of South Korean vulnerability may assist in building domestic consensus, but strong political leadership would be essential in effectively managing internal debates and forging the unity necessary to implement strong, united defense and foreign policy strategies.

An independent South Korean defense posture would be more expensive for Seoul to maintain than South Korea's current posture, which is bolstered by U.S. contributions of 28,500 soldiers and an annual U.S. budget of over $3 billion to the defense of the peninsula.[5] In the event of the degradation of the U.S.–South Korea alliance, South Korea would have to invest in and independently develop a wide range of capabilities previously provided by the United States. For instance, South Korea would have to invest more in air capabilities, intelligence, and reconnaissance capabilities if no deal with the United States could be made to support South Korea's defense needs in those areas.

Following U.S. military withdrawal from the Korean Peninsula, South Korea would have to transition its military posture from one primarily focused on countering the North Korean threat to a 360-degree posture that defends South Korea not only against North Korea but also against the threat from its larger neighbors China and Japan. South Korea has already begun to build the naval and air capabilities necessary to respond to maritime security threats from the south, including the construction of a naval base on Jeju Island. Despite such efforts, South Korea's vulnerability to the risk of maritime conflict from its south and east would grow in the absence of the U.S.–South Korea alliance. Under the alliance framework, U.S. plans for the defense of South Korea have protected rear areas such as Japan through which the United States would flow troops to South Korea in the event of a conflict. An end to the alliance would remove the limits on possible conflict with Japan imposed de facto by the parallel U.S. security commitments to both Japan and South Korea. With the degradation of the U.S.–South Korea alliance, South Koreans may worry more about a possible maritime threat from Japan over the contested Dokdo/Takeshima island feature in the Sea of Japan/East Sea, but the main risk of conflict south of the Korean Peninsula would most likely come from China in the context of its maritime expansion.

To some extent, South Korea has already begun to hedge against perceived security risks from the south and east of South Korea under the Moon administration's Defense Reform 2.0 program. The program projected annual increases in military spending of 7.5 percent through 2023 and increased investments in technology acquisition to offset the demographics-driven military manpower declines already necessitating South Korean defense reforms.[6] The *Financial Times* stated that under Moon's program, "South Korea is broadening its focus from the singular challenge of deterring attacks from North Korea's nuclear-armed Kim regime. It is also reducing its long-held dependence on American troops. The shifts tacitly acknowledge the dual threats of waning US commitment and China's military expansionism."[7] The degradation of the alliance would accelerate South Korean defense spending along the same trajectory.

The Stockholm International Peace Research Institute (SIPRI) estimated that South Korea had the world's tenth largest defense budget in 2020, just behind that of Japan, and in recent years South Korea's ratio of defense spending to GDP has fluctuated in the 2.5 percent range.[8] South Korea's current arsenal of modern F-35A aircraft, military surveillance satellites, and tactical surface-to-surface guided weaponry, submarines, destroyers, early warning radar, and missile defense acquisitions would only grow.[9] The degradation of the U.S.–South Korea alliance would accelerate technology acquisition trends already in place but would likely exacerbate the manpower challenges South Korea already faces resulting from the demographic decline in the number of South Korean males available to serve in the military. It would easily catalyze double-digit increases in South Korean defense spending over multiple years and a defense spending to GDP ratio approaching 3 percent.[10]

An independent South Korean foreign policy would likely pursue equivalent and offsetting cooperation arrangements with its neighbors to hedge against undue influence by any one foreign power. Such an approach would involve the maintenance of a good relationship with China combined with efforts to draw more distant parties into networks that could be used to buffer South Korean independence and embed South Korea in a web of partners that would collectively be capable of resisting undue pressure from more powerful neighbors.

AVOIDING ENTRAPMENT IN U.S.–CHINA RIVALRY

An independent South Korea would likely continue its past efforts to walk the tightrope between the United States and China, but find its position and capacity to do so weaker outside of the U.S.–South Korea alliance. South Korean foreign policy strategists would weigh the following strategies as

South Korea attempted to navigate between U.S. and Chinese pressures: (1) neutrality; (2) dual hedging; (3) alignment with China; (4) solidarity with North Korea; and (5) drawing other powers into a networked independent alignment as a buffer against major power pressures.

In the absence of the U.S.–South Korea alliance, South Korea would grapple with the possibility of seeking a position of neutrality to remain aloof from growing U.S.–China competition. This option, occasionally raised by South Korean foreign policy strategists, advocates for South Korea to play a neutral role in major power competition so as not to be perceived as a threat by China while avoiding entrapment on the U.S. side. The degradation of the U.S.–South Korea alliance would move the strategy of neutrality from the realm of theory to a practical option for policymakers. But the already complex task of navigating the crosscurrents of major power rivalry would become even more challenging for South Korea absent the U.S.–South Korea alliance. Neutrality would be a lonely and fraught pathway for South Korea, which would closely examine the experiences of nations that remained neutral during the Cold War for clues as to how to sustain independence from major power pressures.[11]

An independent South Korea may also consider a policy of dual hedging against both U.S. and Chinese efforts to draw in South Korea as a partner in the context of the U.S.–China rivalry. This pathway resembles the course pursued by the progressive Moon administration, but calibration between the two sides may be more difficult absent the alliance given South Korea's geographic proximity to China, which is actively enlarging its economic and political spheres of influence in Asia. South Korea may struggle to attract sufficient U.S. attention and support in a post-U.S.–South Korea alliance world to counterbalance China's growing influence. The alliance framework would no longer provide security protection against China's increasing maritime and aerial incursions into South Korea's Exclusive Economic Zone and territorial sea. Instead, South Korea's coast guard and navy would bear the brunt of countering China's growing naval capabilities with no U.S. deterrent or prospect of backup.

Nor would the alliance be present to support bilateral U.S.–South Korea economic ties, raising private sector political risk and diminishing prospects for close economic exchanges. As discussed in chapter 7, South Korean companies would also be less likely to enjoy economic opportunities in the context of the rising focus on supply chain resilience, and profiting in both the U.S. and Chinese economic spheres of influence would become more difficult as competition grew. To the extent that dual hedging capitalizes on the cooperative space and economic interdependence between the United States and China, absence of the anchor provided by the U.S.–South Korea alliance framework would complicate or even block that pathway.

In light of the difficulty of pursuing dual hedging, South Korea may instead consider coming into alignment with China through the accommodation pathway. This strategy would acknowledge the geopolitical reality that China is trying to project onto its periphery and establish a Sinocentric regional order. For South Korea, alignment with China would reduce regional tensions and might unlock economic opportunities in the Chinese market, which is on track to become the most sizable and lucrative consumer market in the world. South Korea might consider forms of accommodation with China that do not oppose Chinese prerogatives as it pursues "core interests" in Hong Kong, Xinjiang, Taiwan, and the South China Sea in return for China's political support in dealing with North Korea. In this scenario, South Korea's broader foreign policy orientation would tilt distinctively toward China, with little incentive or opportunity to pursue a counterbalancing strategy of engagement with the United States.

South Korea might also consider two alternative pathways by which to build greater leverage in an effort to avoid being drawn into the U.S.–China strategic competition. The option preferred by South Korean progressives would include investment in inter-Korean coordination and efforts to promote peaceful coexistence with North Korea. A pan-Korean approach that entails greater South Korean cooperation and alignment with the North would seek to elevate Korean interests, leverage, and capabilities as a hedge against external pressures. This approach would serve the interests of both Koreas to the extent that China and the United States are both perceived as impinging on vital Korean interests and that inter-Korean cooperation is perceived as an attractive means for preserving an independent, pan-Korean foreign policy strategy. This is already the preferred strategy of progressives as they seek to insulate South Korea from the pressures generated by the U.S.–China rivalry.

The option preferred by conservatives, and one that becomes more salient to the extent that tensions between the two Koreas hinder prospects for inter-Korean political coordination, would entail South Korean outreach to external partners that serves to neutralize U.S. and Chinese influences and pressures. For example, South Korea might seek greater alignment with ASEAN and its member countries. In the absence of an alliance with the United States, South Korea's foreign policy orientation would likely align closely with ASEAN's strategy of omnidirectional engagement with great powers to ensure that no single great power has a predominant influence.

The most severe challenges facing an independent South Korea would likely derive from pressures emanating from U.S.–China competitive efforts to draw South Korea over to one side or the other. In an effort to avoid such an outcome, independent South Korea would probably find itself using a combination of all the strategies outlined above depending on the specific circumstances South Korea would face as it navigated the difficult crosscurrents and obstacles generated by great power competition.

PURSUING ACCOMMODATION WITH
NORTH KOREA

Aside from the security challenge of establishing effective deterrence in the absence of the U.S.–South Korea alliance, South Korea would also have to develop a new political strategy toward North Korea. In addition to the establishment of mutual deterrence through pursuit of its own nuclear capability, an independent South Korea would have an incentive to pursue accommodation with North Korea as part of a broader effort to ease emergent security pressures resulting from alliance degradation.

As the weakest neighbor in South Korea's post-alliance security environment, North Korea would be the only country with which South Korea would enjoy a relative power advantage in almost every category save North

Korea's nuclear program. While South Korean security planners debate the merits of evening the nuclear playing field with the North by acquiring a nuclear deterrent, South Korea might also pursue strategies designed to buy time and mitigate the risks of nuclear blackmail or nuclear use by the North. South Korea might seek an understanding with North Korea in which the North pledges to refrain from nuclear threats in return for South Korean pledges to limit its development of offensive land-based conventional weaponry that could be used against North Korea. Such an effort might come in the form of peninsular arms control talks designed to build on the 2018 Comprehensive Military Agreement. The next steps beyond this agreement would involve the negotiation of understandings to cap and reduce the number of military troops and armaments in an effort to reduce the risks and costs of military conflict on the Korean Peninsula.[12]

If the risks of North Korean opportunism can be managed, an initial political accommodation between the two Koreas might materialize following the end of the U.S.–South Korea alliance. South Korean conservatives might support such a near-term political and military accommodation to stabilize relations with North Korea. By reducing the likelihood of conflict with the North, conservatives would seek to buy time to manage and prepare for off-peninsula threats from China or Japan. South Korean progressives, on the other hand, might hope that an accommodation would support an institutionalization of peaceful coexistence that would foster inter-Korean integration and lead to a more permanent peninsular peace.

North Korea might also have an interest in near-term accommodation as it assesses South Korean conventional forces and weighs the development of a strategy for pursuing unification on North Korean terms following the long-desired withdrawal of USFK from the Korean Peninsula. A deal that caps further South Korean conventional development in return for North Korean pledges of nuclear restraint would ease the immediate prospects for instability and potentially forestall South Korea's momentum to develop its own nuclear deterrent. More importantly from the North's perspective, it might open the way for North Korea to intensify elements of its political and propaganda campaign to influence the South Korean leadership and public toward greater cooperation and to further pursue political subversion strategies outlined in chapter 5 that would promote South Korean political divisions and enhance North Korean influence in South Korea.

An end to the U.S.–South Korea alliance might heighten prospects for inter-Korean cooperation to mitigate outside interference in peninsular affairs. An independent South Korea might seek greater coordination with North Korea in response to pressure from China or Japan, but unless the two Koreas were able to set aside long-standing inter-Korean rivalries and coordinate external policies, it is difficult to envision pan-Korean cooperation extending beyond joint rhetorical condemnation of intrusion from their larger neighbors. North and South Korea have a common unease about growing Chinese influence and the risks of Chinese economic and political coercion in response to a failure to align with its priorities. These are considerations that Japan also holds because of its long-standing security concern that the orientation of the Korean Peninsula not be hostile to Japan. At the same time, North and South Korea share a historical antipathy to and anxiety regarding Japan's regional influence that would likely continue to inhibit cooperation with Japan to counter China's growing influence.

JAPAN–SOUTH KOREA RELATIONS OUTSIDE OF THE CONTEXT OF THE U.S.–SOUTH KOREA ALLIANCE

With the end of the U.S.–South Korea alliance, Japan and South Korea would no longer be anchored alongside each other in a regional security framework that requires cooperation and bounds the prospects for full-scale competition. But Japan's strategic interest in ensuring that no hostile forces can use the Korean Peninsula as a foothold for endangering Japan's security would persist. As long as North Korea remains implacably hostile and unreconciled with Japan, the Japanese government would have a strategic interest in maintaining some form of cooperation with South Korea. At the same time, South Korea would have an interest in defusing the possibility of renewed hostilities from as many directions as possible, including with Japan. Therefore, both Japan and South Korea would retain an interest in bounding the risk of conflict with each other and in cooperating to manage a security environment that would likely seem more hostile to both a South Korea without U.S. protection and a Japan doubtful of the credibility of U.S. commitments and anxious that South Korea's foreign policy orientation may come under the strategic influence of China.

As long as South Korea remained outside of China's geopolitical sway, Japan and South Korea would have pragmatic reasons to cooperate despite constraints imposed by historical grievances. An independent South Korea engaging in limited cooperation with Japan would be a lesser threat to China than a U.S. security architecture buoyed by parallel alliances with Japan and South Korea, but South Korean noncooperation or resistance could hinder Chinese aspirations to secure geopolitical dominance over the entire Korean Peninsula. A South Korea under Chinese domination would exacerbate security dilemmas between Japan and China.

To the extent that South Korea perceives China as a risk to its security and/or ability to pursue independent security and foreign policies, South Korea may pursue accommodations and engagement with Japan to offset Chinese influence and coercive leverage against South Korea. But if South Korea felt confident in its relationship with China, the prospects for a stable and constructive Japan–South Korea relationship might decline.

South Korea's openness to a new security and economic bargain with Japan would depend on the nature and development of the inter-Korean relationship and the degree of anxiety South Korea felt regarding the possibility of coercive leverage that might be exercised by China. In the event that the inter-Korean relationship remained subject to antagonism and distrust, South Korea might pursue greater stability in relations with Japan to relieve the risk that a deteriorating security relationship with Japan might distract or destabilize South Korea from pursuing other goals. If South Korea could confidently neutralize the risk of security conflict on the peninsula with North Korea, South Korea's strategic focus would turn to measures that could alleviate the risks of security conflicts to the south and west of the peninsula.

ENGAGING INTERNATIONALLY TO ALIGN
WITH GLOBAL NORMS

No longer tied to the security alliance with the United States, an autonomous South Korean foreign policy might face a choice between relative international isolation or the pursuit of a strategy in which South Korea could look to invest in and develop omnidirectional economic, security, and political ties to draw in influential global actors. Though South Korea cannot change its unfavorable geographic position among larger powers, it can use its network power to develop mutually beneficial relationships with a wide range of external actors and build their stake in the preservation of an independent South Korea and a stable Northeast Asia.

South Korea has already built strong economic and political relationships with countries all over the world, but much of that interaction has taken place in a context in which South Korea's security concerns have been enmeshed in the U.S.–South Korea alliance. Without the security platform provided by the U.S.–South Korea alliance, South Korea's challenge would be to maintain and deepen perceptions of an independent South Korea's worth to a broader number of actors and partners in Europe, Southeast Asia, and the Americas. While strengthened economic relationships alone are unlikely to provide the same benefits South Korea has gained from the U.S.–South Korea alliance, South Korea's active ties and extensive record of mutual engagements may constitute a reputational buffer that inhibits drastic actions inimical to South Korea.

Following a degradation of the U.S.–South Korea security alliance, South Korea's security and prosperity would further depend on its ability to navigate and benefit from global rules and norms as they evolve. In the near term, this means that even in the absence of the U.S.–South Korea security alliance, South Korea's choices would be framed by the benefits it derived from a U.S.-led international order. But if those rules are contested or the power to set the rules shifts to other, possibly more illiberal, actors such as China, Russia, and North Korea, a South Korea no longer anchored to the U.S.-led liberal international order would likely have more flexibility, adaptability, and incentive to align itself with new norm setters in the international system.

CONCLUSION: WHAT FUTURE FOR THE U.S.–SOUTH KOREA ALLIANCE?

The degradation of the U.S.–South Korea alliance would free South Korea from the security anchor that has provided protection but prevented it from charting an independent course. Navigating the choppy waters of Northeast Asia absent U.S. protection would expose South Korea more directly to complicated crosscurrents that would require not only a seaworthy vessel but also sufficient skill and unity to stay the course. South Korea certainly has the capacity and resources to manage such a voyage, but it would need to chart a prudent course that avoids emerging obstacles and mitigates the risks inherent in its new security reality.

The main challenges for an independent South Korea involve acquisition and maintenance of the resources and assets necessary to ensure South Korea's protection; management of inter-Korean relations to maintain peaceful coexistence and avoid spiraling provocations; mitigation of the risks associated with China's rising influence and desire to restore a Sinocentric regional order; establishment of a foundation for a stable, future-oriented, and mutually cooperative relationship with Japan; and capitalization on South Korea's network power to draw in external actors as a buffer against getting caught up in great power rivalries or becoming the object of coercion. Prudent security planning, nimble diplomacy, national consensus, and capable political leadership need to work effectively together to ensure that South Korea does not fall victim to the tragedy of great power politics in the absence of its alliance with the United States.

11

SUSTAINING U.S.–SOUTH KOREA ALLIANCE CONTRIBUTIONS TO INTERNATIONAL SECURITY

T he United States and South Korea have worked together for decades to preserve peninsular and regional security against external threats but have thus far not been forced to contend with equally grave internal threats to alliance cohesion that might open the door to a weakening of the alliance. For decades, presidential leadership in both countries has been committed to pro-alliance policies, and the temptation to prioritize national interests to the exclusion of alliance interests has been rare. But under the Trump and Moon administrations, new internal threats to the U.S.–South Korea alliance have emerged from deepening political polarization and new forms of nationalism; that is, variations of America-First and Korea-first ideologies presented in table 1.1 in which a narrow definition of national interests supersedes the manifest pooling of shared interests so as to build and deploy mutual efforts against a common threat. On the U.S. side, "America First" emerged in the form of accusations that South Korea is a security free rider that relies on U.S. investments in a forward-deployed troop presence in the country without contributing a fair share to South Korea's own defense. On the South Korean side, "Korea first" manifested itself primarily through a "North Korea first" approach that elevated an ethnicity-based concept of brotherhood at the risk of ignoring or falling prey to North Korean subversion efforts aimed at achieving North Korean–led unification of the Korean Peninsula, though it is possible to imagine conservative frustrations mounting with a United States unwilling to take risks of instability to either punish North Korea for aggression or to neutralize possible North Korean nuclear extortion or blackmail.[1]

As long as conventional approaches to the bilateral alliance prevail as primary influences on the foreign policies of the two countries, it is likely that the alliance will remain sustainable and resilient. But domestic political polarization in both countries has generated new political dynamics that have given greater space for presidential candidates to pursue platforms and policies influenced by forms of exclusive nationalism. A U.S.–South Korea leadership configuration in which America-First and Korea-first nationalist leaders come to power would once again make the alliance vulnerable to pressures from within.

HOW TO NAVIGATE INTERNAL THREATS TO THE U.S.–SOUTH KOREA ALLIANCE

Given the potential costs and impact of the weakening of the U.S.–South Korea alliance that would result from the rise of America-First and Korea-first policies—which are directly opposed to shared interests that are the foundation for effective alliance cohesion and coordination—how should the United States and South Korea respond to such risks? Both the United States and South Korea should take measures to halt the corrosive and explosive effects that would accompany the degradation of the alliance in the event of the political leadership configuration that would arise when "America First" meets "Korea first."

RECOMMENDATIONS FOR THE UNITED STATES

The Biden administration began from its earliest stages to take steps to save the alliance from the dangers of an America-First narrative in which U.S.

interests were prioritized at the expense of South Korean interests. That narrative has posed the greatest danger from the U.S. side that the alliance has seen in decades. By abandoning inaccurate arguments that South Korea is a security free rider and emphasizing the restoration of the alliance through active consultations based on shared interests, the Biden administration made the necessary course corrections to support the alliance in the near term. The Biden administration expanded the scope of alliance cooperation in its initial interactions with both the Moon and Yoon administrations to a framework that anticipates future U.S.–South Korea cooperation on a global scope encompassing a comprehensive list of shared challenges and opportunities. The Biden administration's reversion to conventional assumptions about and approaches to alliance management does not foreclose the risk that an American public eager to shed international obligations might desire withdrawal rather than continuing to uphold its treaty commitment to protect South Korea. By reframing the alliance conversation as one in which the United States both values South Korea and has expectations for a comprehensive partnership with South Korea that reaffirms the alliance as a valuable instrument in achieving common objectives, the Biden administration reopened a pathway for restoring close relations with South Korea. But it is a pathway that each new government in the United States and South Korea must reaffirm and commit to upon taking office.

To strengthen alliance cooperation with South Korea, the U.S. government should raise American understanding and appreciation of South Korea as an alliance partner and should continue to underscore the mutuality and scope of U.S. shared interests and values with South Korea. The commonality of U.S. and South Korean values and interests has been reinforced by close partnership between the two governments and a wider array of shared economic and cultural interests than ever before as well as the intertwining of U.S. and South Korean markets and deepening appreciation of each other's culture. But there remains an imperative in the course of broadening the alliance agenda to embrace closer economic cooperation including the integration of South Korea into the U.S. supply chain to ensure that such efforts are able to successfully overcome resistance from American domestic protectionist impulses like those represented in the 2022 Inflation

Reduction Act. The effect of greater American public knowledge and awareness about South Korea has been to build public appreciation of South Korea as a positive force and as a partner. Polls by the Chicago Council on Global Affairs show that U.S. public opinion toward South Korea has remained consistently positive, suggesting a strong basis of political support for the alliance.[2] A powerful mechanism by which to sustain high levels of support for the alliance might involve identifying and providing investment incentives designed to encourage a bipartisan and geographically diverse distribution of new South Korean investments in the United States. Such a strategy would be designed to sustain bipartisan support for the alliance in the context of deepening polarization between Democrats and Republicans on so many issues, including on foreign policy. The U.S. government should capitalize on inward South Korean investment flows by highlighting the existing benefits of alliance cooperation in order to cultivate support for the alliance and acknowledge its value to American and global security interests. The United States should guard against costly narrowing of the scope of U.S. national interest based on a transactional approach that pits interests against each other rather than critically evaluating and affirming shared common interests.

As part of its alliance-strengthening efforts, the United States should consistently make the case for forward-deployed influence on the Korean Peninsula through the deepening of institutionalized policy coordination between the two sides, including the maintenance of effective and regular political consultations between the national security councils of the two countries. Such institutional coordination would reinforce prospects for the two governments to take action collectively in pursuit of their shared interests and could serve as a constraint on the emergence of pressures to go at it alone by pursuing actions independent of the alliance. In addition, such investments in the institutionalization of alliance coordination would serve as a form of insurance against catastrophic or detrimental long-term security outcomes that might result from alliance degradation. The United States should regularly critically evaluate domestic South Korean obstacles discussed in chapters 3, 4, and 5 to the perpetuation of the alliance and pursue counters to overcome such obstacles.

Alongside an affirmative approach toward alliance cooperation with South Korea, the United States and South Korea should continue to defend the alliance from external regional threats. The governments of the United States and South Korea should consistently identify and resist North Korean efforts to unilaterally shift the regional security environment in its favor through the expansion of its nuclear and missile capabilities as well as through efforts to infiltrate and subvert South Korea's democratic system and process. The United States and South Korea should maintain joint deterrence strategies against North Korea's political and military wedge-driving efforts. Likewise, the United States and South Korea should prioritize the objective of countering Chinese efforts to weaken and divide alliance partners and respond strongly to Chinese political and economic coercion. This includes ensuring that the United States is prepared to respond effectively to Chinese efforts to impose costs on South Korean allies through economic and political coercion. A U.S. goal should be to build coordination and offer incentives sufficient to ensure that U.S. influence is greater than Chinese influence in South Korea.

To promote greater integration of common economic and security interests, the United States should encourage more technological and economic ties with South Korean firms. Such cooperative efforts would serve as a hedge against alliance degradation and the resulting increase in Chinese influence and as a way of maintaining indirect influence with South Korea during periods of political difficulty between the two governments. For such efforts to be successful, the White House would need to make the case to the American public that trade cooperation with allies is in the U.S. interest and should not be viewed in zero-sum terms. By challenging the prevalent view in South Korea that relations with China are a source of economic opportunity and relations with the United States are essential for South Korea's security, the United States could help realign South Korean security and economic interests with each other and in favor of the United States, thereby providing structural reinforcement to the rationale for deepening U.S.–South Korea alliance cooperation.

Finally, the United States should analyze in greater detail the impact of alliance coordination on South Korea's pursuit of nuclear weapons and should put into place a strategy for managing such an eventuality. Such a strategy would involve technical and political consultations between the United States and South Korea in the context of the U.S.–South Korea Nuclear Cooperation Agreement. It would require careful consideration of the implications of a South Korean pursuit of nuclear weapons for the global nonproliferation regime as well as for U.S. and South Korean strategic interests, respectively. The United States should consider the political, economic, and technical leverage available to dissuade South Korea from pursuing nuclear capabilities and should anticipate South Korea's response to pressures resulting from both U.S.–South Korea alliance degradation and rising regional rivalry among major powers.

RECOMMENDATIONS FOR SOUTH KOREA

The key to sustaining the alliance on the South Korean side lies with the ability of the South Korean public and its institutions to resist and neutralize North Korea–first impulses within South Korea, both by opposing efforts within South Korea's leadership structures to place the ideals of unification above the practical security needs and prosperity of the Korean people and by working together with the United States to the maximum extent possible to protect South Korea from North Korea's nuclear extortion or blackmail. By the same token, the United States must maintain sufficient credibility in its posture and commitment to South Korea's defense that it is not challenged from the right by conservative Korea-first desires to acquire its own independent nuclear weapons capability. These Korea-first influences are a direct threat to the alliance in the same way that America-First influences narrow U.S. conceptions of national interest in ways that exclude cooperation with South Korea. They must be managed and contained if the alliance is to maximize its effectiveness as an instrument for serving mutual interests and objectives between the two countries.

As part of its efforts to strengthen the alliance, South Korean political leadership should reinforce the existing strong domestic public consensus in favor of maintaining the alliance. The consistent positive favorability ratings of the United States compared to any of South Korea's immediate neighbors underscore a deeply held consensus in support of maintaining a close relationship with the United States. It also endorses the long-standing South Korean security logic of a strategy to cultivate friendships with powerful countries that are sufficiently geographically distant to not pose a threat to South Korea's security.

South Korea should also publicly acknowledge and counter the dangers posed by both international (America First) and domestic (Korea first) factors to the alliance and reaffirm the value of the alliance as being based on convergent national security interests. South Korea's commitment to the comprehensive vision of alliance cooperation laid out between South Korean and American presidents represents a substantive foundation for close partnership, in sharp contrast to mercenary, transactional approaches pursued under the name of America First. However, South Korean forms of ethnic nationalism advocated by some progressives converge more with North Korean forms of xenophobic nationalism than with global liberalism, which emphasizes rights-based approaches. It is these rights-based approaches and desires for social reform that increasingly have resonance for young South Koreans in a tolerant, multicultural, and globally integrated South Korea.

In addition, South Korea should encourage the private sector to carefully evaluate the political risks of their business footprint, including the costs and economic risks as well as the need to support a vibrant U.S.–South Korea alliance. This can be done both by enhancing private sector ties with the United States to undergird the alliance and by encouraging Korean businesses to build relationships globally that could blunt the fallout on South Korea's international position and posture that would result from the failure of the alliance.

South Korea should also work to contain the fallout from possible weakening of the U.S.–South Korea alliance by hedging against the security risks that would result from such weakening. To do so, South Korean leadership should try to strengthen public consensus about fundamental security policy objectives and needs in Asia, build a distributed deterrence capability to guard against heightened North Korean adventurism, and pursue a networked outreach to hedge against China's rising influence and build redundancy to the extent possible while the alliance is still in place. South

Korea should assess the regional security environment to determine whether external factors are propitious for a transition to no alliance and plan for how to manage those forces to prevent a possible upset or crisis.

Finally, South Korea should seek stability and clarity in inter-Korean relations to minimize the risk of North Korea resorting to provocations designed to test South Korea's defense capabilities or to induce alliance termination. South Korea should take actions together with the United States to reinforce deterrence while leaving a space for dialogue rather than pursuing dialogue at the risk of deterrence. To the extent that alliance cracks emerge, South Korea should pursue strategies to neutralize North Korean efforts to test and exploit differences between the United States and South Korea resulting from a deterioration of the alliance.

CONCLUSION

The U.S.–South Korea alliance may come under siege from contending and mutually exclusive forms of America-First and Korea-first sentiment that if enabled by nationalist political leadership and domestic polarization, might ultimately lead to the serious weakening of the alliance. The risk and dangers of internal conflict between contending narrow conceptions of self-interest between the United States and South Korea could outweigh the long-time danger that external parties such as China and North Korea may induce the end of the alliance through wedge-driving tactics. The moment for an explosive clash between these American and South Korean forms of nationalism appears to have been averted for the moment, but it clearly still presents as a significant risk and realistic threat in the political consciousness of both alliance partners.

The main beneficiaries of the weakening of the alliance would not be Washington or Seoul but rather Beijing and Pyongyang. Further, the weakening of the U.S.–South Korea alliance could mark a tipping point in a contest between a U.S.-led security architecture that has preserved peace and promoted prosperity in Northeast Asia for decades and a Sinocentric regional order that would benefit China and possibly North Korea but would come at great cost to the interests of the United States, Japan, and South Korea as well as other U.S. allies including Australia, Thailand, the Philippines, and other Southeast Asian partners. Because a world with an ineffective U.S.–South Korea alliance is clearly adverse to both U.S. and South Korean strategic interests, there is a strong basis for eschewing both the America-First approach to the alliance espoused by President Trump and Korea-first approaches represented either by hard-core progressives who have placed brotherhood with North Korea above South Korean national security interests or by South Korean conservatives frustrated with the U.S. emphasis on conflict management rather than willingness to take greater risks to bring about the end to the North Korean threat.

A better approach for the United States and South Korea comes from treating the alliance as a foundation for mutual benefit and as an active contributor to global stability. But the viability of such an approach would depend on the ability of Americans to promote global stability judiciously and on the ability of South Koreans to realistically assess North Korean intentions while determining how to best achieve South Korea's standing, needs, and aspirations in a peninsular, regional, and global context.

NOTES

1. THE THREAT TO THE U.S.–SOUTH KOREA ALLIANCE FROM WITHIN

1. Bob Woodward, *Fear: Trump in the White House* (New York: Simon and Schuster, 2018), xvii–xxi.
2. Byun Duk-kun, "Trump Says He Will 'Blow Up' Korea–U.S. Alliance If Reelected," *Yonhap News Agency*, July 14, 2021.
3. "Nuclear Deal with U.S. Tightens Korea's Shackles," *Chosun Ilbo*, April 27, 2023, https://english.chosun.com/site/data/html_dir/2023/04/27/2023042701635.html.
4. Brett Ashley Leeds and Burcu Savun, "Terminating Alliances: Why Do States Abrogate Agreements?," *Journal of Politics* 69, no. 4 (November 2007): 1118–1132.
5. Stephen M. Walt, "Why Alliances Endure or Collapse," *Survival: Global Politics and Strategy* 39, no. 1 (1997): 156–179, https://doi.org/10.1080/00396339708442901.
6. Alexander Lenoszka, *Military Alliances in the Twenty-First Century* (Cambridge, MA: Polity Press, 2022).
7. Suh Jae-jung, *Power, Interest, and Identity in Military Alliances* (New York: Palgrave Macmillan, 2007).
8. See Andrew Yeo, *Activists, Alliances, and Anti–U.S. Base Protests* (Cambridge: Cambridge University Press, 2011); and Katherine H. S. Moon, *Protesting America: Democracy and the U.S.–Korea Alliance* (Berkeley: University of California Press, 2012).
9. Lenoszka, *Military Alliances*, 163–188.
10. Jae Jeok Park, "The Persistence of the US-led Alliances in the Asia-Pacific: An Order Insurance Explanation," *International Relations of the Asia-Pacific* 13 (2013): 337–368.

11. Susan Lawrence and Wayne Morrison, "Taiwan: Issues for Congress," Congressional Research Service, October 30, 2017, https://sgp.fas.org/crs/row/R44996.pdf.

12. Zachary Abuza, "America Should Be Realistic About Its Alliance with Thailand," War on the Rocks, January 2, 2020, https://warontherocks.com/2020/01/america-should-be -realistic-about-its-alliance-with-thailand/.

13. Xi Jinping, "New Asian Security Concept for New Progress in Security Cooperation," Remarks at the Fourth Summit of the Conference on Interaction and Confidence Building Measures in Asia, May 21, 2014, https://www.fmprc.gov.cn/mfa_eng/zxxx_662805 /t1159951.shtml.

14. Kang Jinwoong, "The Issues and Tasks in the Studies of Korean Nationalism," *Minjok Yeongu* 73 (2019): 4–25, https://doi.org/10.35431/minjok.73.1.

15. Shin Gi-wook, *Ethnic Nationalism in Korea: Genealogy, Politics, and Legacy* (Stanford, CA: Stanford University Press, 2006), 8.

16. Kim Jiyoon, "National Identity Under Transformation: New Challenges to South Korea," in *Asia's Alliance Triangle: U.S. –Japan–South Korea Relations at a Tumultuous Time*, ed. Gilbert Rozman (Houndmills, Basingstoke, Hampshire: Palgrave Macmillan, 2015), 203–218. See also Katharine H. S. Moon, "South Korea's Demographic Changes and Their Political Impact," East Asia Policy Paper 6, Brookings Institution, October 2015, https://www.brookings.edu/wp-content/uploads/2016/06/South-Koreas-demographic -changes-and-their-political-impact.pdf.

17. Within South Korea, the progressive movement historically has drawn support from anti-dictatorship, anti–big business and pro–labor movement activists, powerful left-leaning teachers' unions, and student radicals.

18. B. R. Myers, *North Korea's Juche Myth* (Busan: Sthele Press, 2015).

19. This story became the basis for the making of *The Host*, a 2006 box office success by Bong Joon-ho, who in 2020 would become the first foreign director to win an Oscar for Best Picture—for the film *Parasite*.

20. David Straub, *Anti-Americanism in Democratizing South Korea* (Palo Alto, CA: Stanford University Press, 2015).

21. Nae-young Lee and Han Wool Jeong, "Fluctuating Anti-Americanism and the Korea–-U.S. Alliance," *International Studies Review* 5, no. 2 (October 2004): 23–40.

22. "노무현 대통령후보 영남대 강연," 노무현사료관, September 11, 2002, http://archives .knowhow.or.kr/record/all/view/2046847.

23. Roh Moo-hyun national security policy as referenced in Scott Snyder, *South Korea at the Crossroads* (New York: Council on Foreign Relations, 2018).

24. Governments of the United States and the Republic of Korea, "Statement on the Launch of the Strategic Consultation for Allied Partnership," U.S. Department of State, January 19, 2006, https://2001-2009.state.gov/r/pa/prs/ps/2006/59447.htm.

2. THE INFLUENCE OF THE TRUMP AND MOON ADMINISTRATIONS ON U.S.–SOUTH KOREAN ALLIANCE MANAGEMENT

1. Office of the President, "President Park Geun-hye and U.S. President-Elect Donald Trump Hold a Telephone Conversation on November 10 to Confirm the Steadfast Alli-

ance Between Korea and the United States," November 10, 2016, http://18president.pa
.go.kr/news/newsList2.php?srh%5Bview_mode%5D=detail&srh%5Bseq%5D=18243;
"Daily Opinion 234 (First Week of November 2016)," Gallup Korea, November 3, 2016,
http://www.gallup.co.kr/gallupdb/reportContent.asp?seqNo=787.

2. Euan McKirdy, Paula Hancocks, and K. J. Kwon, "South Korea's Parliament Votes to
Impeach President Park Geun-hye," CNN, December 9, 2016, https://www.cnn.com
/2016/12/09/asia/south-korea-park-geun-hye-impeachment-vote/index.html.

3. Scott Snyder, "Costs and Consequences of South Korea's Political Vacuum," Council on
Foreign Relations, January 10, 2017, https://www.cfr.org/blog/costs-and-consequences
-south-koreas-political-vacuum.

4. Donald Trump, "Full Transcript: Donald Trump's Jobs Plan Speech," Politico, June 28,
2016, https://www.politico.com/story/2016/06/full-transcript-trump-job-plan-speech
-224891; Donald Trump (@realDonaldTrump), "North Korea just stated that it is in the
final stages of developing a nuclear weapon capable of reaching parts of the U.S. It won't
happen!," Twitter, January 2, 2017, https://twitter.com/realDonaldTrump/status
/816057920223846400?lang=en.

5. Jeon Hye-jeong and Choi Seon-yoon, "Kim Choon-jin, 'Acting President Hwang Should
Have Consulted with the National Assembly Before Call with Trump,'" Newsis, January 30, 2017, https://newsis.com/view/?id=NISX20170130_0014672172&cID=10301&pID
=10300.

6. Brian Padden, "Tillerson: 'Strategic Patience' with North Korea Is Over," Voice of America, March 17, 2017, https://www.voanews.com/a/tillerson-strategic-patience-with
-north-korea-is-over-/3770305.html.

7. Cheryl Pellerin, "Pence Thanks South Korean, U.S. Troops at 'Historic Frontier of Freedom,'" U.S. Army, April 18, 2017, https://www.army.mil/article/186246/pence_thanks
_south_korean_us_troops_at_historic_frontier_of_freedom.

8. Anna Fifield, "North Korea Fires Ballistic Missile, First Since Trump Elected in United
States," *Washington Post*, February 11, 2017, https://www.washingtonpost.com/world
/north-korea-fires-ballistic-missile-first-since-trump-elected-in-us/2017/02/11/42d6cb57
-d187-4b2a-bafb-6834c97799b0_story.html.

9. Lally Weymouth, "South Korea's New President: 'Trump and I Have a Common Goal,'"
Washington Post, June 20, 2017, https://www.washingtonpost.com/outlook/south-koreas
-president-trump-and-i-have-a-common-goal-in-dismantling-north-koreas-nuclear
-program/2017/06/20/cd422e08-55bc-11e7-a204-ad70646f1a4f_story.html?utm_term
=.0e1d95471efc.

10. White House, "Joint Statement Between the United States and the Republic of Korea,"
June 30, 2017, https://trumpwhitehouse.archives.gov/briefings-statements/joint
-statement-united-states-republic-korea/.

11. Office of the President, "Address at the Korber Foundation, Germany," July 6, 2017,
http://webarchives.pa.go.kr/19th/english.president.go.kr/BriefingSpeeches/Speeches
/65.

12. H. R. McMaster, *Battlegrounds: The Fight to Defend the Free World* (New York: Harper,
2020), 352–355.

13. Peter Baker and Choe Sang-Hun, "Trump Threatens 'Fire and Fury' Against North
Korea If It Endangers U.S.," *New York Times*, August 8, 2017, https://www.nytimes.com
/2017/08/08/world/asia/north-korea-un-sanctions-nuclear-missile-united-nations.html.

14. Donald Trump, "Full Transcript: Donald Trump's Jobs Plan Speech"; Donald Trump (@realDonaldTrump), "South Korea is finding, as I have told them, that their talk of appeasement with North Korea will not work, they only understand one thing!," Twitter, September 3, 2017, https://twitter.com/realDonaldTrump/status/816057920223846400 ?lang=en.

15. Office of the President, "The President and U.S. President Trump Discuss by Phone How to Respond to North Korea's Nuclear Test," September 4, 2017, http://webarchives .pa.go.kr/19th/english.president.go.kr/BriefingSpeeches/Briefings/72.

16. White House, "Remarks by President Trump to the 72nd Session of the United Nations General Assembly,'" September 19, 2017, https://trumpwhitehouse.archives.gov/briefings -statements/remarks-president-trump-72nd-session-united-nations-general-assembly/.

17. White House, "Announcement of President Donald J. Trump's Upcoming Travel to Asia," September 29, 2017, https://trumpwhitehouse.archives.gov/briefings-statements /announcement-president-donald-j-trumps-upcoming-travel-asia/.

18. Office of the President, "Address by President Moon Jae-in at the National Assembly Proposing the Government's Budget Plan for FY 2018 and Plans for Fiscal Operations," November 1, 2017, http://webarchives.pa.go.kr/19th/english.president.go.kr /BriefingSpeeches/Speeches/19.

19. White House, "Remarks by President Trump and President Moon of the Republic of Korea in Joint Press Conference | Seoul, Republic of Korea," November 7, 2017, https:// trumpwhitehouse.archives.gov/briefings-statements/remarks-president-trump-president -moon-republic-korea-joint-press-conference-seoul-republic-korea/.

20. White House, "Remarks by President Trump to the National Assembly of the Republic of Korea.

21. "DPRK Gov't Statement on Successful Test-Fire of New-Type ICBM," *Rodong Sinmun*, November 29, 2017, https://kcnawatch.org/newstream/1530445459-573105062/dprk-govt -statement-on-successful-test-fire-of-new-type-icbm/.

22. "How Trump Offered Kim a Ride on Air Force One," BBC, February 20, 2021, https:// www.bbc.com/news/world-us-canada-56118936.

23. "Kim Jong Un's 2018 New Year's Address," National Committee on North Korea, January 1, 2018, https://www.ncnk.org/node/1427.

24. Brian Padden, "North, South Korea Agree to Hold Talks to Improve Relations," Voice of America, January 9, 2018, https://www.voanews.com/a/north-korea-to-join-winter -olympics/4199329.html.

25. Ashley Parker, "Pence Was Set to Meet with North Korean Officials During the Olympics Before Last-Minute Cancellation," *Washington Post*, February 20, 2018, https:// www.washingtonpost.com/politics/pence-was-set-to-meet-with-north-korean-officials -during-the-olympics-before-last-minute-cancellation/2018/02/20/89392dfe-1684-11e8 -942d-16a950029788_story.html.

26. Mike Pence, *So Help Me God* (New York: Simon and Schuster, 2022), 282–283.

27. Christy Lee, "Experts: US, South Korea Differ on Expectations for US–North Korea Summit," Voice of America, March 27, 2018, https://www.voanews.com/a/us-south-korea -expactation-us-north-korea-summit/4320245.html.

28. Ministry of Foreign Affairs, "Briefing by Summit Preparatory Committee Chairman Im Jong-seok," April 17, 2018, https://www.mofa.go.kr/www/brd/m_3976/view.do?seq =367987&srchFr=&amp%3BsrchTo=&amp%3BsrchWord=&amp%3BsrchTp

2. THE INFLUENCE OF THE TRUMP AND MOON ADMINISTRATIONS

=&amp%3Bmulti_itm_seq=0&amp%3Bitm_seq_1=0&amp%3Bitm_seq_2=0
&amp%3Bcompany_cd=&amp%3Bcompany_nm=&page=8.

29. Haksoon Paik, "Inter-Korean Path to Peace: Jump-Started but Stalled," in *North Korea's Foreign Policy: The Kim Jong-un Regime in a Hostile World*, ed. Scott Snyder and Kyung-Ae Park (Lanham, MD: Rowman and Littlefield, 2022).

30. "Trump Welcomes Historic North, South Korea Meeting," Reuters, April 27, 2018, https://www.reuters.com/article/uk-northkorea-southkorea-trump-idUKKBN1HY1FA.

31. Mark Landler, "Trump Pulls Out of North Korea Summit Meeting with Kim Jong-un," *New York Times*, May 24, 2018, https://www.nytimes.com/2018/05/24/world/asia/north-korea-trump-summit.html.

32. Will Ripley, Ralph Ellis, and Ben Westcott, "Kim Jong Un Agrees to Meet Donald Trump at DMZ, Source Says," CNN, May 1, 2018, https://www.cnn.com/2018/04/30/asia/trump-kim-summit-dmz/index.html.

33. White House, "Joint Statement of President Donald J. Trump of the United States of America and Chairman Kim Jong Un of the Democratic People's Republic of Korea at the Singapore Summit," June 12, 2018, https://trumpwhitehouse.archives.gov/briefings-statements/joint-statement-president-donald-j-trump-united-states-america-chairman-kim-jong-un-democratic-peoples-republic-korea-singapore-summit/.

34. "Press Conference by President Trump Following June 12, 2018 Summit with Kim Jong Un," June 12, 2018, https://www.ncnk.org/resources/publications/singapore_summit_press_conference.pdf/file_view.

35. "Supreme Leader Kim Jong Un Inspects Wonsan-Kalma Coastal Tourist Area Under Construction," *Rodong Sinmun*, August 17, 2018, https://kcnawatch.org/newstream/1534490532-704394461/supreme-leader-kim-jong-un-inspects-wonsan-kalma-coastal-tourist-area-under-construction/.

36. "President Moon Set to Propose Permanent Liaison Office with North Korea," *Hankyoreh*, April 25, 2018, https://english.hani.co.kr/arti/english_edition/e_northkorea/842029.html.

37. Office of the President, "Address by President Moon Jae-in on Korea's 73rd Liberation Day," August 15, 2018, http://webarchives.pa.go.kr/19th/english.president.go.kr/BriefingSpeeches/Speeches/61.

38. Sukjoon Yoon, "North and South Korea's New Military Agreement," *Diplomat*, October 2, 2018, https://thediplomat.com/2018/10/north-and-south-koreas-new-military-agreement/.

39. Haksoon Paik, "Inter-Korean Path to Peace."

40. Office of the President, "Address by President Moon Jae-in of the Republic of Korea at the 73rd Session of the United Nations General Assembly," September 26, 2018, http://webarchives.pa.go.kr/19th/english.president.go.kr/BriefingSpeeches/Speeches/73; Office of the President, "Remarks by President Moon Jae-in During Special Mass at Vatican for Peace on Korean Peninsula," October 17, 2018, http://webarchives.pa.go.kr/19th/english.president.go.kr/BriefingSpeeches/Speeches/83.

41. Christy Lee, "US, South Korea to Launch Joint Working Group on North Korea," Voice of America, November 3, 2018, https://www.voanews.com/a/us-south-korea-to-launch-joint-working-group-on-north-korea/4641131.html.

42. "South–U.S. Working Group Meets," *JoongAng Ilbo*, November 20, 2018, https://koreajoongangdaily.joins.com/news/article/article.aspx?aid=3055883.
43. "North Sends VIP to U.S. to Get Summit Plans Going," *JoongAng Ilbo*, January 15, 2019, https://koreajoongangdaily.joins.com/news/article/article.aspx?aid=3058227.
44. News Analysis, "Kim Yong-chol's Washington, DC, a Positive Signal for 2nd NK–US Summit," *Hankyoreh*, January 21, 2019, https://english.hani.co.kr/arti/english_edition/e_northkorea/879254.html.
45. Noa Ronkin, "U.S. Special Envoy for North Korea Stephen Biegun Delivers First Public Address on U.S.–DPRK Diplomacy at a Shorenstein APARC Event," Stanford University, January 31, 2019, https://fsi.stanford.edu/news/us-special-envoy-north-korea-stephen-biegun-delivers-first-public-address-us-dprk-diplomacy.
46. Bob Woodward, *Fear: Trump in the White House* (New York: Simon and Schuster, 2019), prologue.
47. Simon Lester, Inu Manak, and Kyuounghwa Kim, "Trump's First Trade Deal: The Slightly Revised Korea–U.S. Free Trade Agreement," *Cato Institute Free Trade Bulletin*, no. 73, June 13, 2019, https://www.cato.org/free-trade-bulletin/trumps-first-trade-deal-slightly-revised-korea-us-free-trade-agreement; White House, "President Donald J. Trump Is Fulfilling His Promise on the U.S.–Korea Free Trade Agreement and on National Security," March 28, 2018, https://trumpwhitehouse.archives.gov/briefings-statements/president-donald-j-trump-fulfilling-promise-u-s-korea-free-trade-agreement-national-security/.
48. Scott Snyder, "Is Trump's Hard Bargaining Fraying U.S.–South Korean Ties?," Council on Foreign Relations, February 21, 2019, https://www.cfr.org/in-brief/trumps-hard-bargaining-fraying-us-south-korean-ties.
49. John Bolton, *The Room Where It Happened: A White House Memoir* (New York: Simon and Schuster, 2020), 356.
50. Kang Seung-woo, "Envoy to US in Hot Seat Over Repeated Controversial Remarks," *Korea Times*, October 13, 2020, https://www.koreatimes.co.kr/www/nation/2020/10/120_297513.html; "A Conversation with Foreign Minister Chung Eui-yong of the Republic of Korea," Council on Foreign Relations, September 22, 2021, https://www.cfr.org/event/conversation-foreign-minister-chung-eui-yong-republic-korea.
51. Byun Duk-kun, "Seoul's Participation in 'Quad' May Jeopardize Regional Security: S. Korean Adviser," Yonhap News Agency, October 28, 2020, https://en.yna.co.kr/view/AEN20201028000200325.
52. Bolton, *Room Where It Happened*, 355–360.
53. U.S. Embassy and Consulate in South Korea, "U.S. & ROK Issue a Joint Factsheet on Their Regional Cooperation Efforts," November 2, 2019, https://kr.usembassy.gov/110219-joint-fact-sheet-by-the-united-states-and-the-republic-of-korea-on-cooperation-between-the-new-southern-policy-and-the-indo-pacific-strategy/.
54. Kim Jiyoon, Kim Kildong, and Kang Chungku, "U.S.–North Korea Summit and South Koreans' Perceptions of Neighboring Countries," Asan Institute for Policy Studies, July 2018, https://en.asaninst.org/contents/u-s-north-korea-summit-and-south-koreans-perceptions-of-neighboring-countries/; Karl Friedhoff, "Americans Positive on South Korea Despite Trump's Views on Alliance," Chicago Council on Global Affairs, October 19, 2020, https://globalaffairs.org/research/public-opinion-survey/americans-positive-south-korea-despite-trumps-views-alliance.

55. Paul O'Shea and Sebastian Maslow, "'Making the Alliance Even Greater': (Mis)managing U.S.–Japan Relations in the Age of Trump," *Asian Security* 17, no. 2 (2021): 195–215, https://doi.org/10.1080/14799855.2020.1838486.

56. Eric Langenbacher and Ruth Wittlinger, "The End of Memory? German-American Relations Under Donald Trump," *German Politics* 27, no. 2 (2018): 174–192.

57. Sarah Turnbull, "A Look Back at Trudeau and Trump's Four-Year-Long Yo-Yo Relationship," CTV News, August 8, 2020, https://www.ctvnews.ca/world/america-votes/a-look-back-at-trudeau-and-trump-s-four-year-long-yo-yo-relationship-1.5033077; Malcolm Turnbull, "Former Australian PM Malcolm Turnbull on Donald Trump: 'You Don't Suck Up to Bullies,'" *Guardian*, April 19, 2020, https://www.theguardian.com/australia-news/2020/apr/20/malcolm-turnbull-on-donald-trump-you-dont-suck-up-to-bullies.

58. Amnon Cavari, "Trump, Israel, and the Shifting Pattern of Support for a Traditional Ally," in *The Trump Doctrine and the Emerging International System*, ed. Stanley A. Renshon and Peter Suedfeld (Cham, Switzerland: Palgrave Macmillan, 2021), 281–315.

59. Mark Beeson and Alan Bloomfield, "The Trump Effect Downunder: U.S. Allies, Australian Strategic Culture, and the Politics of Path Dependence," *Contemporary Security Policy* 40, no. 3 (2019): 335–361.

60. Derek H. Burney, "Canada–US Relations: No Longer Special or Privileged," *American Review of Canadian Studies* 50, no. 1 (2020): 128–132.

61. Kylie MacLellan, "Trump Administration 'Uniquely Dysfunctional,' says UK Ambassador to U.S.," Reuters, July 7, 2019, https://www.reuters.com/article/us-usa-britain/trump-administration-uniquely-dysfunctional-says-uk-ambassador-to-u-s-newspaper-idUSKCN1U2081.

62. White House, "National Security Strategy," October 2022, https://www.whitehouse.gov/wp-content/uploads/2022/10/Biden-Harris-Administrations-National-Security-Strategy-10.2022.pdf.

63. Joshua Berlinger, "The Leaders of South Korea and Japan Are Biden's First Two Visitors to the US, Underscoring Asia's Importance," CNN, May 21, 2021, https://www.cnn.com/2021/05/21/asia/biden-moon-washington-intl-hnk/index.html.

64. U.S. Department of State, "U.S.–Japan Joint Press Statement," March 16, 2021, https://www.state.gov/u-s-japan-joint-press-statement/; U.S. Department of State, "Joint Statement of the 2021 Republic of Korea—United States Foreign and Defense Ministerial Meeting ("2+2")," March 18, 2021, https://www.state.gov/joint-statement-of-the-2021-republic-of-korea-united-states-foreign-and-defense-ministerial-meeting-22/.

65. White House, "U.S.–ROK Leaders' Joint Statement," May 21, 2021, https://www.whitehouse.gov/briefing-room/statements-releases/2021/05/21/u-s-rok-leaders-joint-statement/.

66. White House, "Remarks by President Biden and H. E. Moon Jae-in, President of the Republic of Korea at Press Conference," May 21, 2021, https://www.whitehouse.gov/briefing-room/speeches-remarks/2021/05/21/remarks-by-president-biden-and-h-e-moon-jae-in-president-of-the-republic-of-korea-at-press-conference/.

67. "U.S. Says It May Differ with Moon on End-of-War Idea," *JoongAng Ilbo*, October 27, 2021, https://koreajoongangdaily.joins.com/2021/10/27/national/diplomacy/White-House-endofwar-declaration-Jake-Sullivan/20211027165041553.html.

68. "Yoon Suk-yeol's Diplomatic and Security Pledges, 'Denuclearization of the Korean Peninsula . . . Revitalizing U.S.–South Korea Alliance,'" NewsPim, January 24, 2022, https://www.newspim.com/news/view/20220124000337.

69. Yoon Suk-yeol, "South Korea Needs to Step Up," *Foreign Affairs*, February 8, 2022, https://www.foreignaffairs.com/articles/south-korea/2022-02-08/south-korea-needs -step.

70. Gwon Hyuk-cheol, "Yoon Suk-yeol's Foreign Policy Prioritizes 'Blood Alliance' with the United States . . . Warnings for Inter-Korean and China–South Korea Relations," *Hankyoreh*, March 14, 2022, https://www.hani.co.kr/arti/politics/politics_general /1034680.html.

71. Scott Snyder, "Evolution of U.S.–South Korean Coordination: Parsing Biden's Joint Statements with Moon and Yoon," Council on Foreign Relations, May 24, 2022, https:// www.cfr.org/blog/evolution-us-south-korean-coordination-parsing-bidens-joint -statements-moon-and-yoon.

72. White House, "Remarks by President Biden on Hyundai's Investments in Savannah, Georgia," May 22, 2022, https://www.whitehouse.gov/briefing-room/speeches-remarks /2022/05/22/remarks-by-president-biden-on-hyundais-investments-in-savannah -georgia/.

73. Jennifer Ahn, "Beyond U.S. Credibility Concerns: Factors Driving the Nuclear Weapons Debate in South Korea," Korea Economic Institute, February 17, 2023, https://keia .org/the-peninsula/beyond-u-s-credibility-concerns-factors-driving-the-nuclear -weapons-debate-in-south-korea/.

3. POLITICAL POLARIZATION UNDER THE MOON JAE-IN ADMINISTRATION

1. "Inaugural Address by President Moon Jae-in," Office of the President, May 10, 2017, http://webarchives.pa.go.kr/19th/english.president.go.kr/President/Greetings.

2. Moon Jae-in, "Moon Jae-in's Policy Initiative for a New Republic of Korea," Facebook, January 5, 2017, https://www.facebook.com/moonbyun1/posts/999153240191028/.

3. Shin Gi-wook, "South Korea's Democratic Decay," *Journal of Democracy* 31, no. 3 (July 2020): 100–114.

4. "Minbyun Opinion on the Adjustment of the Prosecutor's and Police's Investigative Authority," Minbyun—Lawyers for a Democratic Society, March 23, 2018, http:// minbyun.or.kr/wp-content/uploads/2018/03/검찰·경찰-수사권-조정-논쟁-등에-관한-민변 -의견서.pdf.

5. The NIS was formerly known as the Agency for National Security Planning until it was renamed in 1999 under the Kim Dae-jung administration as part of a broader attempt to overhaul the agency and reduce its influence in domestic politics.

6. "If Even the Moon Jae-in Administration Fails to Reform the Prosecution, We Will All Regret It," *Hankyoreh*, January 6, 2019, http://m.hani.co.kr/arti/politics/polibar/877153 .html#cb.

7. The KPS investigation of Roh is a factor that may have led him to commit suicide. Editorial, "Obvious Fault of Prosecutors in Roh's Suicide," *Hankyoreh*, May 24, 2009, https://m.hani.co.kr/arti/english_edition/e_editorial/356614.html#cb.

8. "Moon Jae-in's Prosecutorial Reforms Inspired by 'Roh Moo-hyun's Lament' . . . National Assembly Is at a Crossroads," *Hankyoreh*, August 17, 2019, http://www.hani.co.kr/arti/society/society_general/906075.html.

9. "Moon Jae-in's Prosecutorial Reforms Inspired by 'Roh Moo-hyun's Lament.'"

10. "Moon Who Said 'Prosecution Service Is Political' Leads Prosecutorial Reforms to Nowhere," *JoongAng Ilbo*, January 13, 2020, https://www.joongang.co.kr/article/23681366#home.

11. "The Painful Memory of Roh's Passing After Confrontation with Prosecutors . . .'Prosecutorial Reform Is an Inevitable Choice for President Moon," *Hankook Ilbo*, September 10, 2019, https://www.hankookilbo.com/News/Read/201909091836032547.

12. "How Did JTBC Newsroom Obtain the 'Tablet PC?,'" JTBC News, December 9, 2016, http://news.jtbc.joins.com/article/article.aspx?news_id=NB11374134.

13. "Why We Cannot Praise 'Sewol Indictments' by the Special Investigation Unit . . .'Why Not Six Years Ago?,'" Newstapa, February 21, 2020, https://newstapa.org/article/MBPeo.

14. "National Planning Committee Says 'Prosecutors Amassed and Abused Power' . . . Declared Will for Reform," Yonhap News Agency, May 25, 2017, https://www.yna.co.kr/view/AKR20170525131100004.

15. "Turning the Spirit of the Candlelight Revolution into Concrete Policy Outcomes," Korea Policy Briefing, November 12, 2019, http://www.korea.kr/news/contributePolicyView.do?newsId=148866448.

16. "Cho Kuk and His Family Indicted on Eleven Counts, What Is the Current Progress of the Trial?," Newstof, September 3, 2020, http://www.newstof.com/news/articleView.html?idxno=11174.

17. "Police Reform Committee Launched . . . Recommendations Are Not Legally Binding," *Hankyoreh*, June 16, 2017, https://www.hani.co.kr/arti/society/society_general/799142.html#csidx8e788b516df7421bf6e90b1d27d8990.

18. "Moon Government's 'No. 1 Priority' Is 'Eradication of Deep Rooted Evils' . . . Major Investigations Expected," Yonhap News Agency, July 19, 2017, https://www.yna.co.kr/view/AKR20170719050400004?input=1195m.

19. "First Step Taken to Adjust the Investigative Authority of Prosecutors . . . Police Reform Committee Recommends 'Separation of Investigatorial Responsibilities from the Issuance of Indictments,'" *Hankyoreh*, December 7, 2017, https://www.hani.co.kr/arti/society/society_general/822485.html#csidx2d0abfaf9471b9fb46770c9a1d21680.

20. "Opposition Party's Attack on Reform Plan for Power Institutions Is Anachronistic," *Kyunghyang Shinmun*, January 15, 2018, https://www.khan.co.kr/opinion/editorial/article/201801152102035#csidxb32864cb04a63efafa9c53077df3e80.

21. "The Key to Police and Prosecution Reform Is the Removal of Government Influence," *Chosun Ilbo*, January 15, 2018, https://www.chosun.com/site/data/html_dir/2018/01/14/2018011401566.html.

22. "Signing Ceremony of the Agreement on the Adjustment of the Rights of the Prosecution and Police," Korea Policy Briefing, June 21, 2018, https://www.korea.kr/news/pressReleaseView.do?newsId=156276187; "Prosecution and Police Investigation Authority Adjustment," Korea Policy Briefing, February 20, 2020, http://www.korea.kr/special/policyCurationView.do?newsId=148868893.

23. In December 2016, the Liberty Korea Party was established as a successor to the Saenuri Party in the context of a party split over Park Geun-hye's impeachment. The party was

dissolved and replaced by the People Power Party (PPP) as South Korea's main conservative party as a result of a merger of conservative parties in February 2020 in the run-up to the April 2020 National Assembly elections. The author has used the contemporaneous designations for the parties throughout the book. "LKP Launches Indefinite 'Tent Protest': 'Is This a XXX Country?,'" *Kyunghyang Shinmun*, April 17, 2018, https://m .khan.co.kr/view.html?art_id=201804171001001.

24. "Candidate for Justice Minister Cho Kuk Declares 'Prosecutorial and Judicial Reform Will be Accomplished,'" Yonhap News Agency, August 9, 2019, https://www.yna.co.kr /view/AKR20191114065000004.

25. "Candlelight Vigil at Seoul National University and Korea University: 'Resignation of Cho Kuk . . . Investigate Allegations of Illegal Admission to Daughter,'" Yonhap News Agency, August 23, 2019, https://www.yna.co.kr/view/AKR20190823148751004; "Protests Supporting and Opposing Cho Kuk," Yonhap News Agency, August 28, 2019, https:// www.yna.co.kr/view/PYH20190828101200013; "University Students Nationwide Call for Cho Kuk's Resignation," *Korea Herald*, September 22, 2019, http://www.koreaherald.com /view.php?ud=20190922000227; "Candlelight Rally Held in Support of Cho Kuk," *Joon-gAng Daily*, September 29, 2019, https://koreajoongangdaily.joins.com/news/article /article.aspx?aid=3068468.

26. "Candlelight Vigil at Seoul National University and Korea University."

27. "Prosecutors Execute Search Warrant on Pusan National University Medical School and Seoul National University Related to 'Cho Kuk Allegations,'" *Hankyoreh*, August 27, 2019, https://m.hani.co.kr/arti/society/society_general/907258.html#cb.

28. "51% Oppose Appointment of Cho Kuk . . . Support Prosecutorial Reform," KBS, September 12, 2019, https://news.kbs.co.kr/news/view.do?ncd=4282083.

29. "'Prosecution Reform Implementation Task Force' Launched Within Eight Days of Cho Kuk Directive," *Hankyoreh*, September 17, 2019, https://www.hani.co.kr/arti/society /society_general/909830.html.

30. Kim Jun-young, "Netizens Finding Them for Every Allegation . . . Embarrassing 'Cho Kuk Tweets,'" *JoongAng Ilbo*, August 29, 2019, https://www.joongang.co.kr/article /23565022#home.

31. "Top Prosecutor Vows Ceaseless Efforts for Prosecution Reform," *Korea Herald*, December 31, 2019, http://www.koreaherald.com/view.php?ud=20191231000426.

32. Special Investigation Departments (특수부) focus on special criminal cases related to corruption and bribery, but they have abused their power by taking on civil cases. By decreasing the number of those departments, the KPS is focusing on its original mission of investigating government or business-related corruption and crimes. "'Prosecutors Should Provide Opinions, Not Decisions' . . . Cho Kuk Uncomfortable with Yoon Suk-yeol's Shocking Announcement," *JoongAng Ilbo*, October 4, 2019, https://www.joongang .co.kr/article/23595267#home.

33. "'Prosecutors Should Provide Opinions, Not Decisions.'"

34. "South Korean Politician Resigns After Weeks of Protests," *New York Times*, October 14, 2019, https://www.nytimes.com/2019/10/14/world/asia/south-korea-cho-kuk-resigns .html.

35. Criminal Procedure Law, Pub. L. No. 16850 (2019), https://www.law.go.kr/법령/형 사소송법/(20191231,16850,20191231)/제244조의3; Korea Prosecution Service Act, Pub.

L. No. 15522 (2018), https://www.law.go.kr/LSW/lsInfoP.do?efYd=20180921&lsiSeq
=202793#0000.

36. Act on the Establishment and Operation of Corruption Investigation Office for High-
ranking Officials, Pub. L. No. 16863 (2020), https://www.law.go.kr/법령/고위공직자범죄
수사처설치및운영에관한법률/(16863).

37. "Parliament Passes Corruption Probe Unit Bill Amid Opposition Lawmakers' Protest,"
Korea Herald, December 31, 2019, http://www.koreaherald.com/view.php?ud
=20191231000060.

38. "Moon Calls for Continued Reform of Prosecution, Police," Yonhap News Agency, January 21, 2020, https://en.yna.co.kr/view/AEN20200121005900315.

39. "Prosecution and Police Investigation Authority Adjustment," Korea Policy Briefing,
June 21, 2018, https://www.korea.kr/news/pressReleaseView.do?newsId=156276170.

40. "The Day President Moon Declared 'Take Charge of Prosecutorial Reform' . . . Prosecutors Resign," *Dong-A Ilbo*, January 14, 2020, https://www.donga.com/news/Society
/article/all/20200114/99224209/1.

41. "Choo Shuts Down Prosecutor General's Probe," *JoongAng Daily*, July 2, 2020, https://
koreajoongangdaily.joins.com/2020/07/02/national/socialAffairs/Choo-Miae-Yoon
-Seokyoul-prosecutor-general/20200702173900400.html.

42. "The Intention Behind Minister Choo's Invoked Command . . . The Prosecution Must
Demonstrate Impartial Investigation," *Kyunghyang Shinmun*, October 19, 2020, https://
www.khan.co.kr/opinion/editorial/article/202010192159025#csidx5a85d2139047fc09591
ae2c39be1b5d.

43. "'Yoon Suk-yeol Suspension for Two Months' Unprecedented Disciplinary Action on
the Prosecutor General," *Dong-A Ilbo*, December 16, 2020, https://www.donga.com/news
/Society/article/all/20201216/104464427/1; "'Reversal of Yoon Suk-yeol's Suspension' . . .
President's Decision Overturned by Court," *JoongAng Ilbo*, December 24, 2020, https://
www.joongang.co.kr/article/23954301#home.

44. "Amendments to the Police Officials Act," National Assembly Bill Information System,
December 9, 2020, https://likms.assembly.go.kr/bill/billDetail.do?billId=PRC_E2Z0
C1X2K0E2C1B8K4T2H5P1L8K2V5; "Act on the Establishment and Operation of Corruption Investigation Office for High-Ranking Officials," National Assembly Bill Information System, December 10, 2020, https://likms.assembly.go.kr/bill/billDetail.do
?billId=PRC_A2D0L1O2E0O8Q1Y1B2U5J5D9C6H2T0; "Amendments to the National
Intelligence Service Korea Act," National Assembly Bill Information System, December 13, 2020, https://likms.assembly.go.kr/bill/billDetail.do?billId=PRC_U2Y0F1B1Q3
V0B1X5B4E4V3T7T7X0K8.

45. "Hangil Research November Periodic Opinion Poll—Support for State of the Country,
Political Parties, Ruling and Opposition Party Presidential Candidates," Hangil
Research, November 11, 2020. http://hgr1993.com/gnuboard5/bbs/board.php?bo_table
=research_news&wr_id=24&page=2.

46. 19th Presidential Election, "Comparing Campaign Promises: Bureaucracy and Judicial
Reform," Citizen's Coalition for Economic Justice, http://vote.ccej.or.kr/archives/1772.

47. "Cho Kuk's Prosecution Reform, 52% Positive vs. 35% Negative," Hankook Research,
Yonhap News Agency, September 22, 2019, https://www.yna.co.kr/view/AKR201909
22023300001.

48. "Daily Opinion No. 374 (Week of October 3, 2019)—Response to the Resignation of Minister of Justice Cho Kuk," Gallup Korea, October 17, 2019, https://www.gallup.co.kr/gallupdb/reportContent.asp?seqNo=1053.

49. Ha Jun-ho and Han Young-ik, "The Blue House 'Abolition of NIS' National Security Investigatory Powers . . . Opposition Party Revolts Against 'Fifth Republic Police,'" *JoongAng Ilbo*, November 24, 2020, https://www.joongang.co.kr/article/23929102#home.

50. Amendments to the Prosecutor's Office Act, Pub. L. No. 18861 (2022), https://law.go.kr/LSW/lsInfoP.do?lsiSeq=242095&viewCls=lsRvsDocInfoR#; Amendments to the Criminal Procedure Act, Pub. L. No. 18862 (2022), https://www.law.go.kr/LSW/lsRvsDocListP.do?lsId=001671&chrClsCd=010102.

51. Erik Mobrand, *Top-Down Democracy in South Korea* (Seattle: University of Washington Press, 2018).

52. "Constitutional Referendum in Next Year's Local Elections Supported by 78% of Citizens and 89% of National Assembly Members," *JoongAng Ilbo*, September 24, 2017, https://www.joongang.co.kr/article/21965173#home.

53. "Can Moon Keep His 'Constitutional Amendment in June' Promise?," *Dong-A Ilbo*, July 17, 2017, https://www.donga.com/news/Opinion/article/all/20170716/85383468/1.

54. "Moon's Constitutional Amendment Calls for Four-Year Two Term Presidency," *Korea Herald*, March 22, 2018, http://www.koreaherald.com/view.php?ud=20180322000802.

55. "Senior Secretary for Civil Affairs Cho Kuk's Announcement of Constitutional Amendment on Strengthening Fundamental Rights and National Sovereignty," Korea Policy Briefing, March 20, 2018, https://www.korea.kr/briefing/presidentView.do?newsId=148849012&pageIndex=8&startDate=2022-03-20&endDate=2023-03-20&srchWord=.

56. "Senior Secretary for Civil Affairs Cho Kuk's Announcement of Constitutional Amendment on Decentralization of Power and Economy."

57. "Senior Secretary for Civil Affairs Cho Kuk's Announcement of Constitutional Amendment on Structure of Power."

58. "Comments on the National Assembly's Handling of the Constitutional Amendment Bill," Korea Policy Briefing, May 24, 2018, http://www.korea.kr/news/blueHouseView.do?newsId=148850959.

59. "Isn't the Goal of Constitutional Amendment Passage, Not the Proposal," *JoongAng Ilbo*, March 22, 2018, https://www.joongang.co.kr/article/22468182#home; Gwon-ho, "The Blue House Strengthened 'Public Concept of Land' in Draft Constitutional Amendment," *JoongAng Ilbo*, March 13, 2018, https://www.joongang.co.kr/article/22438702#home.

60. "Seven Major Challenges for the New President's First Year: 3. How to Amend the Constitution?," *JoongAng Editorial Magazine*, https://jmagazine.joins.com/monthly/view/316665.

61. "Daily Opinion No. 300 (Week of March 4, 2018)—President's Constitutional Amendment Proposal," Gallup Korea, March 29, 2018, http://www.gallup.co.kr/gallupdb/reportContent.asp?seqNo=917.

62. "'Constitution Amended If More Than a Million People Support' Constitutional Amendment by Popular Support . . . Secretly Listed on the National Register," *NewDaily*, March 27, 2020, https://www.newdaily.co.kr/site/data/html/2020/03/27/2020032700100.html.

63. "'Constitution Amended If More Than a Million People Support' Constitutional Amendment by Popular Support . . . Secretly Listed on the National Register."

64. Yoo Hyo-song and Kang Joo-hun, "The 20th National Assembly Special Committee on Constitutional Amendment Launched . . . Little Progress Amid Debate on Electoral Benefits," Money Today, March 26, 2020, https://news.mt.co.kr/mtview.php?no =2020032511397645986.

65. "Address by President Moon Jae-in on 40th Anniversary of May 18 Gwangju Democratization Movement," Office of the President, May 18, 2020, http://webarchives.pa.go.kr /19th/english.president.go.kr/BriefingSpeeches/Speeches/825.

66. Shin Gi-wook, *Ethnic Nationalism in Korea: Genealogy, Politics, and Legacy* (Stanford, CA: Stanford University Press, 2006), 104–107.

67. One early positive gesture Yoon made less than one week following his election involved his personal participation and that of his party in official memorial ceremonies at Gwangju commemorating the anniversary of the May 18 massacre under Chun Doo-hwan. Through this gesture, Yoon depoliticized Gwangju as a source of political polarization and affirmed the importance of prodemocracy commemorations as a national exercise rather than as an exercise tinged by political partisanship.

4. SOUTH KOREAN PROGRESSIVE FOREIGN POLICY AND TENSIONS IN THE U.S.–SOUTH KOREA ALLIANCE

1. For example, the former progressive President Roh Moo-hyun argued during a Blue House briefing on August 10, 2006, that "The US-ROK relationship is more than 100 years old, and it should not break because of the disagreement between the two countries." He also pointed out that Korean people should not say "yes" to the United States all the time and should exchange opinions and hold our positions on the matter of survival and fate of the country. "OPCON Is Key to National Sovereignty . . . U.S.–South Korea Alliance Will Not Be Shaken Even If It Is Returned," Korea Policy Briefing, August 10, 2006, https://www.korea.kr/news/policyNewsView.do?newsId =148604529.

2. For example, President Roh Moo-hyun emphasized during the 56th National Armed Forces Ceremony that "self-defense and the ROK-US alliance should be the two pillars of national security," SBS, October 1, 2021, https://news.naver.com/main/read.nhn?mode =LSD&mid=sec&sid1=115&oid=055&aid=0000029658.

3. The former representative of the conservative party Hong Joo-pyo criticized the Moon administration by saying that "the administration is being too naïve when it comes to dealing with North Korean matter by believing Kim Jong-un's New Year's remarks that they have opened a path for dialogue with North Korea." *Kyunghayang Shinmun*, January 2, 2018, http://news.khan.co.kr/kh_news/khan_art_view.html?artid=201801022049015 &code=990101.

4. J. James Kim and Kang Chungku, "South Korean Attitudes About ROK–Japan Relations on the Rocks," Asan Institute for Policy Studies, October 14, 2019, https://en.asaninst .org/contents/south-korean-attitudes-about-rok-japan-relations-on-the-rocks/.

5. The former floor leader of the conservative party Na Kyung-won showed her worries by saying that "if Korea drive Japan too extreme, where anti-Korean sentiment is extremely

heightened, Korea will actually deepen concerns about the weakening of the triangular alliance between Korea, Japan and the U.S." "Na Kyung-won: 'Alienating Japan Will Weaken U.S.–Japan–South Korea alliance,'" *E Daily*, January 14, 2019, https://www .edaily.co.kr/news/read?newsId=02502646622357720&mediaCodeNo=257.

6. Brian Kim, "How Biden Can Navigate a New Era in South Korean Politics," *Diplomat*, January 17, 2021, https://thediplomat.com/2021/01/how-biden-can-navigate-a-new-era-in -south-korean-politics/.

7. The progressive thinkers who are most active in developing distinctive views on inter-Korean relations, South Korea's international role, and the alliance with the United States include Moon Chung-in, chairman of the Sejong Institute, former Roh Moo-hyun administration chairman of the advisory committee on Northeast Asian Cooperation Initiative, and former senior advisor to President Moon Jae-in; Jung Se-hyun, chairman of the National Unification Advisory Committee, former minister of unification under Kim Dae-jung, and active progressive commentator on policy toward North Korea and inter-Korean relations; Lee Su-hoon, Moon Jae-in's first ambassador to Japan; Lee Jong-seok, former national security advisor to President Roh Moo-hyun and senior fellow at the Sejong Institute; Kim Yung-chol, former minister of unification; Lee In-young, former minister of unification; and Kim Joon-hyung, chairman of the Korean Diplomatic Academy and former Handong University professor. Editorial contributions of the progressive newspapers *Hankyoreh Shinmun* and *Kyunghyang Shinmun* provide additional texture and understanding to South Korean progressive approaches to foreign policy. References to progressive thinking on foreign policy in this chapter represent an amalgamation of views from these primary sources, among others.

8. "Jeong Se-hyun: 'Alliance Is an Auxiliary Means of Independent National Defense . . . North Korea Is Definitely Changing,'" *Kyunghyang Shinmun*, January 24, 2021, http:// news.khan.co.kr/kh_news/khan_art_view.html?artid=202101241330011&code=910100.

9. "APLN's Chung-in Moon on U.S. Policy Toward Asia and the North Korea Nuclear Threat," Nuclear Threat Initiative, February 7, 2017, https://www.nti.org/analysis/atomic -pulse/aplns-chung-moon-us-policy-toward-asia-and-north-korea-nuclear-threat.

10. Interview, Yun Hee-hun, "Jeong Se-hyun 'Alliance Is an Auxiliary Means of Independent National Defense . . . North Korea Is Definitely Changing,'" *Chosun Ilbo*, January 26, 2020, https://www.chosun.com/site/data/html_dir/2020/01/26/2020012600114 .html.

11. Shin Beom-cheol, "A Realistic Alternative to Joining the Quad," Digital Times, April 29, 2021, http://www.dt.co.kr/contents.html?article_no=2021043002102269660001.

12. Shin Beom-cheol, "Light and Shadow of the U.S.–South Korea Summit," Digital Times, May 24, 2021, http://www.dt.co.kr/contents.html?article_no=20210525021022 69660001.

13. "Gallup Korea Daily Opinion Poll," Gallup Korea, May 2018, https://panel.gallup.co.kr /Contents/GallupKoreaDaily/GallupKoreaDailyOpinion_305(20180504).pdf.

14. "Address at the Korber Foundation, Germany," Office of the President, July 6, 2017, http://webarchives.pa.go.kr/19th/english.president.go.kr/BriefingSpeeches/Speeches /65.

15. Meghan Keneally, "From 'Fire and Fury' to 'Rocket Man,' the Various Barbs Traded Between Trump and Kim Jong Un," ABC News, June 12, 2018, https://abcnews.go.com /International/fire-fury-rocket-man-barbs-traded-trump-kim/story?id=53634996.

16. "Briefing by Inter-Korean Summit Preparation Committee Chairman Lim Jong-suk," Office of the President, April 17, 2018, https://www.korea.kr/news/blueHouseView.do?newsId=148854021.

17. "Address by President Moon Jae-in on Korea's 73rd Liberation Day," Office of the President, August 15, 2018, http://webarchives.pa.go.kr/19th/english.president.go.kr/BriefingSpeeches/Speeches/61.

18. "Agreement on the Implementation of the Historic Panmunjom Declaration in the Military Domain," September 19, 2018, https://www.ncnk.org/sites/default/files/Agreement%20on%20the%20Implementation%20of%20the%20Historic%20Panmunjom%20Declaration%20in%20the%20Military%20Domain.pdf.

19. "Pyongyang Joint Declaration of September 2018," Ministry of Foreign Affairs, September 19, 2018, https://www.mofa.go.kr/eng/brd/m_5476/view.do?seq=319608&srchFr=&amp%3BsrchTo=&amp%3BsrchWord=&amp%3BsrchTp=&amp%3Bmulti_itm_seq=0&amp%3Bitm_seq_1=0&amp%3Bitm_seq_2=0&amp%3Bcompany_cd=&amp%3Bcompany_nm=&page=1&titleNm=.

20. Author conversations with senior Blue House officials and United Nations Command (UNC) officers, October 2018.

21. "The President and French President Emmanuel Macron Hold Summit," Ministry of Foreign Affairs, October 15, 2018, https://www.mofa.go.kr/eng/brd/m_5674/view.do?seq=319776.

22. "1st Meeting of ROK–US Working Group Takes Place," Ministry of Foreign Affairs, Republic of Korea, November 21, 2018, https://www.mofa.go.kr/eng/brd/m_5478/view.do?seq=319134&srchFr=&amp%3BsrchTo=&amp%3BsrchWord=&amp%3BsrchTp=&amp%3Bmulti_itm_seq=0&amp%3Bitm_seq_1=0&amp%3Bitm_seq_2=0&amp%3Bcompany_cd=&amp%3Bcompany_nm=.

23. Notably, the document in question had been removed from public archives, leading to questions about the document's veracity on the one hand while raising questions about the motive for and method of its removal on the other.

24. Inter-Korean Relations Development Act, Act No. 17763 (2020).

25. "On the Amended Provisions of 'Inter-Korean Relations Development Act' for Scattering Leaflets," Ministry of Unification, December 2020, https://www.unikorea.go.kr/eng_unikorea/news/releases/?boardId=bbs_0000000000000034&mode=view&cntId=54255&category=&pageIdx=.

26. "On the Amended Provisions of 'Inter-Korean Relations Development Act' for Scattering Leaflets."

27. Song Young-gil, "Understanding Recent Revisions to the 'Inter-Korean Relations Development Act,'" 38 North, December 21, 2020, https://www.38north.org/2020/12/ysong122120/.

28. "Civil and Political Rights in the Republic of Korea: Implications for Human Rights on the Peninsula," Tom Lantos Human Rights Commission, United States Congress, https://humanrightscommission.house.gov/events/hearings/civil-and-political-rights-republic-korea-implications-human-rights-peninsula-0.

29. North Korean Human Rights Act of 2004, H.R. 4011 No. 108–333, 108th Congress (2004).

30. For information on Women Crossing DMZ and Korea Peace Now, see https://www.womencrossdmz.org/what-we-do/ and https://koreapeacenow.org/category/event/.

31. "Joint Press Conference of South Korean and Japanese Foreign Ministers' Meeting," Ministry of Foreign Affairs, December 28, 2015, https://www.mofa.go.kr/www/brd/m_20140/view.do?seq=302418.

32. Editorial, " 'Comfort Women Humiliation Diplomacy' That Betrays 'Historical Justice,'" *Hankyoreh*, December 29, 2019, https://www.hani.co.kr/arti/opinion/editorial/723948.html#csidx16cabea8a58581ea4b33cde394d4f3a.

33. Celeste Arrington, "South Korea Ended Its Review of Its 'Comfort Women' Deal with Japan. Here's What You Need to Know," *Washington Post*, January 11, 2018, https://www.washingtonpost.com/news/monkey-cage/wp/2018/01/11/south-korea-ended-its-review-of-its-comfort-women-deal-with-japan-heres-what-you-need-to-know/.

34. Choe Sang-Hun, "Ex-Chief Justice of South Korea Is Arrested on Case-Rigging Charges," *New York Times*, January 23, 2019, https://www.nytimes.com/2019/01/23/world/asia/south-korea-chief-justice-japan.html.

35. Cho Ki-weon, "Abe Denounces S. Korea's Decision to Dissolve Reconciliation and Healing Foundation," *Hankyoreh*, November 22, 2018, http://english.hani.co.kr/arti/english_edition/e_international/871356.html.

36. "South Korean Warship Directs Fire-Control Radar at Japan Plane," *Kyodo News*, December 21, 2018, https://english.kyodonews.net/news/2018/12/9a854f9b8e73-urgent-s-korean-warship-directs-fire-control-radar-at-japan-msdf-plane.html.

37. "Update of METI's Licensing Policies and Procedures on Exports of Controlled Items to the Republic of Korea," Ministry of Economy, Trade and Industry of the Government of Japan, July 1, 2019, https://www.meti.go.jp/english/press/2019/0701_001.html.

38. "Exports and Imports by Country," Korean Statistical and Information Service, accessed September 10, 2021, https://kosis.kr/statHtml/statHtml.do?orgId=360&tblId=DT_1R11006_FRM101.

39. "Trends in Annual Visitor Arrivals to Japan by Country/Area," Japan National Tourism Organization, accessed September 10, 2021, https://statistics.jnto.go.jp/en/graph/#graph--breakdown--by--country.

40. Makiko Yamazaki and Ju-min Park, "South Korea Says 'Won't Be Defeated Again' as Japan Trade Row Escalates," Reuters, August 2, 2019, https://news.trust.org/item/20190802063418-9bw8g.

41. "The Comfort Woman Agreement, We Need to Think About Its Tradeoff and Results," *JoongAng Ilbo*, January 5, 2018, https://news.joins.com/article/22260283.

42. "We Did Not Break the Comfort Women Agreement, But Japan Is Not Free from the Responsibility," *Kyunghyang Shinmun*, January 9, 2018, http://news.khan.co.kr/kh_news/khan_art_view.html?artid=201801092048005.

43. "Is the US Taking Side with Japan to Press for 'GSOMIA Overturn?,'" *Hankyoreh Shinmun*, August 28, 2019, http://www.hani.co.kr/arti/opinion/editorial/907521.html.

44. "Seoul-Tokyo Tensions Should Be Addressed as GSOMIA Expires Soon," *Dong-A Ilbo*, November 4, 2019, https://www.donga.com/en/Search/article/all/20191104/1892457/1.

45. Kuk Cho, Facebook, July 20, 2019, https://www.facebook.com/kukcho/posts/10157954631658521.

46. Park Ha-jung, "Lee In-young 'LKP Is Siding with Japan in Bilateral Disputes . . . This Is a New Form of Pro-Japanese Betrayal,'" SBS News, July 21, 2019, https://news.sbs.co.kr/news/endPage.do?news_id=N1005361415; Rhyu Si-min's *Alileo*, episode 28, " 'Abe says~' (Feat. Japanese Trade Sanctions)—Song Ki-ho and Yang Ki-ho," YouTube, July 19, 2019, https://www.youtube.com/watch?v=xNzZvjDYoIY.

47. "Blue House and Ruling Party Intensify Accusations of Pro-Japanese Betrayal . . . Opposition Party 'Are We Traitors for Criticizing the Moon Government?,'" *Segye Ilbo*, July 21, 2019, http://www.segye.com/newsView/20190721505837?OutUrl=naver.

48. "*TV Chosun* defends LKP while focusing on 'Senior Secretary Cho Kuk Attacks,'" Ohmy-News, July 26, 2019, http://www.ohmynews.com/NWS_Web/View/at_pg.aspx?CNTN _CD=A0002557173&CMPT_CD=P0010&utm_source=naver&utm_medium =newsearch&utm_campaign=naver_news.

49. "Cho Kuk's 'Patriotism' and 'Enemy Act,'" *Hankook Ilbo*, July 21, 2019, https://www .hankookilbo.com/News/Read/201907211520742729.

50. "How the LKP Can Avoid Accusations of Pro-Japanese Sympathies," *Hankyoreh*, July 28, 2019, https://www.hani.co.kr/arti/politics/polibar/903606.html.

51. John Bolton, *The Room Where It Happened: A White House Memoir* (New York: Simon and Schuster, 2020), 357.

52. Bolton, *Room Where It Happened*, 93.

53. Bolton, *Room Where It Happened*, 356–360.

5. NORTH KOREAN INFILTRATION AND INFLUENCE OPERATIONS

1. Office of the Secretary of Defense, "Military and Security Developments Involving the Democratic People's Republic of Korea 2017: A Report to Congress Pursuant to the National Defense Authorization Act for Fiscal Year 2012," https://irp.fas.org/world/dprk /dod-2017.pdf.

2. Adam Rawnsley, "North Korea's Special Operations Assassins," Medium, May 26, 2016, https://medium.com/war-is-boring/north-koreas-special-operations-assassins -b9ae884bc12.

3. "North Korean Tactics," Army Technique Publication No. 7-100.2 (July 2020), https:// fas.org/irp/doddir/army/atp7-100-2.pdf.

4. Narushige Michishita, *North Korea's Military-Diplomatic Campaigns, 1966–2008* (New York: Routledge, 2010), 201.

5. "1996 Gangneung Submarine Infiltration Incident," *Encyclopedia of Korean Culture*, Academy of Korean Studies, http://encykorea.aks.ac.kr/Contents/Item/E0075762.

6. "Records from 1996 Gangneung Submarine Infiltration Incident," *Dong-A Ilbo*, September 27, 2009, https://www.donga.com/news/Society/article/all/19961105/7205518/1.

7. "1996 Gangneung Submarine Infiltration Incident," Ministry of Unification, https:// nkinfo.unikorea.go.kr/nkp/term/viewKnwldgDicary.do?dicaryId=192.

8. "Behind the Scenes from the Arrest of Elite North Korean Spy Jeong Kyung-hak," *Kyunghyang Shinmun*, May 12, 2019, https://www.khan.co.kr/national/national-general /article/201905120900011.

9. "North Korean Spy Jeong Kyung-hak Sentenced to Ten Years," Radio Free Asia, December 8, 2006, https://www.rfa.org/korean/in_focus/sk_court_sentence_nk_spy_10_years -20061208.html.

10. "North Korean Spy Jeong Kyung-hak Sentenced to Ten Years."

11. "NIS Arrests 'Direct Spy' for the First Time Under the Roh Administration," Voice of America, August 21, 2006, https://www.voakorea.com/archive/35-2006-08-21-voa3 -91202549.

12. Soo-Hyang Choi and Hyonhee Shin, "North Korea Drone Entered No-Fly Zone Near Yoon's Office, South Says," Reuters, January 5, 2023, https://www.reuters.com/world/asia-pacific/nkorea-drone-entered-no-fly-zone-seoul-during-last-weeks-intrusion-skorea-2023-01-05/.

13. Baek Na-ri, "'Bizarre Life Story' of Female Spy Won Jeong-hwa," Yonhap News Agency, August 27, 2008, https://www.yna.co.kr/view/AKR20080827170200004.

14. Baek Na-ri, "'Bizarre Life Story' of Female Spy Won Jeong-hwa."

15. "Many Undercover North Korean Defectors Working as Spies," Yonhap News Agency, April 21, 2010, https://www.ytn.co.kr/_ln/0103_201004211755397861.

16. "Kim Yo Jong Rebukes S. Korean Authorities for Conniving at Anti-DPRK Hostile Act of 'Defectors from North,'" KCNA Watch, April 6, 2020, https://kcnawatch.org/newstream/1591219896-544350772/kim-yo-jong-rebukes-s-korean-authorities-for-conniving-at-anti-dprk-hostile-act-of-defectors-from-north/.

17. Shin Jong-hwan, "Current Status of Security Incidents Analyzed Through Past Experiences of Major Internet Incidents in Korea," *Internet and Security Focus* 3 (September 2013): 36–53, https://www.kisa.or.kr/uploadfile/201310/201310071957453995.pdf.

18. Choe Sang-hun and John Markoff, "Cyberattacks Jam Government and Commercial Web Sites in U.S. and South Korea," *New York Times*, July 8, 2008, https://www.nytimes.com/2009/07/09/technology/09cyber.html.

19. "2009 DDoS Attacks Against South Korea," *Dong-A Ilbo*, December 11, 2009, https://www.donga.com/news/Society/article/all/20091211/24718743/1.

20. Framework Act on Intelligent Informatization, No. 9369 (2009); 20 Years of Information Protection, "2009 DDoS Attacks Signal Death of South Korea's Internet," Boan News, July 1, 2019, https://www.boannews.com/media/view.asp?idx=81012&kind=0.

21. Choe Sang-hun, "Computer Networks in South Korea Are Paralyzed in Cyberattacks," *New York Times*, March 20, 2013, https://www.nytimes.com/2013/03/21/world/asia/south-korea-computer-network-crashes.html.

22. Zachary Keck, "South Korea Hit by Cyber Attack—North Korea to Blame?," *Diplomat*, March 21, 2013, https://thediplomat.com/2013/03/south-korea-hit-by-cyber-attack-north-korea-to-blame/.

23. "North Korea 'Behind Cyber Attack' on South Websites," BBC, July 16, 2013, https://www.bbc.com/news/world-asia-23324172; Song Jin-shik, "Ministry of Science, ICT, and Future Planning Warns March 20 Cyberattack Can Recur," *Kyunghyang Shinmun*, March 18, 2014, http://biz.khan.co.kr/khan_art_view.html?artid=201403181652121&code=920501&utm_campaign=list_click&utm_source=reporter_article&utm_medium=referral&utm_content=%BC%DB%C1%F8%BD%C4_%B1%E2%C0%DA%C6%E4%C0%CC%C1%F6.

24. Hong Jae-won and Park Hong-du, "'June 25 Cyberattacks' Both South and North Korea Suffered on the Same Day," *Kyunghyang Shinmun*, June 25, 2013, http://news.khan.co.kr/kh_news/khan_art_view.html?artid=201306252215315&code=940202.

25. "North Korea 'Behind Cyber Attack' on South Websites."

26. "Government Establishes 'Comprehensive National Cybersecurity Measure,'" Ministry of Science and ICT, July 4, 2013, https://www.msit.go.kr/bbs/view.do?sCode=user&mId=113&mPid=238&bbsSeqNo=94&nttSeqNo=1212488.

27. "Government Established a 'Cybersecurity Control Tower' as a 'Comprehensive National Cybersecurity Measure,'" *Aju Business Daily*, November 16, 2014, https://www.ajunews.com/view/20141114172757352.

28. Lee Gwang-bin, "North Korea Hacks Calls of Dozens of Diplomats and National Security Officials . . . Concerns About Doxing Attacks," *Yonhap News Agency*, March 18, 2016, https://www.yna.co.kr/view/AKR20160308085751001.

29. Christine Kim, "North Korea Hackers Stole South Korea–U.S. Military Plans to Wipe Out North Korea Leadership: Lawmaker," *Reuters*, October 10, 2017, https://www.reuters.com/article/us-northkorea-cybercrime-southkorea/north-korea-hackers-stole-south-korea-u-s-military-plans-to-wipe-out-north-korea-leadership-lawmaker-idUSKBN1CF1WT.

30. North Korean influence operations differ from infiltration efforts by recruiting sympathizers in South Korea willing to abet North Korean objectives rather than trying to attain them directly.

31. "Suppress Roh Hoe-chan of the 'New Jinbo Party' in 'North Korea Directive' Evidence of Dissolution of the 'Unified Progressive Party,'" *Kukmin Ilbo*, December 25, 2014, http://news.kmib.co.kr/article/view.asp?arcid=0008981914.

32. "Lee Jeong-hee Delivers Speech at the Beomminryon Event," *Dong-A Ilbo*, September 13, 2013, https://www.donga.com/news/View?gid=57636698&date=20130913.

33. Government of the Republic of Korea v. United Progressive Party, Case No. 2013, 25–26 (2014).

34. "Leftist Party Leaders Resign Over Election Scandal," *Korea Times*, May 12, 2012, http://www.koreatimes.co.kr/www/news/nation/2012/05/113_110847.html.

35. The Revolutionary Organization was an alleged group that was following the *Juche* ideology and North Korea's strategy for a revolution in South Korea, although the Constitutional Court concluded that there was not enough evidence to prove that the RO was an established organization with a command structure and its members agreed to pursue violent methods (Court case PDF, 355–357).

36. Government of the Republic of Korea v. United Progressive Party, Case No. 2013, 137 (2014).

37. The Constitution of the Republic of Korea, art. 8, sec. 4.

38. 간첩·간첩방조·국가보안법 위반·법령제5호 위반, 2008제도11 (2011).

39. Government of the Republic of Korea v. United Progressive Party, 8 and 13.

40. "Jusapa: Painful Legacy of Modern History," *Korea Herald*, June 11, 2012, http://www.koreaherald.com/view.php?ud=20120611000977.

41. *Jusapa* was a subgroup within the NL faction known for organizing the "Anti-U.S. Anti-Fascism Democratic Struggle Committee" and was prominent in the June 1987 South Korean prodemocracy demonstrations. "Jusapa," *Encyclopedia of Korean Culture*, Academy of Korean Studies, http://encykorea.aks.ac.kr/Contents/Item/E0066776; Government of the Republic of Korea v. United Progressive Party, 23.

42. Government of the Republic of Korea v. United Progressive Party, 31–43.

43. Government of the Republic of Korea v. United Progressive Party, 49.

44. Government of the Republic of Korea v. United Progressive Party, 49.

45. Government of the Republic of Korea v. United Progressive Party, 112.

46. "Using the National Assembly as a 'Bridgehead of the Socialist Revolution,'" Chosun News Press, October 2013, http://monthly.chosun.com/client/news/viw.asp?ctcd=G&nNewsNumb=201310100015.

47. "Using the National Assembly as a 'Bridgehead of the Socialist Revolution,'" 134.

48. "Ilshimhoe's Jang Min-ho Sentenced to Seven Years," *Yonhap News Agency*, December 13, 2007, https://www.yna.co.kr/view/AKR20071213165600004.

49. Lee Joo-hyun, "What Is the 2006 Ilsimhoe Incident?," *Hankyoreh*, February 4, 2008, http://www.hani.co.kr/arti/politics/politics_general/267894.html.

50. Kim Nam-il, "Supreme Court Rules 'Action and Solidarity Network Is an Enemy-Benefiting Organization,'" *Hankyoreh*, July 23, 2010, https://www.hani.co.kr/arti/society/society_general/431843.html.

51. Lee Sang-yong, "Supreme Court to Affirm Treason Ruling for the Korea Youth Movement Council," Daily NK, February 2, 2002, https://www.dailynk.com/대법-한국청년단체協-이적단체-확정/.

52. Lee Sang-yong, "Supreme Court to Affirm Treason Ruling," 48.

53. Lee Sang-yong, "Supreme Court to Affirm Treason Ruling," 121–124.

54. Jang Ho-chul, "Did South Korea Become Stronger After the 'Party Dissolution' of the Unified Progressive Party," OhmyNews, December 14, 2018, http://www.ohmynews.com/NWS_Web/View/at_pg.aspx?CNTN_CD=A0002496530.

55. "Democratic Party of South Korea's Call to 'Free Lee Suk-ki' at the National Assembly," NewDaily, November 8, 2017, http://www.newdaily.co.kr/site/data/html/2017/11/08/2017110800075.htm.

56. Lee Jun-woo, "Addressing Unequal U.S.–South Korea Relations, Dismantling the Chaebol Monopoly . . . People's Party of South Korea Mirrors the Unified Progressive Party," *Chosun Ilbo*, November 4, 2017, https://www.chosun.com/site/data/html_dir/2017/11/04/2017110400227.html.

57. Notably, the Moon administration at the end of 2021 simultaneously offered pardon and release to both Lee Seok-ki and Park Geun-hye. Despite very different cases and circumstances, the Moon administration's action raised complex questions about treason, subversion, pardon, and comparisons of the historical role and relationship of these two figures to the state.

58. Choe Sang-hun, "Latest Threats May Mean North Korea Wants to Talk," *New York Times*, November 20, 2008, https://www.nytimes.com/2008/11/20/world/asia/20korea.html?ref=todayspaper.

59. Ser Myo-ja and Chae Byung-gun, "North Rejects Idea of Liaisons," *JoongAng Ilbo*, April 28, 2008, http://www.seriworld.org/06/wldNewsV.html?&key=20080428000007.

60. Jennifer Jett and Stella Kim, "North Korea Launches Missile as Envoy Decries U.S. Policies at U.N.," NBC News, September 27, 2021, https://www.nbcnews.com/news/world/north-korea-fires-unidentified-projectile-u-n-envoy-criticizes-u-n1280214.

6. SOUTH KOREA'S ORIENTATION AND CHINA'S RISE

1. Scott A. Snyder, *South Korea at the Crossroads: Autonomy and Alliance in an Era of Rival Powers* (New York: Columbia University Press, 2018), 212–236.

2. "What Really Matters," *Joongang Ilbo*, May 18, 2021, https://koreajoongangdaily.joins.com/2021/05/18/opinion/editorials/What-really-matters/20210518203100270.html.

3. Heung-Kyu Kim, "A South Korean Perspective on the Latest US–China Strategic Competition," Center for East Asian Peace and Cooperation Studies, Ritsumeikan University, December 1, 2020, http://en.ritsumei.ac.jp/research/ceapc/insight/detail/?id=36.

4. Hwang Won-jae, *South Korea's Changing Foreign Policy: The Impact of Democratization and Globalization* (Lanham, MD: Lexington Books, 2017), 13–22.

5. Troy Stangarone, "Did South Korea's Three Noes Matter? Not So Much," *Diplomat*, October 30, 2019, https://thediplomat.com/2019/10/did-south-koreas-three-noes-matter-not-so-much/.

6. Ministry of Foreign Affairs of the People's Republic of China, "Foreign Minister Wang Yi Meets with Delegation of National Assembly Members of the Minjoo Party of the ROK," January 4, 2017, https://www.fmprc.gov.cn/mfa_eng/zxxx_662805/t1428662.shtml.

7. "SK Foreign Minister Refutes Suggestions That THAAD Operations Will Be Restricted," *Hankyoreh*, November 28, 2017, http://english.hani.co.kr/arti/english_edition/e_international/821100.html.

8. "Opposition Party Calls THAAD Deal with China 'Humiliating Diplomacy,'" Yonhap News Agency, November 1, 2017, https://en.yna.co.kr/view/AEN20171101005500315?section=search.

9. Bonnie S. Glaser and Lisa Collins, "China's Rapprochement with South Korea: Who Won the THAAD Dispute?," *Foreign Affairs*, November 7, 2017, https://www.foreignaffairs.com/articles/china/2017-11-07/chinas-rapprochement-south-korea.

10. Editorial, "President Moon's Bizarre China Visit," *Chosun Ilbo*, December 16, 2017, https://www.chosun.com/site/data/html_dir/2017/12/15/2017121503018.html.

11. Editorial, "China Should Abandon Its Arrogance and Welcome Neighbors with Mutual Respect," *Hankyoreh*, December 12, 2017, http://www.hani.co.kr/arti/opinion/editorial/823228.html#csidx6e9d4d7e920f5183a1e3965142ebdc.

12. "Opposition Party's Senseless Attacks About the China–South Korea Summit," *Kyunghyang Shinmun*, December 15, 2017, http://news.khan.co.kr/kh_news/khan_art_view.html?artid=201712152058015&code=990101#csidx70a41e07bfd1d4e8b2b8d3f74f465df.

13. Kim Young-hie, "Trump's Bad News," *Joongang Ilbo*, December 29, 2017, https://koreajoongangdaily.joins.com/2017/12/29/etc/Trumps-bad-news/3042691.html?detailWord=.

14. "US Initiative Against China," *Korea Times*, May 22, 2020, https://www.koreatimes.co.kr/www/opinion/2020/05/137_289986.html.

15. Do Je-hae, "Quadrilateral Alliance and Korea," *Korea Times*, October 9, 2020, https://www.koreatimes.co.kr/www/nation/2020/10/113_297283.html.

16. "Seoul's Participation in 'Quad' Will Antagonize China: Moon's Advisor," *Korea Times*, October 28, 2020, https://www.koreatimes.co.kr/www/nation/2020/10/120_298350.html.

17. Moon Chung-in, "Three Puzzles in S. Korean Diplomacy Discourse," *Hankyoreh*, April 19, 2021, http://english.hani.co.kr/arti/english_edition/english_editorials/991640.html.

18. "'China Is Aware Moon-Biden Statement Targets China Despite No Mention of Beijing': Chinese Amb.," *Korea Herald*, May 25, 2021, http://www.koreaherald.com/view.php?ud=20210525000082.

7. U.S.–CHINA TECHNOLOGY COMPETITION VS. CHINA–SOUTH KOREA ECONOMIC INTERDEPENDENCE

1. James McBride and Andrew Chatzky, "Is 'Made in China 2025' a Threat to Global Trade?," Council on Foreign Relations, May 13, 2019, https://www.cfr.org/backgrounder/made-china-2025-threat-global-trade.

2. "National Import-Exports," Korea International Trade Association, accessed July 6, 2021, https://stat.kita.net/stat/kts/ctr/CtrTotalImpExpDetailPopup.screen.

3. The phrase was coined by Robert Zoellick during the Bush administration. See "Whither China: From Membership to Responsibility?," September 21, 2005, https://2001-2009 .state.gov/s/d/former/zoellick/rem/53682.htm.

4. "South Korea Trade Status," KOTRA, 2021, http://www.kotra.or.kr/bigdata/visualization /korea#search/CN/ALL/2021.

5. Yang Pyungseop, "Causes and Challenges of the Recent Sharp Decrease in Exports to China," *Korea International Institute of Economic Policy* 20, no. 19, July 7, 2020.

6. Jang Jung-hoon, "Crash in China, Two Trillion KRW Deficit Last Year . . . Hyundai's Weapon for a Comeback," *JoongAng Ilbo*, June 6, 2021, https://www.joongang.co.kr /article/24075309#home.

7. Darren Lim, "Chinese Economic Coercion During the THAAD Dispute," Asan Forum, December 28, 2019, https://theasanforum.org/chinese-economic-coercion-during-the -thaad-dispute/.

8. Cho Bit-na and Lee Do-hyung, "Lessons from the THAAD Dispute, How Should Export Strategies to China Change?," *Trade Focus* 48 (December 2017).

9. Hong Kisuk and Ku Kibo, "A Study on the Economic Disadvantage Measures Through China's Refusal to Allow Customs Clearance of Korean Products," Korea Studies Information Service System, March 2021.

10. "Building Resilient Supply Chains, Revitalizing American Manufacturing, and Fostering Broad-Based Growth: 100-day Reviews Under Executive Order 14017," White House, June 2021, https://www.whitehouse.gov/wp-content/uploads/2021/06/100-day-supply -chain-review-report.pdf.

11. "Building Resilient Supply Chains," 6.

12. "FACT SHEET: United States–Republic of Korea Partnership," White House, May 21, 2021, https://whitehouse.gov/briefing-room/statements-releases/2021/05/21/fact-sheet -united-states-republic-of-korea-partnership/; "United States–Republic of Korea Leaders' Joint Statement," White House, May 21, 2022, https://www.whitehouse.gov/briefing-room /statements-releases/2022/05/21/united-states-republic-of-korea-leaders-joint-statement/.

13. "Building Resilient Supply Chains," 7; U.S. Department of Commerce, "Commerce Department Requests Information on Supporting a Strong U.S. Semiconductor Industry," January 24, 2022, https://www.commerce.gov/news/press-releases/2022/01 /commerce-department-requests-information-supporting-strong-us.

14. "China Chasing Korea, United States Keeping Check . . . Opportunity for K-Semiconductors, Not a Crisis," *JoongAng Ilbo*, April 15, 2021, https://www.joongang.co.kr /article/24035519#home.

15. SK Hynix's acquisition from Intel of a $9 billion NAND chip factory in Dalian will increase the Korean share of NAND production. "SK Hynix Completes the First Phase of Intel NAND and SSD Business Acquisition," PR Newswire, December 29, 2021, https://www.prnewswire.com/news-releases/sk-hynix-completes-the-first-phase-of -intel-nand-and-ssd-business-acquisition-301451672.html.

16. "Building Resilient Supply Chains," 40.

17. *The Economist* in 2018 estimated that Qualcomm generated two-thirds of its revenue from China and that Micron generated 57 percent of revenues from China. As stated in "Building Resilient Supply Chains," 39–40.

18. "Building Resilient Supply Chains," 43.

19. Jeong Hyung-geon, "Supply Chain Risks of South Korean Semiconductor Industry and Response Plans," *Korea Institute for International Economic Policy* 21, no. 19 (November 2021), https://www.kiep.go.kr/gallery.es?mid=a10102020000&bid=0003&list_no=9827&act=view.

20. "Building Resilient Supply Chains," 86–87.

21. Kim Bum-hyun, "President Moon: 'Aim to Make [South Korea] First Place in Batteries by 2030,'" Yonhap News Agency, July 8, 2021, https://www.yna.co.kr/view/AKR20210708149800001?input=1195m.

22. "Power That Charges the Future (2030 Rechargeable Battery Industry Growth Strategy)," Ministry of Trade, Industry, and Energy, July 8, 2021, http://www.motie.go.kr/motie/ne/presse/press2/bbs/bbsView.do?bbs_cd_n=81&cate_n=1&bbs_seq_n=164335.

23. "Power That Charges the Future."

24. Eamon Barrett, "New Players Are Piling into the World's Largest Electric Vehicle Market—No Auto Experience Required," Fortune Media, April 9, 2021, https://fortune.com/2021/04/09/china-electric-vehicle-market-evs-tesla-huawei-didi-xiaomi-evergrande/#:~:text=China%20is%20the%20world's%20largest,up%20from%20roughly%205%25%20today.

25. Oh So-young, "Electric Vehicles with Samsung SDI Batteries Receiving Chinese Financial Subsidies," Guru, January 1, 2021, https://www.theguru.co.kr/news/article.html?no=17646.

26. "U.S.–ROK Leaders' Joint Statement," White House, May 21, 2021, https://whitehouse.gov/briefing-room/statements-releases/2021/05/21/u-s-rok-leaders-joint-statement/.

27. "Samsung Biologics Signs Vaccine Production Deal with Moderna," Yonhap News Agency, May 23, 2021, https://en.yna.co.kr/view/AEN20210522008051315; Kim Sung-mo, "South Korea and the U.S. Starting the COVID-19 Vaccine Partnership Expert Group," *DongA*, July 14, 2021, https://www.donga.com/news/It/article/all/20210714/107951727/1.

28. "Briefing on U.S.–South Korea Vaccine Partnership," Ministry of Culture, Sports and Tourism, Republic of Korea, May 23, 2021, https://www.korea.kr/news/policyBriefingView.do?newsId=156452851.

29. "Remarks by President Moon Jae-in at KORUS Global Vaccine Partnership MOU Signing Ceremony," Office of the President, September 21, 2021, https://english1.president.go.kr/Briefingspeeches/Speeches/1066.

30. Choi Song-ah, "U.S. Government-led Vaccine Partnership for the First Time . . . Combination of U.S. Technology and South Korean Manufacturing Abilities," Yonhap News Agency, May 23, 2021, https://www.yna.co.kr/view/AKR20210523025951530.

31. Chris Park, "Potential Dependency Oversight in U.S.–South Korea Chip Policy," Council on Foreign Relations, September 19, 2022, https://www.cfr.org/blog/potential-dependency-oversight-us-south-korea-chip-policy.

32. Jiyoung Sohn, "SK Hynix Gets One-Year Reprieve from U.S. Chip Restrictions on China," *Wall Street Journal*, October 12, 2022, https://www.wsj.com/articles/sk-hynix-gets-one-year-reprieve-from-u-s-rules-limiting-chip-exports-to-china-11665568845.

33. Hee kwon Kyung and Lee Jun, "Implications of Biden's Executive Order That Investigates Semiconductor Supply Chain and South Korea's Response," Korea Institute for Industrial Economics and Trade, March 25, 2021, https://www.kiet.re.kr/research/economyDetailView?detail_no=2167.

34. Antonio Varas and Raj Varadaraian, "How Restrictions to Trade with China Could End US Leadership in Semiconductors," Boston Consulting Group, March 2020, https:// image-src.bcg.com/Images/BCG-How-Restricting-Trade-with-China-Could-End -US-Semiconductor-Mar-2020_tcm9-240526.pdf.

35. Bae Young-ja, "The Outlook of U.S.–China Competition and Korea's Response Strategy: Semiconductors," East Asia Institute Special Report, August 2020, https://www .dbpia.co.kr/journal/articleDetail?nodeId=NODE10477717.

36. Bae Young-ja, "Outlook of U.S.–China Competition."

37. Park Song-yi, "The U.S. Inflation Reduction Act That Is Threatening South Korea," *Kyunghyang Sinmun*, August 28, 2022, https://www.khan.co.kr/economy/economy -general/article/202208280940001.

38. Kim Min-sang, "IRA Concerns Come True . . . Hyundai Motor's Electric Vehicle Sales in the U.S. Fell 14 Percent," *JoongAng Ilbo*, October 5, 2022, https://www.joongang.co.kr /article/25106822#home.

39. Kim Young-bae, "An Electric Car Caught in an Emergency . . . U.S. Treasury Guidance 'Last Chance,'" *Hankyoreh*, October 10, 2022, https://www.hani.co.kr/arti/economy /global/1061977.html; Kim Dong-ha, "Biden Writes Letter to Family, 'Open-Minded Discussion on Inflation Reduction Law,'" *Chosun Ilbo*, October 5, 2022, https://www .chosun.com/politics/diplomacy-defense/2022/10/05/C3T53G2OY5DGVDR7V26 JZD52CE/.

40. Do Won-bin and Kim Kyung-hoon, "Korea's Opportunities and Threats from the Reorganization of the Global Semiconductor Supply Chain," Korea International Trade Association, December 27, 2022, https://www.kita.net/cmmrcInfo/internationalTradeStudies /researchReport/focusBriefDetail.do?pageIndex=1&no=2385&classification=1 &searchReqType=detail&pcRadio=&searchClassification=&searchStartDate =&searchEndDate=&searchCondition=TITLE&searchKeyword=&continent_nm =&continent_cd=&country_nm=&country_cd=&sector_nm=&sector_cd=&itemCd _nm=&itemCd_cd=&searchOpenYn.

8. THE CREDIBILITY OF THE AMERICAN ALLIANCE COMMITMENT

1. "South Koreans and Their Neighbors 2015," Asan Institute for Policy Studies, May 18, 2015, https://en.asaninst.org/contents/south-koreans-and-their-neighbors/; "South Koreans and Their Neighbors 2019," Asan Institute for Policy Studies, April 26, 2019, https://en.asaninst.org/contents/south-koreans-and-their-neighbors-2019/.

2. Victor Cha and Andy Lim, "Database: Donald Trump's Skepticism of U.S. Troops in Korea Since 1990," CSIS Beyond Parallel, February 25, 2019, https://beyondparallel.csis .org/database-donald-trumps-skepticism-u-s-troops-korea-since-1990/.

3. "Remarks by President Trump at the 2020 Governors' Ball," White House, February 9, 2020.

4. Phil Eskeland, "The Truth About KORUS and Jobs," *Diplomat*, October 6, 2018, https:// thediplomat.com/2018/10/the-truth-about-korus-and-jobs/.

5. "Remarks by President Trump in Meeting with State and Local Officials on Infrastructure Initiative," White House, February 12, 2018.

6. "Remarks by President Trump and Prime Minister Abe of Japan After Meeting on Trade | Biarritz, France," White House, August 25, 2019.

7. "Senator Markey: South Korean President Visits a Historic Opportunity to Exert Pressure on North Korea," Office of Senator Markey, June 30, 2017, https://www.markey .senate.gov/news/press-releases/senator-markey-south-korean-president-visit-a -historic-opportunity-to-exert-pressure-on-north-korea.

8. Michael F. Martin, Ben Dolven, Susan V. Lawrence, Mark E. Manyin, and Bruce Vaughn, "The Asia Reassurance Initiative Act (2018)," Congressional Research Service, updated April 4, 2019, https://fas.org/sgp/crs/row/IF11148.pdf.

9. Claudia Grisales, "Trump Objects to New Law That Stops Him from Removing Troops from South Korea," *Stars and Stripes*, August 14, 2018, https://www.stripes.com/news /trump-objects-to-new-law-that-stops-him-from-removing-troops-from-south-korea -1.542636.

10. Lee Haye-ah, "Trump Signs Defense Bill with Provision Against Troop Drawdown in S. Korea," Yonhap News Agency, December 21, 2019, https://en.yna.co.kr/view /AEN20191221000400325.

11. "National Security Challenges and U.S. Military Activities in the Indo-Pacific," House Committee on Armed Services, March 27, 2019, https://www.congress.gov/event/116th -congress/house-event/LC64819/text?s=1&r=4.

12. Bob Woodward, *Fear: Trump in the White House* (New York: Simon and Schuster, 2018), xvii–xxiii, 263–264.

13. Woodward, *Fear*, 280–282.

14. John Bolton, *The Room Where It Happened: A White House Memoir* (New York: Simon and Schuster, 2020).

15. Justin McArthy, "South Korea's Image at New High in U.S.," Gallup, February 20, 2018, https://news.gallup.com/poll/228050/south-korea-image-new-high.aspx.

16. Karl Friedhoff, "Americans Positive on South Korea Despite Trump's Views on Alliance," Chicago Council on Global Affairs, October 19, 2020, https://www .thechicagocouncil.org/research/public-opinion-survey/americans-positive-south -korea-despite-trumps-views-alliance.

17. Troy Stangarone and Juni Kim, "2021 Report on American Attitudes Toward the U.S.– ROK Alliance and North Korea Policy," Korea Economic Institute of America, May 21, 2021, https://keia.org/publication/2021-report-on-american-attitudes-towards-the-u-s -rok-alliance-and-north-korea-policy/.

18. Karl Friedhoff, "Troop Withdrawal Likely to Undermine South Korean Public Support for Alliance with United States," Chicago Council on Global Affairs, August 2020, https://www.thechicagocouncil.org/sites/default/files/2020-12/2020_sma_korea_brief _0.pdf.

19. Byun Duk-kun, "Trump Says He Will 'Blow Up' Korea–U.S. Alliance If Reelected," Yonhap News Agency, July 14, 2021, https://en.yna.co.kr/view/AEN20210714000300325.

20. J. James Kim, Kang Chung-ku, and Ham Geon-hee, "Fundamentals of South Korean Public Opinion on Foreign Policy and National Security," Asan Institute for Policy Studies, September 13, 2021, http://en.asaninst.org/contents/fundamentals-of-south-korean -public-opinion-on-foreign-policy-and-national-security/.

21. Scott Snyder, Ellen Swicord, J. James Kim, Kang Chungku, and Ko Yumi, "South Korean Attitudes Toward the U.S.–ROK Alliance and USFK," Asan Institute for Policy

Studies, February 22, 2019, http://en.asaninst.org/contents/south-korean-attitudes-toward-the-u-s-rok-alliance-and-usfk/.

22. J. James Kim, and Kang Chungku, "South Korean Outlook on the United States and ROK–U.S. Relations in the Biden Era," Asan Institute for Policy Studies, February 10, 2021, http://en.asaninst.org/contents/south-korean-outlook-on-the-united-states-and-rok-u-s-relations-in-the-biden-era/; "South Koreans' Perceptions of President Trump's State Visit and Neighboring Countries," Asan Institute for Policy Studies, December 21, 2017, file:///C:/Users/CFRUSER/Downloads/Asan-ReportSouth-Koreans-Perceptions-of-President-Trumps-State-Visit-and-Neighboring-Countries.pdf.

23. Editorial, "Trump's 'Isolationism,' Must Look Out for Its Effects on the Korean Peninsula," *Hankyoreh*, December 21, 2018, https://www.hani.co.kr/arti/opinion/editorial/875414.html.

24. Park Sung-jin, "A 'Blind U.S.–South Korea Alliance' Unaware of the Number of U.S. Forces in Korea,'" *Kyunghyang Shinmun*, June 21, 2018, https://m.khan.co.kr/opinion/column/article/201806212100015.

25. Kim and Kang, "South Korean Outlook."

26. The Column, Chun Yeong-woo, "Critically Ill U.S.–South Korea Alliance," Chosun Media, September 21, 2020, https://www.chosun.com/opinion/chosun_column/2020/09/21/2HK3ZZHQABDCLHXHUIG4VNL27M/.

27. Franco Ordonez, "Biden Heads to Europe to Convince Allies That the United States Has Their Backs," NPR, June 9, 2021, https://www.npr.org/2021/06/09/1004394359/biden-heads-to-europe-to-convince-allies-the-united-states-has-their-backs.

9. IMAGINING U.S. FOREIGN POLICY TOWARD ASIA ABSENT THE U.S.–SOUTH KOREA ALLIANCE

1. "Benefits and Costs Associated with the U.S. Military Presence in Japan and South Korea," U.S. Government Accountability Office Report to Congress, March 2021, https://www.gao.gov/assets/720/713082.pdf.

2. "Americans Positive on South Korea Despite Trump's Views on Alliance," Chicago Council on Global Affairs, October 19, 2020, https://www.thechicagocouncil.org/research/public-opinion-survey/americans-positive-south-korea-despite-trumps-views-alliance.

3. For instance, this might be a logical concern based on timelines for China's military development produced by the RAND Corporation. Eric Heginbotham, Michael Nixon, Forrest E. Morgan, Jacob L. Heim, Jeff Hagen, Sheng Li, Jeffrey Engstrom, Martin C. Libicki, Paul DeLuca, David A. Shlapak, David R. Frelinger, Burgess Laird, Kyle Brady, and Lyle J. Morris, "The U.S.–China Military Scorecard: Forces, Geography, and the Evolving Balance of Power, 1996–2017," Rand Corporation, April 15, 2015, https://www.rand.org/content/dam/rand/pubs/research_reports/RR300/RR392/RAND_RR392.pdf.

4. Ethan Kessler, "Why the US Should Withdraw Its Troops from Korea," Quincy Institute for Responsible Statecraft, July 27, 2021, https://responsiblestatecraft.org/2021/07/27/why-the-us-should-withdraw-its-troops-from-korea/.

5. Leif-Eric Easley, "Korean Unification and the False Promise of Strategic Bargains with China," *Asian Perspective* 44, no. 4 (2020): 701–723, doi:10.1353/apr.2020.0030.

6. Leif-Eric Easley, "How Proactive? How Pacifist? Charting Japan's Evolving Defense Posture," *Australian Journal of International Affairs* 71, no. 1 (January 2017): 63–87, https://doi.org/10.1080/10357718.2016.1181148.

7. Adam P. Liff, "Japan, Taiwan, the United States, and the 'Free and Open Indo-Pacific,'" Wilson Center and Wilson China Fellowship, https://adampliff.files.wordpress.com/2021/04/liff2021_japan-taiwan-usa-foip.pdf.

8. "Benefits and Costs Associated with the U.S. Military Presence in Japan and South Korea."

9. "Doing Business in Korea: 2019 Country Commercial Guide for U.S. Companies," U.S. Department of Commerce, 2019, https://2016.export.gov/southkorea/build/groups/public/@eg_kr/documents/webcontent/eg_kr_129237.pdf.

10. "U.S.–ROK Leaders' Joint Statement," White House, May 2021.

11. Sheila A. Smith, *Japan Rearmed: The Politics of Military Power* (Cambridge, MA: Harvard University Press, 2019), 99–100.

10. IMAGINING SOUTH KOREAN FOREIGN POLICY ABSENT THE U.S.–SOUTH KOREA ALLIANCE

1. Scott Snyder, *South Korea at the Crossroads* (New York: Columbia University Press, 2018).

2. Mutual Defense Treaty Between the United States and the Republic of Korea, October 1, 1953, https://www.usfk.mil/Portals/105/Documents/SOFA/H_Mutual%20Defense%20Treaty_1953.pdf.

3. George W. Bush and Lee Myung-Bak, "President Bush Participates in Joint Press Availability with President Lee Myung-Bak of the Republic of Korea," transcript of speech delivered at Camp David, April 19, 2008, https://georgewbush-whitehouse.archives.gov/news/releases/2008/04/print/20080419-1.html.

4. "South Koreans and Their Neighbors 2019," Asan Institute for Policy Studies, April 26, 2019, https://en.asaninst.org/contents/south-koreans-and-their-neighbors-2019/.

5. "Benefits and Costs Associated with the U.S. Military Presence in Japan and South Korea," U.S. Government Accountability Office Report to Congress, March 2021, https://www.gao.gov/assets/720/713082.pdf.

6. Ito Kohtaro, "What to Make of South Korea's Growing Defense Spending?," Sasakawa Peace Foundation, March 12, 2020, https://www.spf.org/iina/en/articles/ito_02.html.

7. Edward White, "South Korea Aims for Military Independence as Asia Threats Rise," *Financial Times*, January 6, 2021, https://www.ft.com/content/032a5e2e-8959-4501-89a6-51c27eabc3c3.

8. Diego Lopes Da Silva, Nan Tian, and Alexandra Marksteiner, "Trends in World Military Expenditure, 2020," Stockholm International Peace Research Institute, April 2021, https://www.sipri.org/publications/2021/sipri-fact-sheets/trends-world-military-expenditure-2020.

9. Ito, "What to Make of South Korea's Growing Defense Spending?"

10. Heon-Chul Kwon, "The Value Estimation of the United States Armed Forces in Korea," *Journal of National Defense Studies* 54, no. 2 (August 2011): 23–45.

11. Robert E. Kelly, "China's Support for North Korea Kills Any Chance of Unification," National Interest, April 17, 2017, https://nationalinterest.org/feature/chinas-support-north-korea-kills-any-chance-unification-20227.

12. "Agreement on the Implementation of the Historic Panmunjom Declaration in the Military Domain," September 19, 2018, https://www.ncnk.org/sites/default/files /Agreement%20on%20the%20Implementation%20of%20the%20Historic%20Panmunjom%20Declaration%20in%20the%20Military%20Domain.pdf.

11. SUSTAINING U.S.–SOUTH KOREA ALLIANCE CONTRIBUTIONS TO INTERNATIONAL SECURITY

1. The Moon administration did not pursue such a policy but was influenced by domestic constituencies and individuals sympathetic to such aims.
2. Karl Friedhoff, "Americans Remain Committed to South Korea," Chicago Council on Global Affairs, September 9, 2019, https://www.thechicagocouncil.org/research /public-opinion-survey/americans-remain-committed-south-korea; and Friedhoff, "Americans Positive on South Korea Despite Trump's Views on Alliance," Chicago Council on Global Affairs, October 19, 2020, https://www.thechicagocouncil.org/research/public -opinion-survey/americans-positive-south-korea-despite-trumps-views-alliance.

INDEX